GEORGES LARAQUE

THE STORY OF THE NHL'S
UNLIKELIEST TOUGH GUY

WITH PIERRE THIBEAULT

VIKING
CANADA

VIKING CANADA

Published by the Penguin Group

Penguin Group (Canada), 90 Eglinton Avenue East, Suite 700, Toronto, Ontario,
Canada M4P 2Y3 (a division of Pearson Canada Inc.)

Penguin Group (USA) Inc., 375 Hudson Street, New York, New York 10014, U.S.A.
Penguin Books Ltd, 80 Strand, London WC2R 0RL, England
Penguin Ireland, 25 St Stephen's Green, Dublin 2, Ireland
(a division of Penguin Books Ltd)
Penguin Group (Australia), 250 Camberwell Road, Camberwell, Victoria 3124,
Australia (a division of Pearson Australia Group Pty Ltd)
Penguin Books India Pvt Ltd, 11 Community Centre, Panchsheel Park,
New Delhi – 110 017, India
Penguin Group (NZ), 67 Apollo Drive, Rosedale, Auckland 0632,
New Zealand (a division of Pearson New Zealand Ltd)
Penguin Books (South Africa) (Pty) Ltd, 24 Sturdee Avenue, Rosebank,
Johannesburg 2196, South Africa

Penguin Books Ltd, Registered Offices: 80 Strand, London WC2R 0RL, England

First published 2011

1 2 3 4 5 6 7 8 9 10 (RRD)

LIBRARY AND ARCHIVES CANADA CATALOGUING IN PUBLICATION

Laraque, Georges
Georges Laraque : the story of the NHL's unlikeliest
tough guy / Georges Laraque ; with Pierre Thibeault.

Translation of: La force d'y croire.
ISBN 978-0-670-06590-5

1. Laraque, Georges. 1. Hockey players—Canada—
Biography. I. Thibeault, Pierre, 1965– II. Title.

GV848.5.L37A3 2011a   796.962092   C2011-905491-4

Visit the Penguin Group (Canada) website at **www.penguin.ca**

Special and corporate bulk purchase rates available;
please see **www.penguin.ca/corporatesales**
or call 1-800-810-3104, ext. 2477 or 2474

For Milayna Julia
and Marcus Oliver

CONTENTS

THE "GOOD EXAMPLE"

1

February 1, 1999. Edmonton. Skyreach Centre is crackling with anticipation.

I'm lined up for the faceoff along the boards.

I'm shoulder to shoulder with Tony Twist. He is a beast of a man. Two hundred and forty-five pounds of intimidation and aggression. His job is to scare grown men.

And I'm just a rookie.

The puck drops, and the play moves away from us.

There we stand, nose to nose, our gloves dangling. All eyes are on us now.

In a moment I will drop my gloves and do battle with one of the toughest guys in the NHL.

Why?

That is a question that will take a whole book to answer.

The short answer is that I had dreamed my whole life of making it to the NHL. But that doesn't explain much. That's a dream I shared with millions of other kids.

The longer answer is that dreams are complicated things, and maybe I dreamed mine a little differently from the way my friends and teammates dreamed theirs. Maybe I was a little more competitive. Maybe my dreams had a slightly sharper focus.

And maybe that's because someone called me a nigger.

I heard that word a lot … I heard people shouting it at me. Even when it was whispered, it would create a deafening noise deep inside.

And always, that word was preceded by another word. *Fucking* was the most common among them. Sometimes, people would put it in a degrading short sentence. Above all, it was never pronounced entirely. With contempt, people would modify its last syllable, pronouncing it "nigga."

I've thought about that word a lot. It's not the word itself that needles me—it's what people mean when they use it. Today I've come to understand all the intrinsic beauty and strength of that word. The writings of the founders of Négritude, the literary and ideological movement that preached solidarity in a common black identity in the 1930s, have enlightened me as to what truly constitutes the essence of the word *Negro*. Those extraordinary writers bravely refused the inferior condition into which slavery and colonialism had put them and all black people. Negro means black, and there is nothing insulting about that.

Léopold Sédar Senghor, for instance, who in 1960 would become the first president of a liberated Senegal, wrote an article in 1936 in which he said, "The concept of Négritude includes all the black world cultural values, whether they are expressed in everyday life, in institutions or in works of art created by black people. It is a reality: A knot of realities."

Then came the ceaseless battles led by Malcom X, Martin Luther King, Rosa Parks, and dozens of other great individuals. History may have forgotten most of their names, but their actions were crucial in black history.

Thanks to them, I know for certain that all men are created equal. Thanks to them, I know for certain that all the cruel and racist words that buzzed around my mind during my youth were only meant to soil a beautiful word, a word full of history.

That's what's perverse about the corrosive words I faced when I was young—they weren't just about me. They were about something bigger than me.

But here's the thing—and I've thought about this a lot: if I hadn't heard that word so often when I was young, I wouldn't have been there that night, a scared kid squaring off with a guy whose reputation was enough to intimidate just about every professional hockey player in the world. If I hadn't faced the threats I had growing up, I might not have had the courage to try to make a living facing other people's fears. And if I hadn't been confronted by challenge after challenge as a kid, I know I wouldn't have had the willpower to do what it takes to make it to the world's best hockey league.

So that's why I was about to tangle with Twist in front of 18,000 people that night. Not because he had insulted me, or because I was angry. I wasn't angry at all. I had achieved what I had set out to accomplish. I was where I had dreamed of being since I first fell in love with hockey—under the bright lights of an NHL rink. As a kid, I dreamed of scoring goals to lift my team. I dreamed of being a leader in the dressing room. I dreamed of making big plays to change the game. Even if my dreams didn't take exactly the shape I wished for so passionately as a kid, I would one day do all those things. And though the most cherished moments of my career were still in front of me that night, the fact that Tony Twist was glaring at me was proof of my success.

Even before our gloves came off, I had won the biggest fight of my life.

•

Of course, it's a lot easier to understand these things as a grown man than it was as a kid. It's easier for a grown man to brush off words like that, or to fight through them. But how does a kid make his dream happen in the face of others' suspicions and prejudice? How did the young boy I was back in the 1980s and 1990s manage to stick to his goal despite all the racism he had to suffer? I heard that "nigger" word so many times during my youth that I could have come to believe it was my first name. And yet I never said die.

Not only that. I didn't succeed despite the obstacles others put in my way. I made sure to succeed *because* of them.

For as long as I can remember, I've known I would become a professional athlete. I was taller, stronger, and faster than all the other kids my age. I was good at all sports, from judo to football, from soccer to hockey. Even track and field smiled on me. The question was never whether I would excel at a sport. The only question was which one.

Soccer had always been my favourite, and it still is today. Football was a natural choice, considering the way I was built. Yet hockey was the discipline I devoted most of my energy and time to. I remember those hostile hockey arenas as if it was yesterday. Players, referees, parents, coaches—virtually everyone made me feel as though I didn't belong.

No one ever believed in my dream of getting to the NHL one day. Not because of a lack of talent. No, because of the colour of my skin, a colour that would never be suitable for the whiteness of the ice. How did the ostracized child that I was back in the 1980s, who often wasn't even invited to play in the intercity leagues, manage to never stop pursuing his goal, to never duck his head? I must add that I've always been a very sensitive person, which means that every insult, every act of racism I was the victim of hurt me deep inside. But my pride was stronger. I didn't want anyone to see or even think that the xenophobic comments and attitudes were doing any harm to me. I would keep my anger and sadness inside until, late at night alone in my room, I would cry my eyes out.

But pride wasn't enough. Neither was my strong temper, nor the very strict education I received at home. The courage to follow my dream was the result of what would seem an innocuous event to anyone else but me.

One day I picked up a book from my sister's bookshelf. It was part of a series published by Grolier that had been given to her as a gift, called "Un bon exemple." The objective of that series was to introduce children to men and women who had changed history in a positive way. The range of personalities it covered was large, from athletes like Maurice Richard to inventors like Thomas Edison, and from scientists like Marie Curie to philosophers like Albert Schweitzer.

The book from that series that piqued my curiosity was about the legendary baseball player Jackie Robinson. I devoured every page of it, learning in detail how a small boy from Georgia managed to become the first black man in history ever to play in major league baseball. Coming from a part of the United States where racism was a way of life, Robinson had the nerve to rush headlong into the fray, to fight prejudice, to ceaselessly push back every limit in order to become a better player. On April 15, 1947, when he ran onto Ebbets Field as a Brooklyn Dodger, he also entered history. And nowadays, who can imagine major league baseball without any coloured players?

Historians have written about that Jackie Robinson debut, saying it paved the way for the civil rights revolution that would eventually abolish any form of legal segregation in the United States. And not only was Robinson one of the greatest baseball players of all time, elected to the Team of the Century in 1999, but he also involved himself in black people's causes for years after his career had ended.

When I closed that book, the eight-year-old boy I was knew he wouldn't ever be the same. I had found a role model; I had found the way I would forever approach life.

From that day on, I started praying to God every night, begging him to give me the strength to achieve my goal. Being an NHL player had become the goal of my life. I had the deep impression that it was where I belonged, that it was where I'd be able to play my role.

•

By the time I turned seventeen, it had become obvious to everyone that I'd be a professional athlete. Just one question remained: would it be hockey or would it be football?

At the time, I was playing for the St. Leonard Cougars football team in the north of Montreal. I remember the coach, Danny Maciocia, telling me, "You won't go anywhere in hockey, Georges. No black players in the NHL. And I don't expect to see one in the near future. You should stay with me and become a professional football player. That's where your future lies. And it'll be a bright one, trust me."

He couldn't have known that his words only made me want more than ever to make my mark on the ice. I smiled at him and said, "I'm sorry, Danny, but I'll stick to hockey. I belong there. There are lots of black players in football. If I succeed in that field, I'll just be another black guy playing football. Hockey is different."

A few years later, Danny became the head coach of the Edmonton Eskimos. I was playing for the Oilers at the time, and one morning I went to see him at the Commonwealth Stadium. As soon as he saw me, he smiled and said, "You succeeded, you stubborn, you!" Against all odds, I *had* succeeded. My real mission had now begun.

THE BELT AND THE WELTS

2

One more thing I'd like to add about Jackie Robinson: I may have chosen him as my role model in my youth, but I have to confess that I really hate baseball. This might sound like a contradiction, but it's not. Throughout my life I've always made a big distinction between the public person and the individual. You can respect the baseball player without respecting baseball. This is true not only in Jackie Robinson's case; it also applies to every human being in this world, including me. The book you're holding in your hands was written with the same intention in mind. On the one side is the Georges Laraque you saw in the NHL. And then there's the human being I am off the ice.

Far be it from me, of course, to deny the exceptional talent Robinson showed on the baseball diamond during his career. But beyond the countless feats he performed as a player, it's more the man's personality and determination that guided me throughout my youth. As for my loathing of baseball, it all boils down to two reasons, one being very personal, the other related to the sport itself.

When I was young, as I said earlier, I tried my hand at many sports, not only because I loved them, but also because my father was always pushing me into doing more and more sporting activities. Naturally I did play baseball, but I was so bad at it that I stopped after only one season.

The biggest problem I had was that I was catching and pitching with the same hand, my left one. Every time a ball would land in my glove I had to put it in my other hand, pull the glove off and fling it to the ground, put the ball back in my left hand and finally throw it at my target. Not a very efficient technique, to say the least.

The other reason why I really dislike baseball comes from my observation of the game itself. Half the players look like sumo wrestlers. They eat and chew gum or tobacco all game long and spend more time picking their noses than they do running.

I certainly agree that to be able to hit a fastball coming your way at a hundred miles an hour must be one of the toughest things to do. However, I also know that when David Wells pitched his perfect game for the New York Yankees on May 17, 1998, he was hungover from a boozing session the night before. I'm not the one saying it—he wrote it in his autobiography. That makes it a bit more difficult to take baseball too seriously. And what a paunch, for God's sake!

Not that I have anything against overweight people. It's just that a man with the kind of stoutness Wells carried during his career simply wouldn't have been able to play in any other professional sports league than MLB.

And since I'm talking about paunches, I have to confess that for many years I had a very low opinion of overweight people. Please forgive me, as I was young at the time and had the tendency to take everything my father said at face value. In his eyes, an overweight child meant parental failure, nothing less.

According to my father, only a bad education could lead a child to gain weight. Needless to say, our diet was spartan.

There was absolutely no trace of junk food, either in our kitchen cupboards or in the refrigerator. Same thing went for our lunch-boxes. Soft drinks, cookies, chips, and ice cream were forbidden. Only fruits and vegetables were allowed. When I had friends over at our house they would be in total despair whenever snack time arrived, and they would flood me with questions about our eating habits. Not that I ever managed to explain things in a way they could understand. To kids accustomed to eating whatever they liked, our dietary regime could be met only with incomprehension. Friends would talk to me about Oreo cookies with greedy eyes. I must have been fifteen when I finally tasted one.

Dinners were pretty monotonous. Chicken and rice every evening. My friends would ask their mothers what was for dinner. We didn't have to. We knew for sure what it would be. Chicken and rice again and again …

My father was the one who mainly did the cooking. He didn't experiment a lot, and would basically reproduce Haitian recipes his mother had taught him. And what would Haitian cuisine be without chicken and rice? Still, I don't think we ate those meals to live according to Haitian tradition. I think my parents just didn't feel like cooking anything else.

Though I must say that traditions were important for my parents, and remained deeply rooted in their hearts and customs. Quite a few cousins and close relatives lived near our house, and if someone from outside our family had stepped into one of our parties, that person would have felt as if he'd been teleported two thousand miles away from Quebec to a Port-au-Prince living room. I used to love those parties, as they were the only occasions, besides our birthdays, when we could bend the eating rules and get some chips and cake.

Oh yes, I almost forgot. Once a month we'd have some shepherd's pie for dinner. My heart and stomach were incredibly happy those nights, as I found that meal to be extremely exotic. As you'll see later, I've kind of changed my mind since then.

Still, apart from junk food, we were quite indulged and never missed out on anything as far as material goods were concerned. We lived in a nice, cozy district called Les Boisés d'Angoulême and had quite a big house with four bedrooms, two bathrooms, and a huge yard, in the centre of which was a large in-ground pool. During the ten years we lived there, from 1982 to 1992, kids from all around the neighbourhood would come and enjoy the yard and take dives in the water.

When I was eight years old, my father started giving me chores, like mowing the lawn or shovelling the driveway. I was paid seven dollars every time I accomplished one. Kids usually hate those jobs. I loved them, so much so that I'd often knock on our neighbours' doors and offer them the same services.

Sounds like a pretty idyllic suburban childhood (minus the Oreos), no? I suppose that in some ways I had the perfect upbringing to get me where I wanted to go, as will soon become clear.

•

However, if there's one thing that defined my childhood, for better and for worse, it was my father's tyrannical regime. My father's inflexibility ruled that house. And we had to abide by it at all times. Needless to say, we would escape it whenever we could, which wasn't often. School, sports, and even games were subject to the rules and regulations that my father invented and imposed. He ruled over his children like an army sergeant over his soldiers.

My earliest memories of my father are of him instilling his fierce version of discipline in his kids, and bending us to his will. And aging hasn't softened his attitude towards people. In other words, he hasn't changed a bit—he's still every inch the autocrat.

Between my father and his kids, there was absolutely no room for any kind of discussion. We had to obey without grumbling; even a mild look of resentment on our faces was treated the same as open rebellion. The slightest mistake any of his kids would make was sure to be severely punished. We had to suffer his chastisement every time he thought we'd gone off the right track he had planned for us. And by "chastisement" I mean the physical kind, the kind most of us nowadays think is inappropriate. Unless, of course, someone thinks that hitting a kid's hand fifty times with a belt is a proper punishment.

I know this type of behaviour seems to come straight from another era. But those punishment sessions took place as recently as the 1980s and 1990s right here in Quebec, since I was born on December 7, 1976, in Montreal, my sister, Daphney, on May 17, 1978, in Brossard, and my brother, Jules Edy, on August 23, 1980, in Sept-Îles. When it came to raising his kids, there were no alternatives to belt-smacking for my father. He was simply repeating what he had gone through during his own childhood in Haiti.

Raised the hard way by his own parents, my father spent his young years in the hostile environment created in his native land by the Duvalier regime. He understood very quickly that he would have to count on no one else but himself to get out of that climate of pervasive fear. From those years he inherited three well-defined character traits. First, a disproportionate pride; second, a will to control everything; and third, a very stubborn mind. Although my father and I never talked about it, I'm convinced that what he expected was the same perfection from his kids he felt he had attained himself. We needed to get everything right simply because he thought he'd been getting everything right since his younger days.

Leaving Haiti when he wasn't even twenty years old, he came by himself to establish his new home in the cold northern metropolis of Montreal. In his first months in North America, this six-foot, two-hundred-pound colossus had no choice but to avail himself of food banks simply to survive. But he managed to graduate with a mechanical engineering diploma from Montreal's prestigious École Polytechnique and with a Bachelor of Architectural Studies from the University of Montreal.

Despite the humiliation, the financial setbacks, and the pain of exile, he succeeded in starting a family and in giving his kids everything he'd lacked as a child. Since he was convinced— and still is—that roughness was what had allowed him to pull through, he couldn't see his children's education better served by any other means than the use of his belt on our hands.

Not that I'm trying to excuse the way he punished us, but I must say that lots of kids from an immigrant background were— and still are—raised in a similar fashion, using similar methods. Nowadays I have quite a few friends whose parents come from the Maghreb, the Middle East, and of course Haiti. When we talk about the way we were respectively raised, it's disconcerting to me to find so many broad similarities between us.

Parents with an older Canadian background are a lot less hard on their kids than freshly arrived ones, and so I can understand their indignation at that kind of treatment. Besides, and you can trust me on this, never will my twin children ever have to suffer the belt-smacking torture. I'll never terrorize them that way. I strongly believe in different and better ways to raise my kids than getting the strap out every time something in their attitude doesn't comply with my standards.

But without trying to minimize the impact of violent practices against children, it's not always easy or even possible for newly arrived immigrant parents to learn and comprehend what behaviours are acceptable or not according to the host society's customs. And this applies not only to children's education, but to all the spheres of their new social life. It really seems to me that those who are newly arrived are often left in the dark. I'm certainly not here to shed light on the reasons for this situation, but it appears obvious to me that a prevailing type of multiculturalism in Canadian society has been to confine new migrants to a certain form of ghettoization. That tends to make it difficult for those people to adjust their social behaviour to the customs and practices endorsed by the majority in Canada. And that includes Quebec, of course.

I can clearly see evidence of this in the fact that my father, despite having been educated according to Western standards, never hesitated to beat us even when we had friends over. I'll never forget one particular afternoon.

I was in the basement of our home in Sorel-Tracy with about twenty of my "old-stock" Quebecer buddies. The music was loud and so were our conversations. However, the only thing we could clearly hear on that afternoon were the cries and howlings of my brother getting beaten up by my father on the upper floor.

Lack of understanding is often the fastest route to racism. And the way my father was acting, he was sure getting my friends thinking that we, black people, were strange, to say the least. Freaks, to say the worst.

I could read the fear in my friends' eyes. If the hockey arena was the theatre of the worst xenophobic attitudes, I'd managed to keep that kind of animosity out of my regular life. Away from the rink, the colour of my skin wasn't a barrier. I was a jovial, friendly kid who got along with everyone. And there was my father, conjuring negative stereotypes out of thin air with his barbarism. I was so ashamed of him that it was almost unbearable. I hated him more for the affronts he inflicted on us in front of others than for the actual punishments we were given.

All three of us experienced our father's brutal severity, but I must admit I had the "pleasure" to feel it a bit more often than my brother and sister did. Not only was I a hyperactive child, but I was also the one succeeding in everything I was doing. I was the oldest, the tallest, the strongest, and the fastest. These things should have protected me and even prevented me from being punished. But since I was the least likely to make mistakes, my father was a lot less inclined to let me get away with anything than he was with his two other children. In a certain way, I was supposed to be the one embodying my father's pride, the incarnation of his success as a self-made man.

At home, we only had toys with an educational value to play with. Puzzles, Lego blocks, and other building sets were the rule in the house. My father was against any type of passive toy, as he would call them. No television or video game console was allowed to enter our lives. We always had to play a sport, whether it involved our body or mind. Needless to say I was thrilled to visit friends, simply to get away from that rule.

But the hyperactive in me would lead me to do things that my father would find reprehensible. I just couldn't stand still. For instance, I loved to play Superman or any other superheroes. I'd be jumping everywhere, falling on the floor, hurting myself quite often, and all that action would usually end up with me breaking something in the house or one of my toys. This would, of course, provoke my father's ire.

On the other hand, there was school. Success at school wasn't just encouraged in the Laraque household. It was mandatory. Luckily, though, it was pretty easy for me. I would even say too easy, as I was always one of the first in the class to complete exams. Since I was a hyperactive child, I would then start to clown around, disturbing the other pupils, making them laugh. The teachers would send me to the principal's office, and my father would get a call. I'm sure I don't have to relate to you here what would happen when I'd get home.

I could recount hundreds of anecdotes that all ended up with the belt-smacking sessions. But there's one in particular that comes to my mind, one that can sum up and symbolize what our father expected from us, how he wanted us to be upright and exemplary at all times. The whole family was visiting one of our friends. I must have been nine years old at the time, not more for sure. In the corner of the living room stood an upright piano. I had never seen one so close up before and I was so tempted to touch it, to press my fingers on one of its keys just to hear the sound of its strings. After a couple of minutes, incapable of restraining ourselves anymore, my brother and I simply pressed three of its keys. My father didn't say anything right away. But the look on his face left little to interpretation. Those three keys were worth fifty belt hits, and we sure got them. And so did my sister, simply because she'd made noises with her mouth while finishing her glass of juice.

I haven't spoken about my mother in these pages yet. I certainly will in upcoming chapters. She never approved of my father's use of violence against her kids, although she rarely interceded. And when she did, it was only to ask my father not to hit so hard or to tell him that fifty blows were maybe a bit too many. He never listened to her, as he never listened to anyone anyway. He was always right and he knew everything.

We, the kids, often talked about the way our father was treating us. I was often outraged and angry about it. I sometimes hated him in my heart of hearts. But never ever did I find the nerve to protest. His revenge would have been even more terrible. So I spent my youth getting smacked and smacked again. Then one night it stopped.

I perfectly remember the last time my father raised his hand against me. I was fifteen and a half and was working night shifts at a convenience store. It was in July 1992, two years after my parents had divorced, an event I'll talk about in the next chapter. My father had already gotten married again to his second wife, named Irma, although they weren't living together yet. We were in the Anjou district in the north of Montreal and she was living pretty near our place, in the Laval suburbs. My father would sometimes go to her house to spend the night, and for the three of us kids, those nights were synonymous with heaven on earth, a true fiesta. Especially for me, as I was the oldest. I would often take those special occasions to go out with friends, bravely ignoring the curfew imposed by my father. But he had a head on his shoulders, and I was about to discover that he was harder to deceive than I'd thought.

I believe that what tipped him off about my nocturnal outings was the fact that I'd get out of bed around ten or eleven in the morning after his nights away from the house. My main problem was that I was an early riser on any other morning.

That particular night, my father left as usual while I was still at work. Knowing he wouldn't be back until the next morning,

I decided to meet up with some friends after my shift. We went to downtown Montreal to see a free outdoor show that was part of the Just for Laughs Festival. When the event ended, my friends and I went back to our respective houses. I was walking alone on the streets that led to our house when I suddenly saw lights glowing in our windows. That, for me, was a spine-chilling sight. My father was home.

Beads of sweat stood out on my brow. I was scared out of my mind. I was so paralyzed by fear that I had to wait ten minutes before finally finding the courage to unlock the door and go inside the house. My father was of course waiting for me at the top of the stairs. He was seething. No doubt he could read the fear in my eyes. His hands were trembling and so were mine. But not for the same reasons.

He started to yell, sputtering his venom at me, shouting that he knew I was going out every time he turned around, that he knew he would nick me one day. Then he grabbed a chair and threw it at me with all his might from the top of the stairs. I tried to block it, and catch it with my hands, but it cut me deeply just above my nose. I still have a scar from that today.

Something changed in me. I rushed up the stairs like a madman, holding the chair in one of my hands while he kept going with his litany of insults. My fear had metamorphosed itself into pure hate. Years of frustration, hundreds of violent acts were propelling me towards him. I reached the top of the stairs in no time. I was all rage and hate. He kept yelling at me, asking me where I'd been, shouting at me that he'd gone to the store to ask my colleagues what time I had left. Then he paused, and with a humiliating grin on his face, told me that my fellow workers were laughing at me when he went there. I was looking at him straight in the eyes, just ready to explode.

That's the moment he chose to grab a plastic garbage can next to him. He waved it over my head and then violently whacked me with it. The garbage can exploded against the arm I'd lifted over my head to protect myself. The look I gave him then was cruel and arrogant—as much of an affront as the assault with the garbage can had been. He took up a boxer's stance and invited me to fight.

Still staring at him, I said, "I won't fight with you because you're my dad. But right now, here, I could kill you!"

Then I slowly went to my room. He didn't follow me.

He never touched me again.

LIFE SENTENCE   3

My parents got divorced when I was thirteen years old. Daphney, Jules, and I had known for a long time it was bound to happen. Our parents' relationship had always been so tumultuous and erratic that, in my mind, it was only a matter of time before they ended up facing the point of no return.

I don't know of one child on this planet who would be happy to see his or her parents separate. But frankly, in my case, I wanted it to happen as soon as possible. For me, the sooner the better was my motto, even though I felt sad thinking about that inevitable split.

They were arguing so violently that even though they did it behind closed doors, their anger was obvious to us. Their voices were tuned to the "screamer" button on an imaginary mixer. We'd hear them fighting all the time, sometimes over some trifle, but for my mother it was mostly on her kids' behalf.

My mother was a quiet woman, but she could not tolerate his tyranny. If my dad wasn't exactly the pinnacle of fatherhood, he didn't excel at being a husband either. A few years after these epic fights, my dad would confess to us that although he had married our mother on September 11, 1975, renewing his vows in front of a priest on August 28, 1976, it was only because he'd known from the start that she'd be the best mother in the world. All these years later, that's one thing I can say he was absolutely right about.

I tried for many years to understand why my mother forced herself to accept my father's temper. I understood it only recently. That very same pattern my parents were following when I was a kid could, and still can, be observed in numerous immigrant families. The wife is aware of her husband's imperfections and she's trying to close her eyes to them, sometimes successfully, repeating to herself, as if it was a mantra, that the road to exile had been an arduous and demanding one and that, after all, she's better off in her current situation than she would be if she had stayed in her homeland. For a lot of immigrant women, their children's future is more important than marital bliss. And for many years, that's exactly what my mother tried to convince herself of.

In vain.

One night she surprised my father in charming company in a hotel room. I guess that was the last straw. She decided to leave the family home we'd had since I was five, on D'Argenson Street in the city of Sorel-Tracy, and rent an apartment quite close to our house.

The following months were awful in every way. Far from soothing the animosity that had crackled in the Laraque household for so long, separation had the exact opposite effect. It was as if somebody had poured oil on the fire that was already ravaging their relationship. From that moment on, not only did they keep fighting about the things they had always fought about, they now had the details of their separation to fight over. Custody of the children was the most important battle, of course, but they also went to war over the house, the car, the kitchen appliances, everything they shared. They even fought over who would keep the shower curtain.

Only a few days after my mother had left the house, lawyers from both sides came into play. In my father's case, this was the straw that broke the camel's back. He was completely set ablaze. Life at home became unbearable, the atmosphere nauseating. The drama was everywhere around us. There was not one minute of respite.

The attorneys were fighting each other like mad dogs, drawing my parents deeper and deeper into unnecessary expenses. And the more the bills piled up, the angrier my parents got. Hatred was making them go blind. At that point, nothing could have stopped their crazy combat. Their only goals now were to hurt, humiliate, ruin, ridicule, and destroy the other.

My parents' strife ultimately unfolded in front of a judge, who was at sixes and sevens as he tried to sort out my family's situation. Neither of my parents was even close to being rational, animated as they were by some kind of almost murderous emotionalism.

Daphney, Jules, and I were only the spectators at that tormented ball. We were totally disoriented. Our only wish was to wake up from that fever and return to normal. We felt totally powerless. And yet, although I was only thirteen, the decision-making power to put an end to that turmoil, an almost inhumane responsibility, was thrust into my hands.

One morning, my father and mother appeared in a courtroom in Montreal, one on each side of it, of course. We, the children, were too young to attend the hearing and were asked to wait in another room. The judge was going to render some very important decisions that day. Among them, custody was the crucial one. Both my parents were asking to be granted sole custody. Neither of them was ready to mix water with wine, even though it tasted like vinegar.

I knew that the two lawyers were probably clashing shamelessly, arrogantly questioning my father and my mother. Showing no mercy, I'm sure they weren't looking for any kind of compromise. Their one and only goal was to make one or the other collapse in a total knockout.

A court clerk came to see me in the private children's waiting room. She told me that since I was the oldest child, the judge wanted to see me in private. I followed her down the hallways of the courthouse. I really had no idea what the judge wanted to see me for.

We finally arrived at a glass door. The clerk opened it and invited me in. I entered the small room, and there seated in front of a table was the judge. I was impressed. He gently asked me to sit down on a chair facing him. His face was full of empathy, which reassured me. I sat down. He remained silent for a few seconds.

He finally took a deep breath and said, "Boy, I wanted to see you here this morning because I have a question for you. Only one. You're the oldest of the three children. In a few minutes I will have a very important decision to render and it's not an easy one. I have to decide where you and your brother and sister will be living from now on. And I don't want to render it before having talked to the people concerned. This is all about your future. So here's my question for you: where do you think the three of you should be living for the years to come? At your mom's or at your dad's place?"

I was stunned. Never had I expected this to happen. For months now my parents had been fighting like crazy, spending fortunes on legal fees, and there I was, sitting in that small room in front of a judge, being asked to settle that storm for good. I had my family's destiny in my hands.

He clearly saw the commotion his words had created inside me. In a soft voice he asked me to take my time before answering. He even told me I didn't have to answer now, that I could wait a couple of days before doing so. I was sweating, head down, my muggy hands all tangled up between my legs. After only a few seconds, I lifted my head up and looked at the judge straight in the eyes. It was my turn to take a deep breath: "I want us to go with my father." He looked at me and asked if I was sure about that. I answered that I was. He said I could go back to the waiting room.

I followed the court clerk again. Back in the room with my sister and brother, I remained quiet, still disturbed by what I had just told the judge. I was also very anxious. Would he follow my words or make another decision? I couldn't wait any longer, but I had to.

The judge went back to the courtroom. He knew what both parties had to say, and now he knew my thoughts too. I could only guess what he was going to say when he rendered his decision, and it was only later that I pieced together in my imagination what his words were:

"With what I know, and after having spoken in private with Georges, the oldest child of Mrs. Évelyne Toussaint and Mr. Edy Laraque, I've decided to give full custody of Daphney Laraque, Jules Edy Laraque, and Georges Edy Laraque to Mr. Edy Laraque. My decision also gives Mrs. Toussaint extended visiting rights with respect to her three children."

For years afterward, I would imagine how my father might have expressed his satisfaction. And I could not escape the thought of what my mother's dismay must have been in that courtroom. I felt so bad about the sorrow I caused her. I still do.

How in the world was that possible? How could I have told the judge I wanted us to live with our father? Some might have thought back then that I was some kind of masochistic teenager. Given what I've already said about my father's parenting style, my mother's reaction makes perfect sense.

The ride back home to my father's place was pretty silent. Yes, I often hated our father. No, he had almost never demonstrated any affection for us. He had practically never even complimented us on anything. The only things we ever got from him were reprimands and belt-smacking sessions. My family thought I was insane, and it's easy to see why.

Still, I was deeply convinced that I had just made the right decision for our future.

•

As a discipline freak, my father would push us, as I've said, into practising all sorts of sports. In my case, it was even more mandatory. Since I was breaking everything in the house, he wanted me out as much as possible.

Almost every weekend we would compete in various tournaments all over Quebec. All of us would jump into the car and drive a hundred kilometres to Granby simply to compete against other kids in track and field events. Since I had inherited my father's spirit of competition, I just loved those meets.

To get us in shape for those events he would take us several weekends a month to a running track in Sorel-Tracy. There, he would force us to run. Sometimes it would be sprints, other times long-distance runs. He would leave us there, but would come back from time to time to make sure we were practising hard. All of that was done in order to inculcate the love of discipline, effort, and determination in us. But frankly, I also think he did it to prevent us from becoming fat.

My sister was truly gifted when it came to track and field. Her only competition came from much older girls, and even then she was accustomed to winning. Daphney was a little bit like me. She was taller, stronger, and faster than any girl her age. She was fifteen and nearly six feet tall. She had a bright future awaiting her in the track and field disciplines and could have chosen among a dozen of them. At least until my father's obsession with excellence blunted her love of sport.

At the age of sixteen she chose to quit track and field. Track and field had become a battleground between them, and rather than argue with him, Daphney chose to hang up her cleats— and some of her dreams along with them.

From a distance, I now can say I'm a bit sad for her. Daphney was truly *the* talented kid in that family. But when I recall the circumstances under which she decided to give it all up, I can only say she made the right decision. My dad had put more pressure on her than she could tolerate and watched her like a coach. He always expected her to win and regularly challenged her to quit if she didn't. He wanted to motivate Daphney, but he ended up disenchanting her. He wanted her to dream, but he killed every possibility of doing so.

As for my brother, he had a totally different frame. My sister and I were tall and slim while he was short and stocky. At five-foot-six and 160 pounds, he was built like a bull. He played hockey as much as I did, but he didn't go as far. He made it to the Quebec Major Junior Hockey League (QMJHL) and could have entered the American League, but I encouraged him to stop at that point, for two reasons. First, due to his small size he hardly had any chance to play in the NHL where I was already playing; and second, guys in the American League were already challenging him, trying to get him into fights just to see if he was as strong as his brother was. Still, he was a fast player and almost impossible to push off the puck. It wouldn't have been hard for him to have the softest hands in the family.

As for me, let's just say that competition wasn't something I was scared of. On the contrary, I loved it. I was seeking victory everywhere and at all times. My father was very pleased about that. Honestly, I never received any punishment from him regarding my performances in sports or at school. As I said before, he really had passed his spirit of competition down to me. I was always trying to be the best, the fastest, the brightest.

In addition to that, I was lucky enough to be naturally strong as an ox. I did a lot of cardio training during my youth and in the NHL, but I almost never had to work on strength. As strange as it may sound, in all my life I've practically never lifted weights.

And I've already mentioned how important school was to my father. It was our priority number one; we *had* to succeed in our studies. There was just no way around that. Even before my parents got divorced, my father was the one reviewing our homework. He was always verifying if we had learned our lessons, if we knew by heart the texts we had to study. At the slightest mistake he would send us back to our rooms. If my father wasn't satisfied, we had to redo the exercises. And perfection was the only thing that would satisfy him.

Needless to say, with that kind of discipline, I got great grades throughout my primary school years. And reading books was not an incidental or optional activity in my father's eyes. As soon as we were able to decipher a few words, which means after a couple of months in primary school, we were forced to read almost one book a week. He would take us to the public library, and even though we could choose our books ourselves, he would indicate in which section we were allowed to look for them. Comic books were of course prohibited, and as we got older the length of the books grew at the same pace we did.

Those Fridays, before we were given permission to go out and play with our friends, my father would subject us to a test. We had to give him our book of the week and then go to our rooms for a few minutes until he called us back. During that time he would pinpoint some passages in the book, and then he would ask us to come and see him so that he could question us on those passages. It was his own personal way to make sure we had read the book from the first to the last page.

With such a precise interview technique it was virtually impossible for us to cheat. I tried once, though. I had decided to read only what was written on the back cover of the book. I wanted to test him and his methods, and was hoping I could get away with it. This sure was the wrong move. The technique I'd improvised that very week turned out to be very bad and led me to a miserable failure. I spent that beautiful summer weekend locked up in my room, reading that damned book. I could hear the laughter of my friends playing outside, and for the hyperactive child I was, it was a tough time. Do I really have to tell you I never tried to cheat again? From that time on, I never missed a single page, a single word of those mandatory paternal readings.

As you will have gathered, we had absolutely no room to manoeuvre when my father was around, nor when we were involved in regulated activities such as school or sports. But as soon as I could get away from my father's supervision, everything would change. I just wouldn't be the same. I was, I am, and I always will be an all-or-nothing type of person. I don't know half measures. When I get involved in something, I put in all my energies, heart and soul. And when I was younger, as I said earlier, I would always try to win at everything. At dinner, I had to be the first one to finish my plate. It wasn't enough for me to have the best marks in school, I had to be the first one in the whole classroom to finish the exam.

That almost pathological need to win, to be ahead of everyone at all times, went along with a character trait I haven't always been very proud of. I have to confess that I was the worst bad loser the world had ever seen. I hated to lose, but even more, I hated not to win. I was the incarnation of the exact opposite of what Pierre de Coubertin, the founder of the modern Olympic Games, used to advocate: "The most important thing is not winning but taking part."

To play or to compete just for fun made no sense to me. Every aspect of my life was a competition in which I fiercely needed to succeed. I had to win by any means necessary. When playing a game of Monopoly, for instance, if I had the sense that I was about to lose, I would start arguing, grumbling about everything. I'd push my opponent to such limits that he'd finally say, "Okay! That's it! I quit! You win! Are you happy now?" And I sure was! Anyone in my shoes would probably have said no, if they were honest with themselves. Not me. If I won, I was happy.

During those years, I had another character trait that guided my actions. I had the need to stand out in the crowd. At the time, I really enjoyed being the centre of attention, the one everybody would talk about. And to achieve that, I would sometimes play with fire.

Knowing how extreme I was, I never wanted to try drugs, for instance, because I'm quite certain I would have become the biggest junkie of all. At home, my parents didn't keep any alcohol, not even wine. I'm really glad they didn't for the same reasons as above. I would probably have been a champion boozer if they had.

I know I could have stooped to a very low level had I let myself go down certain paths. To be totally honest, by the age of twelve, I'd lost confidence in myself and didn't know where my extremism was going to lead me. Frankly, I was scared of what I was capable of doing.

In those days I had invented a winter game that I'd play with some of my friends. We would hide on top of a small hill overlooking a street. Every time a car would pass under us we would pepper it with the biggest snowballs we could throw. Sometimes the car would stop and its driver would start running after us. We never got caught, although it came close quite a few times. And we wouldn't discriminate against any car. Even police cruisers were our targets. A couple of times we escaped arrest by the skin of our teeth.

I remember a particular day playing that game. Stopped under us was a small convertible car. I lifted a huge icy snowball over my head and threw it as hard as I could. The projectile missed its aim by only a few inches. And thank God it did. Had it hit the car, it would certainly have gone through the roof and severely hurt the driver inside. And this was just one of the many adolescent stupidities I was playing at back then. I loved the adrenalin rush they would give me, and to keep it going I had to push the limits a little bit further every time.

But I wasn't blind. I knew perfectly well that these activities could take me over the edge if I kept on doing them. On the other hand, I needed them like I needed oxygen.

So this is the reason why I told the judge that morning that we should go live with my father. My mother was softness incarnate, a source of tenderness and comfort. But I knew for certain that she wouldn't have the strength to keep me, my sister, and my brother out of trouble in the years to come.

Staying with her would of course have been a lot easier. On the other hand, I had the feeling even then that living according to my reckless adolescent impulses could only mean trouble. With my father, there was no way I could do that. I preferred my mother by far. I hated my father's attitude and the way he was raising me. But if my goal was to reach the NHL one day, it could only be achieved under his severe supervision. Between the cuddling comfort my mother would have given me and the pathological harshness of my father, I had chosen. And even though I would regret that decision at least a million times in the years to come, I'm totally convinced today that it was the only one possible.

FROM RACISM TO
THE FIRST DRAFT

4

Throughout my childhood and teenage years, I experienced a big paradox in my relationships with others. As much as I was the victim of the most odious racism when I put on my skates in an arena, outside that environment I was very popular and surrounded by friends. At school, in the playgrounds, and in the streets of Sorel-Tracy, I had no problem socializing with other kids even though I was the only black one. I was laughing all the time and was always the first to throw in a joke in every situation, drawing others in like flies to a fly strip.

Racism wasn't totally absent from my everyday life, but it remained a rare thing. And yet it was in a non-hockey context that I received my first face-to-face xenophobic comment. I was about nine at the time, and I was fooling around with my friends while waiting for the school bus. When the bus door opened, the driver, whom we had nicknamed Mustard, shouted at me, "Come on, nigger, hurry up!" I climbed into the bus in a state of shock. I didn't know how to react.

When I got home, I went straight to my father and told him what had just happened. The next morning he came with me to the bus stop. He jumped into the bus and took the driver by the collar. He clearly explained to him that if that kind of comment were to be repeated, he wouldn't be soft with him.

We never saw Mustard again.

I had mixed emotions about what my father did that morning. On the one hand, I really did appreciate his move. On the other, I was pretty embarrassed. He was instilling fear not just in Mustard, but in my friends too. Plus, he had a tendency to see racism everywhere, even when there was none. When you added his blunt nature and stubbornness to that, let's just say he didn't have the best recipe to live a simple life.

And he lost a lot of jobs because of it. When one of his bosses would give him a specific task, he would always try to find a better way of carrying it out than what was prescribed by the company. If the boss asked him to follow the company rules, he'd argue and fight to the point where he would simply quit the job.

My dad recently lived in Edmonton. And I suspect that he left the city after only a few years because he couldn't find a job anymore. Actually, he rarely kept a job for more than a few months. And every time, he would of course pretend that he'd been the victim of racism. But when he was telling me how things had happened, it was often obvious it was nowhere to be seen.

That also reminds me of a game I played while I was in Midget AAA. My father was in attendance, and not far from him was the home team mascot. This one was dancing, fidgeting, acting like a clown. That's what mascots do, after all. At one point when I was in the penalty box, the mascot climbed onto the glass behind me to goad me. Again, that's the kind of goofing off a mascot does. That's not the way my father saw things, though. What he saw was racist taunting—not the sort of thing he took lightly. After a few minutes he stood up fiercely, stormed up to the mascot, and literally pulled the poor thing down from the glass behind the penalty box. Security guards rushed over to my father and ushered him out of the arena. I was so ashamed that I had problems finishing the game. I would rather have had a mascot laughing at me over the glass than see my father wrestling with a stuffed animal.

This sort of attitude was typical of my father—and it's what he would teach his children. When we'd get hit or when someone would insult us, he wanted us to defend ourselves. Turning the other cheek was not part of his philosophy of life. He was more an eye-for-an-eye, tooth-for-a-tooth type of man.

The way I was built helped me throughout my youth; I was too big to be challenged. It was quite different for my sister and brother, who had to answer to all kinds of provocations. My father was very proud of them. One day, though, my sister came home from school crying. One of her schoolmates had insulted her—and Daphney hadn't stood up for herself. Instead of trying to comfort and console her, my father exploded. The way he saw things, it was her own fault for putting up with those insults. If she wanted them to end, it was up to her to put a stop to them.

•

But let's get back to hockey. For obvious reasons, my parents were not big fans of the sport. Coming from Haiti, their favourite had to be soccer. But the indifference they felt at first for the game of hockey slowly metamorphosed into pure disgust as the racist acts against me grew in number. They soon stopped taking me to the arena altogether. I had to look out for myself and manage to make my way there, whether it was on my feet or on my bike, carrying all my gear on my back.

When people talk about racism, it's often in relation to disparaging words. But racism isn't made up only of demonstrable actions; it can be a lot more insidious. Let's take my hockey years in Sorel-Tracy, for instance. Every single season, I was one of the best players in my age group, yet I was never chosen to play with the intercity team. My whole family, including me, knew the reason for that. My father was disheartened to see me play in these conditions, and often tried to dissuade me from playing the game. But since I was getting very good grades in school, he didn't have any reason to force me to quit.

But just before entering grade six, I suffered a new blow to my dream of making it to the NHL. I attended the Pee-Wee AA training camp for the Sorel Riverains, as they were called in those days. By all reports, people watching the tryouts were very impressed by my performance. Even though it was rare to see a first-year peewee player join the ranks of the elite team, I really believed I had a chance at it. I was so proud of what I'd accomplished, and everyone was so enthusiastic about my strong showing during the camp, that I couldn't see myself anywhere else but with the big team. I was floating on air. All the harder, then, would the fall be ...

Once the camp came to an end, the trainers released a list of the players who had made the team. My name was not on it. My father tried to get some explanation from the team manager, but all he was told was that, although I'd had a good training camp, it was obvious to them that I didn't understand a single thing about the spirit of the game. My father was furious. And I was heartbroken.

I would often hear my parents discussing my case. They were really worried about all that hatred surrounding me, wondering how it would affect me in the future. And after that decision, I remember my father questioning me a lot. He wanted to know what was motivating me, why I was still banging my head against the wall to make my way in a sport that didn't want me. He told me I should move to some other sport where racism didn't exist.

I would consistently answer him that to quit the game at that moment would only prove those people right. The only way I could possibly prove them wrong was to succeed, to find a way to fulfill my personal dream of being an NHL player one day. He would always shrug that off and start laughing. Even my father, who had such high expectations of me, never thought I had the slightest chance of making my way up to the NHL.

Even worse, he didn't want me to see that dream as a possibility. The only thing he wanted me to do was to study as hard and as long as I could in order to find myself a "real job" one day. In a certain sense I couldn't blame him. The route I'd been following since the beginning of my hockey years had nothing to do with the one a typical would-be NHL player would follow.

That year, despite my recriminations and entreaties, my father decided that organized hockey was definitely over for me. If I still wanted to play the game, from now on it would only happen in the streets, with my friends. I was shattered, staggered, and most of all, totally powerless in the face of paternal authority. But I hadn't had my last word yet.

•

High school was approaching. Because of my grades, every school in Quebec had opened its doors to me.

All but one, that is. My sister was going to a school called Notre Dame, and it would have been convenient for me to go there as well. But my cousin Patrick was on the hockey team at a school called Brébeuf. Guess where I decided to go? Strictly speaking, it was not my decision, of course. But how I performed on the entrance exams was very much my decision. Somehow I failed the Notre Dame exam and passed the Brébeuf exam with flying colours.

After thinking long and hard, my dad decided I would go to Brébeuf, a private school. For him, no doubt, it was the best he could dream of. The only snag was that Sorel-Tracy was about an hour away from Brébeuf.

So the decision was made that I would attend Brébeuf as a resident student. During that whole year my parents would take me to Montreal every Sunday night and then come back and pick me up after the last class on Fridays. On the hockey side, the season was a disaster as far as my development was concerned, since the school team I played on wasn't as competitive as what I was used to.

•

It was during the summer of 1988 that we finally moved to Longueuil, just south of Montreal. My father couldn't bear the racist atmosphere of Sorel-Tracy anymore, and he had found a job as an engineer for Pratt & Whitney. I was about to start my second year in high school, and just thinking that I'd have to play again for Brébeuf in the high school league was depressing me. I had the feeling that my dream was slipping away from me a little more each week. I wasn't giving it up, but school and family circumstances seemed to always keep it just beyond my reach.

I tried once again to go back on the offensive. I asked my father to register me in a public school so that I could play in a better league. I didn't want to go back to Brébeuf. I explained to him that it was impossible for me to make any progress in the hockey world if I was to keep on playing against weaker players. Talk about speaking to a wall.

Studies, studies, and studies again—nothing else would find favour in his eyes. Still, I managed to weaken his legendary inflexibility a bit. I convinced him to let me attend a Bantam AA training camp in Longueuil. Once again I performed very well; once again I didn't make the team; and once again my father saw racism in that decision.

I was, however, invited to play in the Bantam A league. Not the highest level, of course, but it sure had to be better than the high school league. The prospect of getting back in touch with some real competition helped me spend the last days of summer in a climate of serenity.

I started school that year with the impression that I had achieved the impossible. I had managed to bring my father to accept a compromise. Needless to say, that was something I would never have dreamed of even a few days before I attended the Bantam AA training camp.

But after only a few weeks of school, my spirit wasn't that serene anymore. The high school league was no better than the previous season, while the Bantam A league was just slightly better. I had the impression of skating alone on the ice, shooting in empty nets; I would score nearly at will. It was ridiculous.

In October, the Bantam AA coach, the same one who'd told me I couldn't make his team just a month before, said he was now ready to give me a chance. I was dumbfounded to hear myself say no to him. Two things motivated that answer. First, I have to admit it, pure pride; and second, I knew exactly what my father's reaction would have been if I had said yes.

But when the coach left, I started insulting myself inwardly. My goal was to get to the NHL one day and I'd just said no to the best opportunity that had ever been given to me to move towards it. At least that decision of mine made one person happy: my Bantam A coach. That season I got over two hundred points and about a hundred goals.

I was in a dead-end situation. I really had the impression that I was wasting my talent, along with some precious developing years. I felt like I was in a kind of quicksand that was slowly swallowing my one and only dream. So once again I tried to go back to my father, but he was such a mountain of incomprehension that I had the feeling I'd never ever be able to climb it. And the previous months had made his inflexibility even worse. He was totally happy and proud of his son; after all, I'd been voted one of the best sporting students in the school in my first year at Brébeuf. A brilliant son getting good grades and being the best at sports—wasn't that the ideal situation for a father? It sure was for him, anyway. He wanted me to keep on with what I was doing just as much as I wanted to get out of it.

Since he thought he was better than everyone else, that his determination and inflexibility would win out over everything, for him my future was settled. My destiny wasn't to be questioned for the years to come. But he was about to discover how strong he'd made my own determination.

After that last discussion I had with the wall my father was, I went back to my room and started thinking about my options. And that's when a Machiavellian plan popped into my head. Since Brébeuf high school was clearly the main obstacle standing in the way of my dream, I had to find a way to get out of it. And I sure did.

I started to act as if everything was going just perfectly. I pretended that I agreed with my father's views and that I would wait until the end of high school to see if hockey was still something that meant something to me. If so, I would have the right to try my luck at it.

Behind his back, though, it was a totally different story. I started getting bad grades in geography, physics, and math. For the first time in my life, I was on the verge of failing— something intolerable to him, but part of my plan nonetheless. And he didn't understand why I wasn't doing well, since I was perfect at home when studying with him. Probably racism again ... Boy, was he naive.

Then came the final exams. I had to ace them just to avoid failing my courses. But I failed those too.

My father was in total despair for one obvious reason: education meant everything to him. To see a son who was accustomed to getting As suddenly fail two courses was catastrophic in his eyes. I was out of Brébeuf.

Furious that he'd wasted money on my now supposedly failed education, my father reacted fiercely to the situation. He didn't like the idea of letting me go to a public school. But the only solution was for me to attend the Anjou school north of Montreal, where we'd moved at the end of spring. In the meantime, I had to attend six weeks of summer classes at a school called St. Exupéry and pass the exams I'd failed at Brébeuf to get into the Anjou school. Which I did.

After getting my exam results, St. Exupéry's principal called my father and me in for a meeting. While we were driving to the school, I had a sense that my plan might have gone a little off the rails, but I had no way of knowing what was awaiting me. As for my father, he was wondering what kind of fix I had gotten myself into again. He knew from the principal that I hadn't failed my exams, but the question remained: why was the principal asking to see us both?

After a brief discussion between my father and the principal, it became clear to both of them that I had intentionally failed my exams in order to be pulled out of Brébeuf. After all, I had just scored 100 percent on the make-up exam. What other explanation could there be?

I wanted to disappear into a crack in the floor. I was looking at my father from the side, and the way he was biting his lips made it pretty clear that his fury was about to consume him. Words coming out of the principal's mouth weren't reaching his ears. His inner rage had cut him off from the outside world. We left the school without exchanging a single word or glance.

On our way back home, I decided I wasn't going to hide anything anymore. I took what was left of my courage in both hands and got everything off my chest: my deliberately failed exams, my deep will to leave Brébeuf, my firm intention to go back to competitive hockey. My father was seething with rage, but he didn't say anything.

The day after, my dad accepted the deal I put on the table. I would go to the Anjou school and he would let me play in the league of my choice as long as my grades averaged 90 percent or more.

Thus, I started my third year of high school along with the Bantam CC training camp. It wasn't the level at which I wanted to play, but considering the two preceding years, it was clear progress. My determination had never weakened, and now I could feel the zest of life back in me.

Right at the beginning of training camp, the coach, Pierre Cournoyer, spotted me. He had a great influence on me, helping me improve some aspects of my game while working hard psychologically to bring my confidence to its pinnacle. I was totally convinced I had all the skills needed to play with teenagers at that level. But I couldn't deny that the two years I'd spent at Brébeuf, far from all competitiveness, had somewhat damaged my confidence.

After only four games with the Bantam CC team, I had accumulated sixteen points. Alain Faucher, the head coach of the Bantam AA Bourassa Express, approached me. He'd seen me play a couple of times and said he wanted me to join his team. Playing in the Bantam AA league was a totally different kettle of fish. It would mean more training, more personal involvement, and more travelling. And that would mean less time for school. There was no way my father would approve. I didn't have to talk to him to know he would oppose this plan of mine.

My only solution: play with the Bourassa Express without telling my father.

Everything went well during the season. I was one of the best players on the team. My grades were skyrocketing to an all-time high. I was fulfilled. And so was my father, completely unaware of the subterfuge going on.

I couldn't hide my secret hockey life from him forever, though. It was at the end of February 1992. The team was supposed to enter a big provincial tournament in Trois-Rivières later in March. That would mean I'd have to miss a couple of school days in order to be part of it. And Lord knows I wanted to be there. The Cité de Laviolette Classic, as the tournament is called, was one of the major Bantam events throughout the province of Quebec. But I was doomed. My father would never understand or accept it.

As a last and desperate resort, I went to see my coach and told him everything about my situation. He promised me he would talk to my father. I shrugged, telling myself Faucher didn't have the slightest idea of what he was getting himself into. I wasn't expecting anything to come of their meeting, other than another encounter with my father's volcanic temper for having played with the Express without letting my father know. So when I learned, two days later, that my coach had finally managed to convince my father to let me go to that tournament, I nearly fainted.

Even better, I didn't get punished for lying. I was floored. And when I got over my surprise, I had to think the whole situation through again. I realized my father had probably known about it all since the beginning but had never said a word because I was getting exceptional grades.

In addition to all this good news, my coach informed me that he knew scouts from the Quebec Major Junior Hockey League (QMJHL) had an eye on me. I was drunk with delight.

Three weeks later, a journalist from the daily paper *La Presse* called and told me he'd been asked by his boss to write a short article portraying me in their sports pages. Here's an excerpt from what I told him in this article, published on March 18, 1992: "It's quite a strange feeling to draw the attention of both the fans and the scouts to myself; I was never used to that ... My coach Alain is very demanding, but I believe it's the only way to improve oneself. Even when our team wins, if he's not satisfied with some aspects of our game, we're sure to know it."

We won the Trois-Rivières tournament. I was voted the most valuable player of the whole event. The Bourassa Express also got to the semifinals in the Montreal/Metro Circuit and in the provincial championships of the Ice Hockey Quebec Federation.

The QMJHL's draft was just around the corner, and rumours circulated that I was to be among the happy few. Not that bad for a young boy who'd never really got to play in an intercity league before. I remembered that at the same time the previous year, I was spinning my wheels in a mediocre high school league and for a Bantam A team ...

•

The big day finally arrived: May 30, 1992. The draft was held at the Maurice Richard Arena in Montreal. Seated with my father and brother at a table right in the middle of the assembly, my hands were all sweaty and I was trembling with excitement. Would I be drafted this very year, even before entering the Midget League? Faucher really did believe in my chances. So did I, but I remained cautiously optimistic. After all, the previous years had brought their fair share of frustrations, and I knew I'd be a fool to assume anything.

While sitting in that hall, I also couldn't help thinking about racism. Even though it had almost completely disappeared from my life since we'd left Sorel, I was suddenly nervous about it. Was it going to reappear right here, right now, when least expected?

Like a weathervane, I was feverishly looking all around me. The decorum and the scale of that event were quite impressive for a sixteen-year-old boy. I couldn't believe that it was actually I, Georges Laraque, sitting here among the ones who would one day shine in the QMJHL. I was also wondering how many of us would ever make it to the NHL. And would I be one of them?

Sitting next to me, my father didn't quite understand what was truly going on. His eyes were filled with incredulity. I knew he was asking himself what all those people were here for. Coaches, general managers, parents, scouts, players' friends and girlfriends, onlookers—a cross-section of the Quebec hockey world was crowded into that room. I was looking at him. He was proud, I could tell. Was he the guy who had nearly crushed my dream?

The first four rounds went by without my name being called. Anxiety was now my first name. I was slumping into resignation, slowly beginning to accept that I had come this far only to fail. A draft-eligible sixteen-year-old has to be taken in the first five rounds, and I was running out of teams that might call my name. But just when I was ready to pack my things up and leave the place, the St. Jean Lynx chose me. An amazingly huge weight went off my shoulders. I proudly raised my head. I stood up. So did my dad. We looked at each other straight in the eyes for a few seconds. He took my hand, shook it, and with a gentle pat on my back, sent me to the stage where people from the Lynx were waiting for me. It was the most beautiful day of my life.

TORMENTORS, THANK YOU!

5

That summer I sacrificed everything in the name of my dream. Friends, family, and even just hanging out like any other teenager—I no longer had time for any of that. I was totally concentrated on hockey, and that's what I spent my time on. There was no way I was going to disappoint my new team or the coach who was waiting for me in major junior. And above all, there was no way I was going to disappoint myself.

As I've already mentioned, I never had to train a lot to keep on muscle mass. So I didn't have to spend my summer grunting and pumping iron in the gym to get ready for the season like a lot of guys whose role is to throw their weight around on the ice. Instead, I've always worked on my cardio, and in the summer of 1992 I played soccer at quite a high level. Combined with my regular training program, soccer helped me show up at camp in August in the best of shape to start my first season.

First off was a series of physical tests. The team wanted to know what kind of shape I was in. I suppose those tests could tell them not only what kind of physical specimens they had to work with, but also who had taken things seriously enough to get ready for the season. In any case, I wanted to make an impression, and I think I did. The head coach and the physical trainers seemed pretty impressed by my results. Never before had I felt so strong and in such great shape.

Even though I was only sixteen at that time, it quickly became obvious that I'd be making the team that year. I hardly have to say that it was yet another dream come true. But like previous dreams come true, this one came with a headache. Since I was still a minor, my father had to sign a release for me to be able to join the team. The release had to do with the type of visor I would be wearing.

Since my first days in organized hockey, I had always worn a full shield or cage, like every other kid. Now that I was about to play major junior, I'd be able to wear a visor for the first time (that is, only half my face would be covered, from my forehead to my nose). That's just what players wear in junior. Watch any major junior game—the only guys not wearing visors are the goalies. So it seemed pretty obvious that my father would sign the release. Why wouldn't he?

It wasn't as though he had to go out and buy me a visor. Everything was now going to be supplied by the team. As soon as a QMJHL team drafted you, they paid for everything you needed to play the game. All my gear, from the helmet to the skates, along with my travel expenses, my rent, my food—everything would now be paid by the St. Jean Lynx. I was even going to receive a $40-a-week stipend.

The only thing my father had to do so that I could become a full member in the QMJHL was sign that little release. I was going to be a part of the elite young players in the province. My life was just about to change for the better, and it would have been hard to determine which was racing more, my heart or my mind. I was about to climb the first of the last steps of that stairway to my dream, as I used to call it.

But things were never that simple if my father had a role to play.

The release my dad had to sign wasn't a complicated document. He just had to agree not to bring legal action against the QMJHL if ever I was to be the victim of an accident on the ice. That was it. Only a few words. But those few words implied enough threat to keep him from putting his signature on that piece of paper.

According to him, the moment I took off my cage, the part of my face not covered by the visor would be exposed to every slapshot fired anywhere near me. I could be mutilated, disfigured, concussed. Who knows? Maybe killed. Mutilation and death weren't written into the release, but that's sure what he read.

In his mind, that was it. That was the end of the matter. He wasn't going to sign that piece of paper, no matter what it meant to me. What had I done to gracious God to deserve a father like this? It is impossible to exaggerate how exasperating he could be. I think I've already made it clear how racism could infuriate me by frustrating my dreams. But the racism I had to suffer throughout my youth couldn't hold a candle to my dad when it was time to put a screwdriver in the spokes of my progress.

There I was. All set. Ready to play. The Lynx wanted me on the team right now. I was about to begin my very first season in the "Q." The only thing missing to make that dream come true was just a little signature at the bottom of a release.

That piece of paper was never signed.

When my father announced his decision, my jaw dropped to the ground. I was devastated. I went up to see my coach—or at least the guy who *would* be my coach—and explained the situation to him. His name was Normand Flynn. Six months earlier,

Alain Faucher had managed to convince my father to let me go to the tournament in Trois-Rivières. If Faucher could accomplish the impossible, maybe Flynn could too. I tried to remain positive. History would repeat itself.

As I've said, my father was authority embodied. To his kids, he was an almighty figure. Coaches and teachers came in second—there was no way around that. He wasn't accountable to me. He didn't have to listen to a word I had to say, and he never did.

Still, I thought my coaches would at least appear to him as responsible adults. They couldn't bend him to their will, but maybe one or two of them might be capable of making him see things differently. After all, those people played an important part in my life in some activities he didn't have a clue about. Alain Faucher was able to corner him six months before; Normand Flynn would succeed in doing so too.

Well, he tried anyway. He told my father that the disclaimer he had to sign was just a small detail. Everybody signed it. He added that the gruesome accidents my father was worried about never happened.

My father asked him why I couldn't just play with a full-face shield. Not a crazy question, but also not a question you'd ask if you had watched a lot of major junior games. Flynn told him that with the size I was, as a guy who was in the lineup to play a tough game, I would be the laughingstock of the whole league.

I guess that wasn't the right answer to soothe my father's concerns. History didn't repeat itself.

Even one of my would-be teammates, Samuel Groleau, approached my father and tried to convince him. In vain.

Nothing would budge my father from his position. I was crazy with anger. I told him I didn't need his approval, that my mother would sign the release. But I was bluffing, since the league needed both signatures anyway. He had veto power over my first year of junior. And he used it.

I had no other option but to go back to Anjou and play Midget AAA for the team that was affiliated with the sport study program of the Édouard Montpetit high school.

•

Things didn't go great for me that year, as I really didn't get along with my coach, Pierre Pelletier. And life at home was even more complicated. My father and I would argue all the time. And I mean *all* the time. I just couldn't get my mind off the fact that he hadn't signed that disclaimer. This was the guy who had prevented me from playing major junior. I knew for sure I would have made much better progress if I had joined the Lynx. No matter how things went at school or on the ice, that year was filled with bitterness and rancour for me as I thought of where I *should* have been.

The summer after, I trained even harder. Getting ready for my second camp was my only goal. I had made the team the year before, and this time around I wanted to be an even better player. But I was still a minor. Was I training for nothing? Was my father going to sign the disclaimer this year? That question hung over me for months.

Then ... he signed it. I couldn't believe it. Of course I was happy to finally be able to play major junior, but I had mixed feelings about his decision. Why in the world did he sign it now and not last year? By signing it a year later, he was pretty much conceding that there had been no good reason to refuse to sign it the year before. He seemed to be admitting that I had missed out on a year of junior for *nothing*. I got even madder at him.

I couldn't understand his reasoning, and I still haven't understood it.

I moved to St.-Jean-sur-le-Richelieu at the end of August. I was ready to start my last high school year, but even more ready to play my first season with the Lynx. I was very nervous, but also totally confident that I had everything it took to make it all happen.

The intensity and speed of the game at the junior level really surprised me, though. The jump from Midget AAA to the Q is huge. In my last year as a midget I had stood out. Now I was on the ice with a bunch of other guys who had stood out just as I had. These guys could all skate and pass and shoot the way only the very elite midget players could. But there was one thing I could do that almost no one else could. I understood almost immediately that to make my dream come true, I would have to start fighting.

If I fought, I was on the team. If I fought, I was on the ice. And if I was on the ice, I could also contribute to the team's success by scoring goals.

That season I managed to get 22 points in 70 games, scoring 11 goals. My stats also showed an impressive 142 minutes in penalties. For the first time in my life, I wasn't one of the best players on my team. But I did succeed in finding my place among my teammates. Normand Flynn had a big role in helping me do that. He found exactly how to use the player I was to his full potential.

Would that be enough to manage my way up to the NHL one day? I couldn't tell at that time, but Flynn sure thought I had everything to make it that far. For that, I will always be grateful to him.

Right at the beginning of this first season, he explained to me the kind of player I would have to become to reach the top. He's the one who groomed me, who opened the doors leading to what my career would be. Looking back, I find it hard to remember the exact words he used to explain to a kid like me that I'd have to become a tough guy to fulfill my dream. But I quickly understood that he was putting me on another route to the place I wanted to be.

It's not an easy thing to communicate, telling a star-struck kid that he's not going to be the next Hart Trophy winner— everyone wants to be the guy putting the puck in the net. During my younger years, never would I have thought I'd have to become a tough guy to reach the NHL. Just a year earlier, I had been a leading scorer in my league. That's not to say that lighting up goalies in minor hockey means you're going to do the same when you move up a league—unless your name is Sidney Crosby or Alexander Ovechkin. However, you don't get tired of scoring goals, and you don't arrive at camp in junior thinking you're about to say goodbye to that part of the game. I'm sure it's the same for every guy who has ever dropped his gloves in the NHL—I bet every one of them was a sniper at some point in their minor hockey careers.

Still, I wasn't naive. It was during my Midget AAA year that I started to understand I would have to use my muscles in the future. Even though I had maintained an average of nearly a point per game, I noticed that puberty had kicked in for everybody and some of my teammates had grown to be faster and more dexterous than I was. I wasn't going to win with speed anymore. Luckily, there were other ways to win.

When I got to the QMJHL, I stopped comparing myself to the best scorers and started to watch what the other tough guys were doing. I don't just mean fighting. I mean I watched to see how many points they were getting. I didn't have to out-score the snipers. Those weren't the guys I had to beat. I had to out-fight the fighters. I knew that it would be those guys I'd have to outshine using my skills but also my fists to get to the NHL.

•

In order to put the odds on my side, I started looking for an agent who would look after my best interests. I must admit that this quest did little to boost my confidence. Nobody (and I mean *nobody*) wanted to represent me. There was simply no one out there who believed in my chances.

I knocked on a lot of doors that year, but they all remained closed. All but one. I finally met a guy named Fred Simpson who told me I had every chance in the world to play in the NHL one day. That was all I needed to hear.

A few years later, Fred would experience a lot of difficulties. His boiling temper and the unorthodox way he managed his businesses got him into trouble with some of the players he was working for. He ended up being sued for fraud and burned lots of bridges. Fred was no saint.

Nevertheless, the man really helped me in my first junior years. He had a great and positive influence on my development as a player and as a human being. At the end of my first season with the Lynx, it was Fred who suggested I participate in two summer training camps. I followed his advice, and that decision changed my career and my life.

First, I went to Ville Ste. Catherine, where I spent a month attending Claude Ruel's hockey camp. Ruel had been a coach for the Montreal Canadiens and was now working as a scout for the team. He was very old school in the way he ran his workouts and exercises, which was good, since he was focusing on the basic principles of the game.

It was simple stuff: stick-handling, positioning, getting our passes right on the tape. We also worked on handling the puck with our heads up, and practised the right way to take a hit—sometimes it's more dangerous to try to avoid a check than to absorb it. (If you've ever seen a lumbering defenceman bounce off a little forward he thought he was going to drill into the glass, you'll know how important it is to get your weight and balance just right when that bodycheck is about to be delivered.) None of it was fancy, but I wasn't preparing for the skills competition at the All Stars. And working on the simple things made a huge difference in my game. I may have scored a lot of goals in minor hockey, but I never said I had soft hands. For a player like me, going back to Hockey 101 as I did during that month had a very positive effect on the rest of my career.

The second half of that summer was even more memorable. After having gone back to the basics of hockey, I went to a camp held by former speed-skating Olympic medallist Mario Vincent. For almost a month I didn't touch a puck, but God did I ever skate! Edge control, lengthening my stride, acceleration from a standing start—my thighs were burning all day. But that's the kind of pain an athlete enjoys.

The techniques I picked up transformed my skating. I may not have been the second coming of Jean Béliveau, but I was getting around the ice a lot better. And that made a huge difference in my game. Ever wonder why it's often the best players who are the best open-ice hitters? You have to be a pretty great skater to time a big hit—in fact, that's more important than brute strength. You can't hit a guy if you can't get close to him. I didn't want to be chasing guys around the ice—I wanted to be making impact plays, and that meant being in the right place at the right time. Every summer after that I would go back to take power-skating lessons, even while I was in the NHL.

•

Fall 1993 had arrived. I entered the St. Jean Cegep to attend Social Studies classes. Not many people know that if hockey hadn't chosen me, I would have tried to become a lawyer. At the time, though, my second season was all I wanted to think about. I wasn't the same player I'd been a few months before— still in great shape, as big and strong as ever, but with new skills I never thought I could get. I may not have turned myself into Wayne Gretzky, but I'd learned so much that summer that everybody could see how much better a player I now was.

Normand Flynn, who was soon to be fired, congratulated me on my progress. His successor, Claude Therrien, gave me the same role as Flynn did. I had to make sure that our best players could play safely, without being annoyed by tough guys from other teams. As long as our players were safe, I was given ice to make a difference on the scoring sheet. I had the best of both worlds, and just loved it!

I'll take one game as an example. On October 21, 1994, we were playing against the Collège Français Titans. Not only did I score the second goal in a 3–0 win, but I also had the "plea-sure" of sending their tough guy, David Haynes, to the ground. I doubt there's any role on a hockey team more satisfying than in a game like that.

I had a very good start that season. It went so well, actually, that Mario Tremblay, former player and future head coach for the Canadiens, and journalist Yves Mallette wrote an article about me, entitled "When Lil' Georges Acts Like Lil' Guy." They were, of course, referring to the great Guy Lafleur. They quoted my former coach, Normand Flynn: "Georges is all stirred up these days! He plays inspired hockey. He has become one of the most respected players in the league. If he goes on playing like that, he sure will be one of the top prospects in next year's NHL draft. For now, he's the most popular player among the Lynx!"

A few days later, I had another great game. My teammates then did something that really touched me. As a surprise, they put up a crown over my rack in the team's locker room. I had just become the king of the St. Jean Colisée. I can tell you, no compliment a hockey player can get feels better than one that comes from his teammates.

Big daily newspapers started writing articles about me on a regular basis. My name kept showing up in the local papers. And I was reading everything that was written about me. I was also very curious about what those journalists had to say about the other tough guys in the league. I really wanted to know how I was doing compared to them. After all, they'd be the ones I would have to outshine in the next NHL draft.

What captivated me more than anything else during those years were the NHL Central Scouting Services (CSS) reports. I would devour them.

The CSS is directly affiliated with the NHL. Its goal is to follow every junior player around the world and rank them according to a number of criteria. The CSS analyzes not only the players' skills but also their potential to play a distinct role in the NHL. In other words, the CSS doesn't really rank players according to how *good* they are. It ranks them according to how valuable they can be to the team that drafts them.

Throughout the 1994–95 season, my CSS ratings kept going up. One night, as we were playing against the Sherbrooke Faucons, a dozen NHL scouts made the trip to St. Jean to evaluate me as well as one of our opponents, Christian Dubé.

When asked about my performance that night, Alain Chainey from the Anaheim Mighty Ducks said the following: "A guy like him won't be available after the second round. Scouts have an eye on him. If one team needs a player like him, they should move fast." All this attention was greatly motivating me to give my best, night after night, on the ice.

My stats showed an even better record than they had the season before. I played 62 games and scored 19 times for a total of 41 points. At six-four and 240 pounds, I had a lot of room to manoeuvre on the ice. I also didn't lose a single fight that year, winning most of them by KO.

The agents who had ignored me the season before were all knocking at my door now. But I wouldn't have been able to look at myself in the mirror if I'd abandoned Fred Simpson at that point—it was out of the question for me. He had been by my side since day one and knew from the start that I'd be drafted. And Central Scouting had proved him right. I was ranked among the top forty most promising young players. When the season ended, only one thing was left to do: wait for the July 8 NHL entry draft.

●

We went to Edmonton a couple of days before the actual draft. More than a dozen teams wanted to meet me before the special day. Fred had explained to me how important those meetings were. I was very anxious about them, but not because of my hockey skills. The thing that scared me back then was my ability to converse in English.

I had learned the language during my school years in Quebec. In other words, I stammered it more than I could speak it. Would I be able to understand what the people from the teams were saying to me? I didn't have a clue. But I managed pretty well, even though when I was asked if I had brothers and sisters I proudly answered, "Eighteen." The person looked at me with incredulous eyes. I thought he had asked my age. He laughed out loud when he realized my mistake.

Half of the teams I met then had a psychologist among their crew. Those doctors would ask us all sorts of rambling questions that, in my mind, were pointless. I answered them without thinking. I really couldn't understand what use they could make of the answers I gave them.

My agent told me afterwards that I should have paid more attention to those questions before answering them. Between two players of equal strength, teams would sometimes turn to the psychologists to come up with their decision.

I was of course tested in order to detect if I had taken any performance-enhancing drugs during my junior career. There were streams of rumours that I was using steroids. Nobody seemed to believe that I could carry that kind of mass without putting any illegal substances in my body. I wasn't annoyed by that testing frenzy at all. As a matter of fact, I took it as a compliment. I was also fascinated by all the high-class technology the teams were using to test me.

After every meeting, it was easy for me to know whether a team was interested in me or not—not only by the length of the interview process, but also by the way people would talk to me. The longest interview I had was with the Oilers staff. It lasted about an hour and a half. In succession, I met the legendary general manager, Glen Sather, the head scout, Kevin Prendergast, and finally the former Oilers tough guy, Dave Semenko. I was really impressed with the latter. Even now, Semenko's name is remembered with awe and respect, and when I met him the Gretzky years weren't so far away in time.

I came out of that meeting with great confidence, but Fred brought me back down to earth pretty quickly. Nothing was settled yet, and only on draft day would things be significant. I understood how right he was at the end of the day on July 8.

The NHL draft is an electrifying event, even on television. If you're there, it's still more dramatic. And if you're an eighteen-year-old kid from Anjou, playing in St. Jean, waiting to have your fate decided, it's like facing a jury.

Think of the devastation on a lot of guys' faces. A young player can be full of promise, ranked well by the CSS, and yet nothing guarantees that he'll be drafted, or when. I won't mention any names, simply because they wouldn't ring any bells for you, but I do remember some young players who were there for the draft in Edmonton. They came to Alberta with all their relatives. They arrived full of hope. They were so anxious to hear one or the other teams pronounce their names that the total distress and the cries that would go with it after the last round had ended without their names being called was really a pitiful thing to see.

For some of them it was the end of the road, the closing of their dream. Even before knowing how to write, they had started sacrificing everything to hockey. And now, on this very day, the game they loved so much and to which they had given everything was turning its back on them. Appalled, totally dispossessed of their sole ambition, they would have to invent for themselves a new destiny. The time had come to venture a totally new start in their life. New dreams, new hopes were now to be found. But when you've never dreamed of anything else but hockey, how are you supposed to do that?

As for myself, I was cautiously confident. I really had felt the Oilers' interest, but they weren't the only team that had showed they were favourably disposed towards me. Among these were the Montreal Canadiens. I was terrified they would draft me. Does this sound scandalous coming from a Québécois player? I must admit here that I *really* didn't want to play for the Habs. In my mind it was any team *but* the Canadiens.

I was very young and I knew I still had a lot of work to do in order to develop my potential to its fullest. My only goal for the years to come was to concentrate on working hard to progress as a player. And I really wanted to do it far from the media limelight. I didn't want to have to handle the Canadiens' heavy media pressure while trying to establish myself as a regular NHL player.

I was aware that nothing was worse for a Quebecer than to start his career with the Canadiens. To understand my point, just look at the departures of Maxim Lapierre, Guillaume Latendresse, and Pierre Dagenais, or even those of José Théodore and Mike Ribeiro.

This negative feeling I had towards the team was largely shared by most of the young players born in Quebec. And it still is. Of course, none of them would admit it loudly. On the contrary, they would all declare with a big smile on their face that their dream was to play for the Canadiens one day. Deep inside of them, though, it was the last thing they wanted.

When I openly said, just days before the draft, that I really didn't feel like playing for them, the Quebec media went berserk.

Behind the scenes, though, all the other players from Quebec would shake my hand and congratulate me for having the nerve to say aloud what they were all thinking.

To succeed in Montreal, a young player must be skilled for sure, but that's not enough. He has to have exceptional character and a very strong backbone. Patrick Roy had all of that. He had fame, he had success, he had everything a hockey player could want as a Canadien. And even in his case, it took only one game to send him packing in frustration. If a legend can be treated that way in Montreal, imagine what it's like for a young player taking his first steps in the NHL.

The Montreal Canadiens were and still are in a big dilemma. The fans, supported by the press, have always asked for more Quebecers among the team. And the organization was and still is working hard to satisfy that appetite, but it's facing huge problems, the main one being the fact that Quebecers don't want to play with the team.

•

I also had the sense that, besides Edmonton and Montreal, the Detroit Red Wings were interested in me. So, when the draft began, I was getting very nervous every time one of those three teams' picks was approaching. I was sitting there with my dad, my agent, and a good friend of mine, Patrick Côté, who was also managed by Fred. Minutes seemed like hours. The anxiety was nearly indescribable.

First came the Oilers' initial pick. Steve Kelly was called, a centre from Prince Albert, Saskatchewan. After that, the Canadiens chose Terry Ryan. I breathed a sigh of relief. The Red Wings were the last ones to draft a player in the first round.

They selected a very promising young Russian defenceman, Maxim Kuznetsov.

My heart was pounding. An irrational fright took control of my whole body and mind. There were eight rounds still to go, but I started panicking like crazy. What if I wasn't drafted? What if I'd been deluding myself all these years? What if those people who had been mocking my dream were right in the end? My whole youth was starting to look like a stupid gamble.

I looked at my father. He had never believed in my dream either. The fact that the St. Jean Lynx drafted me two years ago sure made him proud of his son. But did he start believing in my goal back then, or was he simply happy that hockey wouldn't cost him a dime anymore? In short, I was sitting there freaking out!

A few seconds after that turmoil started, Fred gently elbowed me in the ribs. I turned to him with distress in my eyes. He smiled at me, and with no further warning he said, "You're going to Edmonton, kiddo!"

"What?!? What makes you say this?!?" was all I could squeak.

He was so calm, just the opposite of me. He told me that the Oilers' staff knew exactly where we were sitting in the hall and that they had just made a sign to him. Minutes seemed now like days.

The Mighty Ducks chose right winger Brian Wesenberg. One more pick to go and the Oilers would take their turn. The Lightning then drafted defenceman Mike McBain. I held my breath. Was Fred right? Had he bluffed? My mind was all foggy and I couldn't concentrate on anything anymore. Allow me to repeat myself here: I was freaking out!

The sound of my own name jolted me out of my panicky reverie. When the Oilers took the microphone, I heard "Georges

Laraque!" and I literally snapped to attention. I looked all around me. My father, Fred, Patrick Côté. (Patrick was drafted six picks later, by the Dallas Stars.)

I still wasn't totally sure. Was it really my name I'd just heard coming from the upper stage? The noise of people clapping was intense. The rink was booming. We were in Edmonton and the Oilers had just drafted me as their second pick. They were cheering for me!

After a couple of seconds of feeling numb, and right before I was about to faint, I stood up and ran to the stage. I put the Oilers sweater on and started smiling blissfully. That smile didn't leave my face for the next several hours. I had just climbed the second of the last steps leading to my dream. Still, I wasn't there yet.

I knew I had to keep my feet on the ground. And Fred sorted me out: "If you think you're there, then you'll never get there." It was great to be drafted; it was one giant step, but it sure wasn't the last one. Despite all of Fred's flaws, his experience was exactly what I needed right then. He'd seen so many young players ruin their careers because they thought things would happen naturally after an NHL team drafted them. Fred explained to me that to be chosen by a team was more a great sign of confidence than a guarantee. "Scouts know you're not an NHL player yet. By drafting you, the Oilers simply told you they think you can rise up to that level. It's your choice now to prove them right by working and training like crazy." These were the wisest words I heard that day.

•

The 1995 draft saw a few soon-to-be stars get called. Among them were Jarome Iginla (Dallas Stars), Wade Redden (New

York Islanders), Bryan Berard (Ottawa Senators), Petr Sykora (New Jersey Devils), and Radek Dvořák (Florida Panthers).

Besides those happy few, more than two hundred players were called. Most of them have totally disappeared from the hockey world today. If we need any reminder of that, we need only look at some of the players drafted by the Canadiens that year: Miloslav Guren, Martin Hohenberger, Jonathan Delisle, Niklas Anger, Boyd Olson, Greg Hart, and Éric Houde. Toronto took Jeff Ware, Ryan Pepperall, Doug Bonner, and Marek Melanovsky. None of them would even have been in the draft if they weren't very, very talented players. These guys all had something special enough that an NHL team thought they could make the team better. But that wasn't enough. Interestingly, the Habs' best pick that year, Stéphane Robidas, who went on to play more than seven hundred games in the NHL, was still available in the seventh round, which means that the Canadiens had passed him over six times already—as had every other NHL team. Toronto's best pick that year was Danny Markov—and he was still available in the ninth round. Obviously, not many hockey executives thought he would make it, but he did, when more than a hundred guys taken ahead of him never played a game in the NHL. That goes to show that what you do after the draft means a lot more than what you do before.

•

We took the traditional photos. Glen Sather was standing in the middle, with Steve Kelly and me on either side. I was on cloud nine. Thousands of images were crowding in my mind.

I was remembering all the haters and dream-breakers that had crossed my path. I also took a moment to think about racism.

It was during that draft night that I finally realized how xenophobia had been the most powerful and efficient fuel to ever fill up my motivation tank. Without racism, I would never have become a professional hockey player.

So to those who insulted me during my youth, the ones who treated me like a slum-dog nigger, I only had one thing to say on July 8, 1995: Thank you!

PLAYING WITH THE
REAL MEN ... MAYBE

6

Everyone went out to the Malibu Club in Edmonton that night. The party was on among the drafted guys, and it went on. And on. There was a lot to celebrate, and maybe even more stress to blow off. So some guys went at it pretty hard until the wee hours of the morning. I didn't drink much and I won't name the guys who did, of course. But we had a good time—I'll say that much.

Steve Kelly had drunk a bit more than me. We went back to the hotel together, talking about our future aspirations. You won't find two happier, more confident guys than a couple of high draft picks wandering back from the bar on the day they were picked by a storied franchise.

The next morning, Steve and I had an early appointment with the Oilers' general manager, Glen Sather. That is, Oilers legend and Stanley Cup architect Glen Sather. We managed to arrive on time, but we must not have looked like the future of the franchise. We were in a pitiful state, nearly comatose. We thought we were in for yet another routine speech and a handshake, and we were already thinking of lurching back to the hotel to sink into bed.

But Sather had other plans for us.

As soon as we got into the GM's office, he introduced us to one of the Oilers' physical trainers, Curtis Brackenbury. He'd played about a hundred games in the NHL, with the Blues, the Oilers, and the Nordiques. Most of his playing career was spent in the now-defunct World Hockey Association (where he rang up 255 penalty minutes one season with the Minnesota Fighting Saints). After he retired from hockey, he became a very impressive triathlete. He was even able to complete the famous Hawaii Ironman in 1995.

Right after we shook hands, he asked us to follow him. I thought he was going to show us around the facilities and that we'd soon be on our way to pack our things and go back to our families and friends to celebrate the good news. Boy was I ever wrong. I was about to undergo the most intense boot camp I had ever experienced.

I couldn't help but think about all the other drafted players who were on their way back to the comfort of their homes to show off their new colours to their relatives. Maybe even the Habs' draft picks had their feet up. Meanwhile, Steve and I were about to sweat blood and tears for a whole week. And I'm not exaggerating here. That Brackenbury man was psychotic.

When he climbed onto his exercise bike, for instance, he would ride it for many hours as if he were being pursued by bears. He had to keep a small garbage can next to him when he worked out. Every now and then, under the virulence of the effort, he would vomit in it without even slowing down on the pedals. How would you like a guy like that for a personal trainer?

Brackenbury made us suffer as no one else ever had. Never had I pushed my physical limits so far. For instance, he would have us run fifty sprints of thirty metres each, which should be enough to leave most athletes begging for mercy and a long nap.

But for us that was just the warm-up to a Brackenbury-style ride on the exercise bike.

Even though we were then close to fainting, we would have to run several more kilometres up and down through the hills. Steve and I were in good shape when we showed up at the draft, but there was no way our bodies were up for what the Oilers threw at us. We couldn't believe what he was asking us to do. I went to bed every night before 8 P.M. during that camp.

We never asked anyone from the Oilers why they had subjected us to such a mad treatment and a mad man. It was probably Sather's idea. He must have known what we'd be going through under Brackenbury's supervision. I guess he wanted us to experience the pain and discipline you need to endure in order to play in the NHL—and what an experience it was! Just thinking about it today brings back memories of physical pain.

In the plane on the way back to Montreal, I admit I was a bit scared about what had just happened. I remember thinking that if those were the kind of workouts and training I had to submit to in order to play with the Oilers, I might as well quit the team right away. My body wouldn't be able to take it.

•

By the summer of 1995, my father felt he had endured enough of the Quebec winter and moved to Florida. I then went to live with my mother in Laval, on Montreal's north shore. I spent those two months cut off from the world, alone with my brother—the two of us were both training relentlessly. Six to eight hours a day, we did nothing but work out. I wanted to be in the best physical condition possible when the Oilers training camp started. Let's just also say the Brackenbury experience didn't leave me in an indolent state of mind. I didn't train with a bucket at my side that summer, but I sure didn't want to show up at camp and find out I was the only guy who needed one.

I didn't socialize much that summer. The only social activities I participated in were with my family. I noticed immediately how people had changed towards me. I'm not talking here about my mother, my brother, and my sister. All three of them were joyful about my new situation and kept congratulating me. But with the rest of the family, the attitudes were quite different. The very same people who'd been shrugging off my ambitions just a few months earlier were now looking at me with a mix of pride and envy. No one was shaking their head and telling me to come back to earth anymore. All of a sudden they were congratulating me, telling me they knew I would make it to the top. The best part was when they started giving me advice on how I should now behave to really make my dream come true.

In their eyes I'd been a lout and a good-for-nothing boy when I decided to leave Brébeuf to pursue my studies in a public high school. And now they were telling me I had made the right decision. The whole thing was such a joke, and since I was around my family so much that summer, I heard it everywhere I went. It was my own private joke, and I admit I enjoyed more than a few laughs.

Summer went by at the speed of light, even though I'd been counting the days before camp. During the day I was training like crazy, and at night I would lock myself up in my room to indulge in the most wonderful dreams. I was so anxious for it all to finally begin that it would give me butterflies in the stomach. Excitement, sure, but also apprehension—sometimes I had to try to think about something else just to lower my pulse.

•

The big day finally arrived. I took the plane to Edmonton, and some guys from the Oilers staff came to pick me up at the airport. They drove me to the hotel where I was to stay during the whole training camp.

The next morning would be my first meeting with all my new teammates and the technical crew. It was going to be held at the Edmonton Coliseum (now called Rexall Place), where the Oilers play their home games. I was so agitated that I lay on my bed for a few hours before finally falling asleep.

When I first entered the Oilers locker room, I was blown away. It was definitely one of the most intimidating moments of my entire life. I was used to seeing these guys on television, not in the same locker room as me. I knew I was going to be rubbing shoulders with NHL players, and I'd tried to prepare myself for this special occasion, but I must admit I couldn't believe I was now among them, sharing the same room.

All the Oilers' regular players were totally relaxed and laid-back. Especially Doug Weight, who kept joking around. I was inside an NHL locker room, not as an onlooker but as a player. I was shaking like a leaf and feeling so small in my skates. And yet the feeling was amazing.

I put my gear on and followed the other players down the hallway leading to the ice. For the first time in my life I was going to jump on the ice with no visor on. At this very moment, I really felt I had become a man.

And that meant nothing was going to be easy anymore.

Since my very first days in organized hockey I'd never really had to try to make a team. Sure, I'd been cut from teams in the intercity league more than once, but that had nothing to do with my skills. Until I started playing at the Midget AAA level, I'd always been one of the best players in the league, if not the best. If it hadn't been for plain and pure racism, I would probably have excelled even in the intercity leagues. During my junior years, even though I wasn't among the top players anymore, I knew my role and I knew I could do it efficiently. I was the toughest guy in the league.

But now the game was going to be very different. I understood that as soon as I saw the number of players on the ice. They were big, and fast, and skilled, and as focused as any of the players I'd ever shared the ice with—and there were a lot of them. Far more than the Oilers needed on opening night.

I would have to show no mercy. If I wanted to be a part of the twenty-two men who would start the season with the Oilers, I realized now that I would have to take another guy's spot. For the duration of training camp, I would have to adopt the every-man-for-himself approach.

That was a completely unknown feeling for me. I had always played hockey as a team sport, and my job was to help my teammates. The knowledge that the rules had changed in an important way, and that I now had to beat guys on my own team—and not only beat them, but come between them and their dreams—made me very uncomfortable. But there was no way around it. I knew every one of those guys was in camp to do the very same as me. It wasn't personal. Someone had to make the team. I was the youngest on the ice and would have to push some older players to the side.

The camp went very well for me, every day bringing its little bit of additional confidence. The pre-season games were getting near and I still hadn't been cut from the team. I started to believe I might be involved in at least one of them. I just wanted to sample the feeling of an NHL game, even if it was only the pre-season. And it happened, not once but three times: once against the Winnipeg Jets and twice facing the San Jose Sharks.

It was both exciting and intimidating. The very first time head coach Ron Low slapped my back gently to make me understand I was to be on the next shift, I'm positive my heart missed a beat. I was as ready as I could ever be—but I also wanted to disappear.

I saw the players coming back to the bench, I jumped over the boards, and a split second later, there I was on the ice. The feeling was incredible. The sheer scale of the building and the size of the crowd were things I could never have anticipated. The fastest and most physical ballet was spinning around me. I can't remember, even today, if I got to touch the puck on that first shift.

To be honest, playing as a right winger on the fourth line was suiting me perfectly. I saw no drawback in the fact that I was playing only four to five minutes a game. I felt like the luckiest guy in the world. I had the best seat in the rink, and got to hop over the boards from time to time. But I admit, I enjoyed those games watching from the comfort of the bench much more than when I was on the ice.

Every shift made me nervous. I never knew what was going to happen. Was I going to have to fight? Fights are pretty common in the pre-season, as young guys are trying to make an impression and the score doesn't mean as much. Whenever I was on the ice, I had to keep looking over my shoulder, watching for the guy who could challenge or attack me at any moment. In other words, every time I was on the ice, I couldn't wait to get back on the bench.

•

The first trip I made with the Oilers was to Winnipeg to play the Jets. Since we were a Canadian team, and not the most well off among them, we would travel by plane, of course, but on regular flights.

For the Winnipeg trip, we would leave Edmonton in the morning to come back the morning after the game. When I arrived at the airport, the other players looked at me in a strange way. They all had a small shoulder bag with them in which they had put the strict minimum for the trip.

I hadn't thought for a moment how brief our trip would be. So I had filled my huge, ugly brown suitcase and lugged it along. All my clothes were in there. Since I couldn't bring it on the plane, I was the only one who had to check his luggage. My teammates joyfully mocked my suitcase and me. But the laughter faded in the Winnipeg airport, where the team had to wait while my suitcase made its way to the luggage carousel. I was feeling pretty stupid, and my teammates were in no mood to change my mind.

When we came back after the game, I fell asleep on the plane for a couple of minutes. When I woke up, I immediately noticed that people on the plane were staring at me with big smiles on their faces. Others were whispering to each other before guffawing. I couldn't understand what was going on, so I was stupidly smiling back at them. There I sat for more than an hour like the big, dorky kid I was, grinning like an idiot before the urge to scratch my head allowed me to finally let the cat out of the bag.

While I had been napping, Bryan Marchment had covered my head with whipped cream. It looked like I had some sort of cushion on my thick frizzy hair. It was his way of taking his revenge on me for the suitcase incident and the wait it had forced the whole team to go through. All the passengers and the plane crew then burst out laughing. It was probably my first time blushing.

•

After three weeks, the training camp was winding down, and to my great surprise I was still an Oiler. I had also made some very good friends among the players. My fists had often been used to their fullest potential during the three pre-season games I played. I was greeted with wild applause quite a few times, and I could sense that the core of the Edmonton fans had already adopted me. I guess they'd missed the presence of a real tough guy on their team since Dave Semenko had retired.

The local newspapers were writing nice things about me. Journalists would say that I had real potential as a tough guy but that I could also help the team without dropping my gloves. That was exactly what I wanted to do, and exactly what I wanted to hear. In short, the momentum was great and I sure wasn't complaining about it.

Yet Ron Low still had one last round of cuts to make, and I was pretty sure I would be among the ones leaving. He met every player individually to let us know our fates. For a player, whether you're a rookie or a guy who's been around the league for a while and is fighting for a spot, to have your future laid out in an interview like that is humbling and terrifying. Up to that point you've been in control of your own destiny. But now it's in someone else's hands.

At least that's the way it usually works. When my turn came, I wasn't expecting anything. I'd had a great camp but I was still very young. I really had no idea of the kind of plans Low had for me. But one thing was certain: whatever they were, I had already made up my mind where I wanted to play that season, and there wasn't a lot Low could say that would change it.

He started our meeting by complimenting me. He congratulated me on my performance in camp. He said I had made progress in every aspect of the game, that I had a good work ethic, and that I was quick at understanding what he expected from me. What player doesn't want to hear that? He ended his long series of compliments by telling me he wanted me to start the season with the team.

And what player wouldn't want to hear *that*?

Well, me. I heard myself respond to his invitation to suit up for the Oilers on opening night by saying that I would prefer to go back to junior. I told him I wanted to refine my technique, that I wanted to gain in maturity before putting on an Oilers sweater.

He was stunned. He really couldn't believe it. He had just shattered the dreams of dozens of guys who would do just about anything to make the team. And here was a kid saying thanks but no thanks.

I wanted to go back to the junior league. He accepted my decision, but I could see he thought I was crazy. I've never talked about that discussion with anyone, nor have I ever told anyone the *real* reason why I turned down Low's offer.

All the things I told him to justify myself were in fact pure lies to hide the real truth. There was only one reason I wasn't going to play in the NHL that year and it had nothing to do with the excuses I gave him. That reason?

Fear.

I mean real terror. It took hold of me during one of the pre-season games and never left me.

Those games didn't mean anything to the teams as far as their standings were concerned. For guys like me, though, they meant everything. I had to "seduce" my coach every time I was on the ice. I was there to impress him, and for a young tough guy like me, that meant proving I was fearless.

On the night I learned about pure fear, we were facing the San Jose Sharks on our home ice. I went through their statistics, just to know what tough guys I would be lining up against. Maybe I shouldn't have looked. Because I saw a name that sent chills down my spine.

Dave Brown.

I couldn't help but remember the night when, as an Oiler, he broke Calgary Flames tough guy Stu Grimson's face. That's Stu Grimson, himself a legendary heavyweight. What an awful fight that was. If Brown could do that against The Grim Reaper, what was he going to do when he squared off against me?

Game time seemed to approach like an oncoming train. There was no getting out of the way. There I was, shaking on the bench, waiting for my first shift. Then came the coach's tap. I had to go over the boards and make my way to the faceoff.

I lined up shoulder to shoulder with Dave Brown. I could feel his breath on my face. I'm sure he thought I would provoke him. After all, I was a young, wannabe tough guy. I was trying to take my place in the NHL and the best way to do it was to fight guys like him.

If only he knew. I was so scared of him I could barely breathe. I was drenched in sweat. I stared at the ice between my skates, hoping he wouldn't notice me; I was bent over so far, waiting for the referee to drop the puck, that I could see my own goaltender between my legs. I couldn't fight him! It was impossible for me to grapple with such a monster.

I managed to get out of the situation by fighting a young guy like me, a Swedish player named Fredrik Oduya. I received a big round of applause for that fight, which was settled with only one punch.

But I didn't feel like a winner. My job was to intimidate the Sharks, and yet Dave Brown hadn't even had to look at me to intimidate me. I had to reconsider what I'd been aiming for all this time. Was I really built to be an NHL tough guy? Did I really want to spend my life fighting these guys? After facing off against Dave Brown, I couldn't even think about being one of them anymore.

Anyway, one of the mysteries of Ron Low's coaching career has just been solved. Reading these words, he now knows why I refused his offer that year.

In junior, my reputation was more than established. I was the toughest guy around. I was the most dangerous player to deal with. Guys may have felt about me the way I felt about Dave Brown. But in the NHL, the name on the back of my sweater didn't scare anyone. And having been on both sides, I knew better than ever that a reputation was more intimidating than a heavy fist. And a reputation is not an easy thing to get. Was I really ready to go through the battles it would take to make tough guys think about the name on my sweater?

I was even starting to miss wearing a visor ...

The pre-season was a reality check. I already knew that getting drafted meant nothing. It means you have talent, but it takes more than talent to stick around. Oduya was one of those guys, for instance. Was that going to be my fate, too?

My mind was all smeared with doubts after that game. If Dave Brown had provoked me that night, trust me, I simply would have fallen to the ice and turtled.

So I went back to junior, where I could feel secure. Would I ever come back to the NHL?

I frankly didn't think so.

OUT OF THE NIGHTMARE 7

Even though I had refused to start the 1995–96 season with the Oilers, I got to sign my very first professional contract just a few hours after that decisive meeting with Ron Low. Three years and $1.2 million. It also came with a signing bonus of $275,000—and a lot of gossip when I got back to Laval.

The draft had changed my family's perception of me, no doubt about that. However, it was nothing compared to the effect that huge amount of money was going to have.

I changed, too. Even before going to Laval, where I was to join my new team, the Titan, I knew my life had just taken a new and irreversible turn. The good and carefree life I had experienced in my junior years was over. For the second time in a month, I felt I had become a man.

On paper, I was now a hockey millionaire. Members from my wider family were now trying to get closer to me. Acquaintances tried to become best friends. I wasn't the same Georges Laraque anymore. The nice, funny guy who used to make $40 a week playing junior hockey had turned into a man sought after for all the wrong reasons, and I really wasn't sure I liked that new status. The one place I didn't have to worry about all that was in the gym. It was a good thing I had to train like crazy in order to keep progressing. The more time I spent working out, the farther I managed to stay from the vultures.

My first purchase was a Chevrolet Jimmy. Not a really glamorous vehicle, I admit, but I felt pretty hot being able to buy myself a new car with my own money. And even hotter after having paid for it in cash and the balance of my bank account didn't seem to have moved.

As a total teenage moron, I equipped it with a ridiculously powerful sound system. I don't remember exactly, but I'm pretty sure it cost me more than the truck itself. It was stuffed with amplifiers and speakers. They were everywhere, under the seats, on the dashboard, on the doors, even on the ceiling. I had to install a second battery under the hood just to have enough power to make all this stuff work. Added to that, I put in five or six fans to keep all that equipment from overheating. Ridiculous.

When my brother and I would cruise down the streets of Laval or Montreal, we had to wear earplugs so we could stand the noise. The sound and vibrations of the bass would literally penetrate our bodies. We were so cool, we thought. When stopped at a red light, drivers around us probably thought the bolts and rivets were about to vibrate right out of their cars. My mother would hear me coming back from miles. Eighteen, pockets bulging with money, completely unaware of what a jackass I must have seemed.

•

When it came to hockey, though, I was all business. I played only 11 games with the Laval Titan, scoring 8 goals for a total of 21 points and spending 76 minutes in the penalty box. And I'd managed to get those statistics despite a sharp pain in one of my knees that made me limp. I had to take painkillers before every practice and game to be able to skate.

I was then traded to the St. Hyacinthe Laser. As soon as I got there, I went to see a doctor to have my knee checked. After a series of tests, they finally found out that I had a ripped meniscus. Since I was under contract with the Oilers, the team flew me to Edmonton to have my knee operated on. I then came back to St. Hyacinthe for physio. I missed a little bit more than two weeks of hockey because of that.

The Laser was going nowhere during that season, and I started thinking I was wasting my time. It became obvious pretty quickly that we would have to fight just to make the play-offs. And thinking about playing at the bottom of the Q when I could just as easily have been playing for the Oilers didn't make it any easier to swallow some of the disappointments our team went through. But all I had to do was think about Dave Brown to calm myself down and soothe my regrets.

The trade deadline was quickly approaching. I wanted to move away from St. Hyacinthe to join a better team. I wanted to play with a team that could take a run at the league championship and maybe challenge for the Memorial Cup. Only two teams had a hope of either: the Hull Olympiques and the Granby Prédateurs.

The first one had no need for a player like me since they had one of the toughest guys in the whole league, Peter Worrell. The Prédateurs kept the door open, but they didn't make the move immediately. Yet if Worrell made me unattractive to Hull, he was probably the guy who kept Granby interested in me. A lot of journalists and analysts thought Granby couldn't beat Hull precisely because of Worrell. If Granby was going to advance, they would have to be Worrell-proof.

When the deadline date arrived, though, I still was playing for the Laser. We were leaving for Val-d'Or to meet up with the Foreurs. I figured I'd be spending the rest of the season with the Laser, and took the bus with my teammates. I never arrived.

Halfway there, in the town of Mont Laurier, we stopped for lunch. Just as we were about to get back on the road, a phone call came in. I had been traded to the Prédateurs.

I said goodbye to all my teammates, telling them that I hoped to see them again in the NHL. They left for Val-d'Or, abandoning me in Mont Laurier. Somebody from the Prédateurs organization was supposed to come and pick me up to take me to Drummondville, where Granby had a game the very same night.

I was on the road most of the day and the temperature was awful. When I finally arrived in Drummondville the game had already started. In fact, the second period was about to end. I was totally burned out. My legs felt like marshmallow. I certainly didn't have my mind set to hockey.

I was sitting on a bench in the locker room when I heard the siren announcing the end of the period. My sweaty new teammates entered the room. They all seemed very happy to see me and warmly welcomed me. The coach, Michel Therrien, did the same.

Just as I was about to go back on the bench to let them recover a bit and discuss the strategies they would use in the remaining period, Michel Therrien asked me to put on my new uniform. In his eyes, my presence on the bench could make a real difference. He told me that the guys had been really happy when they learned I'd be playing the rest of the season with them. As he explained it, he figured that having me on the bench during the third period would be a spark for the guys.

I dressed in no time while the other players were looking at me. Granby had a great team that year, with players like Francis Bouillon, Jason Doig, and Benoit Gratton. Therrien then repeated to me what I'd previously heard from journalists: that the team really needed a tough guy like me to protect the skill players and to make sure our opponents respected them. He mentioned the Hull Olympiques and Peter Worrell. I suddenly realized that I'd never played against him or fought him.

In any case, we made our way out to the ice and I came out of the gate in the sweater of my fourth team that season. I was looking forward to taking in the third period from the comfort of the bench. But Therrien had tricked me—he had no intention of leaving me on the bench. I was on the ice for the opening faceoff. While we were skating around our zone before the beginning of the period, I saw one of my good friends at the other end of the arena: Joël Thériault, who was playing for Drummondville.

Joël and I had spent quite a lot of time together during the summers. He'd been drafted the same year as me, chosen by the Washington Capitals. He was also a tough guy, but we had never fought each other, mainly because we were friends.

The summer before, though, he'd told me that we'd have to fight sometime during the upcoming season. Members of the Capitals organization had told him that they thought he was scared of me and that that was the real reason why he'd never dropped his gloves against me. I told Joël that if it could help him in his career, I would do it. As strange as it sounds, I promised to do him the favour of punching him in the face. But I never would have thought he'd choose that particular game to provoke me.

He skated up to the face-off circle to get ready for the puck to drop. I joined him there, thinking he wanted to say hello. Well, he sure did say hello, but right after the courtesies he told me to get ready to drop the gloves because some Washington scouts were sitting in the stands. I was totally stunned. How could he do that to me, knowing the day I'd just had?

I became very nervous. Joël was definitely one of the toughest players in the whole league, and I was far more interested in taking a nap than throwing the dukes. More than that, the game was shown on television—and who wants to get beaten up on TV? I really wanted to give a good impression for my first game with Granby, but given the way I felt, I really didn't know if I'd be able to compete against Joël.

As soon as the ref dropped the puck we both backed up a bit, took off our helmets, and dropped our gloves, while the stands buzzed with anticipation.

It went very well for me. We were never the same friends afterwards.

•

With the Prédateurs I felt I'd come back to life. We had a terrific team—a mix of very complementary players and a team spirit solid as a rock. As for Therrien, he was one of the best coaches I'd ever had. He was such a great motivator. And what he did before our first game against the Olympiques after I joined the team was eloquent proof of his ability to lash his troops.

My teammates had been waiting for that moment for a long time. As good as Granby was, Hull was the one team they could never manage to beat, mostly because Worrell seemed to be able to call all the shots. Our players spent the games against Hull looking over their shoulders for the menace of Worrell. My teammates really believed I was the solution.

Two days prior to that confrontation between the two teams and right before a practice, Michel Therrien called me into his office. Adopting the most solemn tone of voice, he said the following: "I don't want you to fight Peter Worrell."

I was stunned by his words. I shouted back, "WHAT! Everybody is saying that you traded for me specifically for that reason!"

He looked sheepish and a bit embarrassed as he said, "I know, Georges, you're right, but the risks are too high. Because if you lose your fight against Worrell, the troop's morale won't be able to deal with it."

A little bit more stunned than earlier, I yelled again, "WHAT! If I lose?!? What do you mean, if I lose?!? It's absolutely out of the question. I'm going to give him the biggest lesson he's ever received!"

He looked at me, smiling: "Tell it to the guys then."

My mind switched on. He had all but scripted this whole conversation. It was a tactic. He'd made me angry simply in order to motivate me so that I could motivate the guys afterwards.

At practice, he didn't mention our little meeting at all. But when the workout ended, he gathered everybody at centre ice and told my teammates that I had a message for them. I started yelling, "Guys, tomorrow we're playing the Olympiques! And what I have to tell you is that I'm going to break Peter Worrell's face so good, his mother won't recognize him afterwards!"

I started smashing my hockey stick on the ice. My teammates began yelling at the top of their lungs while I was pounding my stick to bits. That's what I call Motivation 101.

Game day was February 11, 1996. Newspapers knew it was a preview of the league finals, and most of the articles I read couldn't help talking about the inevitable heavyweight bout that was meant to happen between Worrell and me.

The stands were jam-packed. The atmosphere was electrifying. Fans were all standing up. Thirty-four hundred people shouting, holding up signs, hundreds of them massed along the glass.

I didn't want to waste a second. On my first shift, less than two minutes into the game, I headed straight for Worrell and provoked him. He knew it was coming. He was ready. But the fight was pretty short. Let's just say everything went fine for me.

I want to open a small parenthesis here. I'll talk a bit more in a later chapter about what it's like to be a tough guy in the junior league as well as in the NHL. However, I want my readers to know that there's a huge level of respect between the tough guys. That's why I'll never write that I've won a fight or that I've destroyed another tough guy, even if it was the case. I'll simply note that things went well for me. I'll never gloat. You'll make the link yourself. End of parenthesis.

More important than my fight against Worrell was the fact that not only did we finally beat Hull, we shelled them. We put seven pucks past José Théodore, who was in net for the Olympiques. Hull managed only two goals, with Frédéric Deschênes being exceptional that night in our net.

That victory put an end to a four-game losing streak against the Olympiques, coached by Robert Mongrain, and ended Hull's fourteen-game winning streak on the road. Speaking to the media after the match, Michel Therrien summed up his state of mind with this: "I feel like kissing the boys!"

Since my arrival with the Prédateurs, we'd become almost unbeatable, losing just a few games before the end of the season. We went on to end the QMJHL regular season at the top of the standings by defeating the Halifax Mooseheads 4–3 in front of our fans at the Léonard Grondin arena. And on our way there, we set several team records.

•

The Coupe du Président playoffs were also held at the Léonard Grondin arena, and our confidence was sky-high. We liquidated the Chicoutimi Saguenéens before winning in the finals against the Beauport Harfangs, then coached by Alain Vigneault. (The Harfangs had beaten the Olympiques in the semis.) I had great statistics during that series. But guys like me don't always have their biggest impact on the score sheet. After one loss against the Saguenéens, a game I missed because I'd injured my hand in a previous game, Michel Therrien told the press that my absence had made some of our players three feet smaller.

Far be it from me to say it was solely my presence that won us the championship and the Coupe du Président. But because I was with the team, our best players weren't worried anymore and could finally play their game. And that team had no shortage of talent. It takes more than one kind of player to build a championship team.

Being the champions and proud winners of the Cup, our next step was the Memorial Cup. We were invited to participate in the seventy-eighth edition of the tournament. The last time a team from Quebec had won was twenty-five years before, in 1971, when the Quebec Remparts had defeated the Edmonton Oil Kings.

The 1996 edition was to be held in Peterborough, Ontario. As well as the Petes, the host team, we would be competing against the Guelph Storm from the Ontario league and the Brandon Wheat Kings from the West. Because my injured hand hadn't completely healed, I wasn't able to fight. None of our opponents knew that, but still, I was worried about it.

We started as lions, even though, according to a TSN poll, we had no chance whatsoever to even think about winning the competition. But then we thumped Guelph 8–0. I had three assists in that game. The press and the public began to take us a bit more seriously.

Probably overconfident after that win, we got trapped by the Peterborough Petes in our second game. Since we'd scored so many goals in our first match, we simply forgot to protect our net and kept trying to beat the Petes playing river hockey. They beat us 6–3.

That loss was like a slap in the face that woke us all up. Our next game was against the Brandon monsters, as we called them. This team was loaded with the beefy farm boys who liked to throw their weight around. That was fine, though. We weren't going to run away—we had to beat them to get to the finals, and we were ready. Our 3–1 victory meant a berth in the final game.

It was a rematch with the Petes. We really wanted to bring that Memorial Cup back to Quebec after a quarter century of absence.

Two things were going to play in our favour in that game. First, we had learned from our mistakes in the first loss to the Petes; second, the local team was definitively overconfident. Add to that the exceptional performance our goalie, Frédéric Deschênes, gave that night, and you end up with a 4–0 win over them. It was a wild night, with fog blanketing the ice and moisture dripping from the glass. But both teams had to skate through it, and the Petes never used the conditions as an excuse. And anyway, we didn't care about the fog or the water in the goalie's crease. All we cared about was the fact that the Granby Prédateurs had just succeeded where the Olympiques had failed the year before.

A few days later, on May 20, the whole city of Granby gave us the warmest and most joyful welcome during a truly festive parade that I'll never forget in all my life. It was as if we had just won the Stanley Cup. Our fans treated us as heroes, and so did the rest of the province. Finally, a team was bringing the trophy back to Quebec.

That Memorial Cup victory was the crowning achievement of the most wonderful hockey season I had ever experienced. From the training camp with the Oilers to that trophy and from the signature on my contract to the Coupe du Président, everything I went through during the 1995–96 season bore the stamp of success.

I was ending my junior years in the most joyful state of mind possible. I had played 202 games and scored 58 goals for 122 points. The total amount of minutes I spent in the penalty box reached a total of 814.

I had conquered every challenge the hockey world had put in front of me.

Except the fear.

TWENTY-FIVE SECONDS AND THE WORLD WOULD CHANGE

8

The summer of 1996 was very short. I spent it resting a few injuries, training furiously—and feeling afraid of what the autumn would bring. And when I wasn't doing any of those things, I'd be cruising in the Jimmy with my brother by my side.

I did get some great news that summer. Dave Brown announced he was retiring from hockey. Brown, who'd succeeded Dave Semenko as the Oilers tough guy after years with the Flyers, had gone back to that same team before ending his career with the Sharks. His body wasn't in such great shape anymore after years of going toe to toe with the strongest, toughest players in the game, and he chose to hang up his skates instead of trying to push the limits too far.

I remember smiling at the idea that I'd never have to fight him. That was one guy I would never have to worry about. But then again, there were still guys like Bob Probert. And they weren't ready to retire ...

•

← I'm three years old …

↓ Five years old, my first steps on skates …

1

→ With my sister, Daphney, and my father, Edy, just before a track and field session …

↓ With my brother, Jules Edy

→ With my mother, Évelyne Toussaint, in 2010

↑ With Erin Kathan, the mother of Milayna Julia and Marcus Oliver (Debbie Boccabella)

← Laughing with the kids … (Perry Mah)

↓ Yes, my kids drive SUVs … electric ones, that is! (Perry Mah)

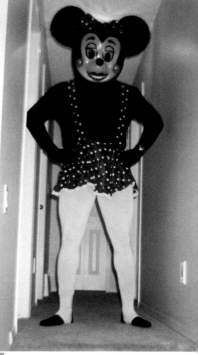

I've always loved Halloween!

↑ After the 1995 draft, with
Glen Sather and the Oilers' first
pick, Steve Kelly

5

Les Prédateurs et Georges Laraque font un maître

Le match n'était vieux que de 110 secondes lorsque Georges Laraque et Peter Worrell en sont venus aux coups. La victoire du 27 des Prédateurs devait d'ailleurs donner le ton au match.

"The game was only 110 seconds old when Georges Laraque and Peter Worrell came to blows. Laraque's victory set the tone for the game." (*Journal la voix d'est*)

↑ In 2010, the Granby Inouk (previously the Predateurs) honoured me for my days skating in the Q

With David Brosseau and Michel Massie and the Memorial Cup   →

6

←↓ With my teammate Dennis
Bonvie in Hamilton

The first Heritage Classic, on November 22, 2003 (Jeff Vinnick/Getty Images Sport/Getty Images)

I proudly wore the Oilers
uniform for eight years
(above: Perry Mah/
right: Gerry Thomas)

27

POSITION: Forward

**GEORGES
LARAQUE**
BORN: December 7, 1976
Monteal, Quebec
SHOOTS: Right   HT: 6'3"   WT: 235 lbs.

I started my second training camp with the Oilers in great shape. Physically, I was on top of the world. Mentally, it was a different thing, though. A year later, I had still not shaken off the fear that had chased me out of the NHL. In fact, the second time around I had even more to worry about. The year before, I'd had no expectations whatsoever when I arrived in Edmonton. I was young, with still one year to play in the junior league ahead of me. In short, I had no pressure. But in September 1996, everything was different.

I'd been flattered when Ron Low asked me to start the season with the Oilers. But one year later, that invitation was starting to look like a curse. I had impressed the team very favourably in 1995. What were their expectations for me in 1996? Plus, junior wasn't an alternative anymore. If I received another terrifying invitation to play for the Oilers, it would be impossible for me to tell them I needed one more season in some other league before joining the team. I was now a full-fledged professional with no exit possible.

That is, I worried that I might not live up to the team's expectations, and I worried at the same time that I might meet expectations so well that I would make the team.

So despite the excellent physical condition I was in, all that turmoil in my head finally began to harm my performance on the ice. I didn't have the greatest camp and I was soon sent to the Oilers farm team in the American league, the Hamilton Bulldogs.

My fear was still nagging me, even with the Bulldogs. The fact that my ex-captain with the Prédateurs, Francis Bouillon, had been invited to play in Hamilton despite not being drafted by the Oilers reassured me a bit, but even a familiar face in the dressing room wasn't enough to make the fear disappear.

We played our first pre-season game against the St. John Flames. During the warm-up before the game, I stared down the ice to appraise my opponents and tried to see how I stacked up against them. For some reason, the fright vanished. In fact, I started taking them lightly. After all, if these guys were so good, why weren't they playing in the NHL? My old swagger started to return.

Not for long, though. Those were the last moments of confidence I'd enjoy for a while.

I fought twice during that game. The first time was against a young player my age, Rocky Thompson. It was a unanimous loss for me by decision. During the third period, I went at it again, this time against an older player named Sasha Lakovic. His nickname was Pitbull. Trust me, in this bout, the Bulldog was no match for the Pitbull. My face took a beating. It wasn't a pretty sight.

When I got back on the team bus after the game I made my way to the very back. I was groggy and totally depressed. Everything had gone so well for me the year before, and now here I was thinking about quitting it all and going back home. The way I figured it, I had just lost two fights back to back against guys who were big, sure, but not as big or as tough as the guys who dropped their gloves for a living in the NHL. The logic was simple. If two guys from the American league could beat me, what was going to happen the day I faced Bob Probert or Stu Grimson? Was I going to keep dreaming of getting to the NHL just so I could turtle the minute a real tough guy invited me to dance? I figured my dream was done. My career was to end even before it started.

Francis Bouillon came to see me at the back of the bus to cheer me up. "What's going on, Georges? You were the toughest guy in the league last year!" He had never seen me beaten up like that and was doing his best to reassure me, to remind me of all the fights I had won not so long ago. But his words just dragged me further down—all that glory seemed lost in the past.

I was used to skating around as if I were untouchable. Other teams' tough guys would avoid eye contact with me in junior. One pugilist's trick is to smear Vaseline on your face to make the punches slide off harmlessly, and I used to laugh a little looking at the faces of other teams' tough guys shining from across the rink. And remember, junior hockey is a small world. I knew a lot of the other teams' players from around Montreal, and from time to time guys would tell me that their teams' enforcers were afraid of me.

But those were just kids.

The guys I was playing against now were men. Some of them were ten or fifteen years older than I was. And that's a lot of experience. I mean, they had facial hair. And when you're a kid, even that is intimidating. But what really made me nervous was seeing a guy with leather loops in his helmet for the chin strap to attach to. That can mean only one thing—that guy is a real fighter.

Anyone would rather punch his opponent in the head than in the helmet, so if a couple of tough guys get in close, they'll usually try to get the other guy's lid off. Since most helmets have plastic loops, all it takes is a stiff tug, and the helmet is off. So to keep his helmet on, a tough guy will replace the plastic with leather.

In other words, if you see a guy with leather straps, you know he's planning to get into a scrap and doesn't care who knows it.

And those guys were looking at me the way I used to look at the other kids in the Q. Just a few months before, I could look into a player's eyes, see fear, and know that I'd pretty much already won. Not anymore. No one was afraid of me now.

My reputation wasn't worth a dime. When you're a tough guy, if you don't have a reputation, you're in trouble.

I knew I was in trouble.

But there's always another game. And I was lucky. I wasn't the only tough guy on the team. I wasn't even the toughest guy on that team. There were quite a few guys in the Bulldogs that season who could take care of themselves, like Dennis Bonvie, for instance. Just to give you a small idea of the game he played, he ended that season with a total of 522 penalty minutes in only 73 games. As for me, I would accumulate 179 minutes.

In other words, the Hamilton Bulldogs were a scary team and not a lot of other players would take liberties with us that season. And when it did happen, I wasn't the only player who was supposed to sort things out. Knowing that all that responsibility wasn't on my shoulders, that other pugilists weren't skating around looking only for me, helped me rebuild my confidence. Game after game, it started to return.

It didn't hurt either that I started to win fights.

We didn't have what you can call a great season, with only 28 wins, 39 losses, 9 ties, and 4 losses in overtime. As for me, I'd scored 14 goals for a total of 34 points.

Beyond those stats, the main feature of the 1996–97 season was the huge rivalry that built up between us and the St. John Flames. From the very first pre-season game during which I was knocked down twice, to the series in which we beat them three games to two, every game was the scene of an avalanche of hits, scrums after the whistle, and stickwork that went unseen by the refs. And, of course, there was no shortage of fights.

A great percentage of the penalty minutes Dennis Bonvie, Martin Laître, and I accumulated that season had been earned during Bulldogs–Flames games, and to an equal extent against the St. John's Maple Leafs. The antagonism between the two Albertan farm teams had always existed and still does, but according to a lot of analysts and journalists, including Don Cherry, never had we seen such animosity between the players as we saw that year. I specifically remember one game during which even the coaches, Lorne Molleken and Paul Baxter, almost went at it themselves. One must say that neither of those two is a real stranger to the rough stuff. I want to take a moment to really thank Lorne for being so important in helping me develop into the player I was going to be. He had a major impact on my career.

The playoffs gave us the opportunity to make amends for our mediocre regular season. We managed to go all the way to the finals, where we lost in five games to the Hershey Bears. I played fifteen of the twenty-two playoff games, scoring only one goal for three points and twelve penalty minutes. But I didn't miss games because I was sitting in the press box. I'd been called up by the Oilers to fill out their roster during their own series.

It was a long way from that first game, when I was trembling at the back of the bus, fearing what I'd wanted my whole life. By the end of that season, I wasn't the same player anymore. Fear would still torment me, that was for sure, but I didn't lose a single fight after the first two against the Flames. And my reputation? By the end of that season, if a guy wanted to square off with me, he knew what he was getting into.

●

After the playoffs, I went back to Laval for the summer. It was much like the summer before. I still spent my hours working out, still cruised around, pumping out the bass in my truck. The one difference was that, even though I was still nagged by fear, I was now a bit more confident that I could possibly make it. I wanted my shot. The next step would be to fight some of the NHL "killers." I trained like crazy. The next season I wanted to play with the Oilers, not the Bulldogs.

That was the only goal I had in mind going into that third training camp with Edmonton. There were about seventy players at first, but after a few weeks, that number had been reduced to forty. I knew I had to make some progress in order not to be included in the next round of cuts.

I didn't make it. As hard as I tried, I was one of the last guys to be sent down, along with Jason Bonsignore. The latter had been the fourth overall pick in the 1994 NHL draft, a supposedly can't-miss prospect. He was big and talented enough to be compared with Mario Lemieux—he even looked like Mario. But I can tell you, Bonsignore was easily the best player I have ever seen in practice. He could do whatever he wanted with the puck. And he'd managed to play a few games with the Oilers in his first year as a pro. But here he was, on his way back down to the minors with me. He didn't whine or complain like a lot of other high draft picks might, but I could tell he wasn't happy. Bonsignore was an example of what I said earlier: that being a high draft pick is no guarantee of success. That scared me a bit. If a guy the scouts had once touted as a future superstar was having a hard time cracking the lineup, what were the odds that I was going to make it?

I also thought about Steve Kelly. The Oilers had picked him ahead of me, and he still wasn't with the big team full-time yet—he'd played only eight games the year before. I couldn't know it then—no one could, not even professional scouts—but Bonsignore and Kelly, both high picks and elite players, would never crack the Oilers roster and would spend most of their careers in the minors. That's how fine the line is between success and failure.

Sitting in the airport taxi on the way back to Hamilton, I started to cry. From sadness, of course, but mostly from rage. I was mad at myself, at the team, at the whole universe. I was beginning to think I would spend my entire career in the American league. Worse, I was already thinking about next year's training camp. It was going to be the last one of my three-year contract. I wanted to be there right away, to skip the season that was to begin in a couple of days. I'd already written off a year of my life by thinking only of what I would do differently the next year. In the meantime, I was scared to death just thinking I might fail.

After a few games with Hamilton, though, I received the phone call every minor-league player longs for. On November 13, 1997, the Bulldogs' big boss, Scott Howson, phoned to say I had to rush to the airport to make an afternoon flight to Edmonton. The Oilers needed me for their November 15 game against the Calgary Flames. He added that my stay with the big team would go on as long as they needed me.

At first, I thought he was joking. The reason for that is simple. Jokes were part of the Bulldogs culture. Virtually everybody was playing tricks on everybody. But Howson repeated what he'd said and told me I really had to rush if I didn't want to miss my plane. His insistence persuaded me that he really was telling the truth.

I packed my things in no time and went straight to the airport. I arrived in Edmonton a few hours later and met with the team at what used to be called the Northlands Coliseum when the Oilers were winning Stanley Cups, but was then called the Edmonton Coliseum. I had chosen the number I would wear beforehand: 27. It had always been my lucky number since my first days in organized hockey. When I was in Granby, I even bought it from another player. In fact, the only team I played for without wearing it was the Bulldogs. Scott Ferguson had chosen it before my arrival with the team and refused to let it go.

Ron Low gave me my new shirt as soon as I arrived in the locker room. He looked at the number and then smiled and gave me a wink. I didn't understand why he'd done that, not realizing that 27 was the number Dave Semenko had worn when he was riding shotgun for Gretzky, Messier, and Kurri. That number was powerfully symbolic and emotional for the Oilers and their fans.

And even though that had been a pure coincidence, the press and the public saw a lot more to it. Some even talked about fate. When journalists would ask me about it, I'd simply say that I hoped I would honour that number and be good enough to wear it. I would also tell them that my goal was to help the team the same way Semenko had a few years earlier.

My first regular-season game as an Oiler came against the Flames—always a physical game for the Oilers. I was all in knots before the game, but the worst thing I could have done was go out there and play tentatively. I wanted to get in on the forecheck and make the Flames defencemen hear my footsteps. And it was the forecheck that led to my very first NHL fight.

I came in at full speed on Jamie Allison and caught him totally flat-footed. I got my shoulder into him and sent him reeling. Todd Simpson, the Flames' captain, probably thought that was no way for a rookie to treat his defence partner, and he quickly demanded that I answer the bell. I knew he would, of course. So I was ready.

He was a big, strong guy and really knew what he was doing. He also seemed totally fearless. He didn't try to hug me or tie up my sweater, and the two of us went at it recklessly in a long, very tough bout. It was exactly what a hockey fight should be. The fans thought so too. The building was electric.

As a first fight in the league, it was perfect.

I stayed with the Oilers a couple of weeks, playing on the fourth line with two other players who'd been called back from Hamilton. Mike Watt was playing centre and Joe Hulbig was the left winger. The fact that we knew each other sure made it easier for us on the ice, and no competition existed between us—we weren't there to take each other's jobs.

Eventually I went back to the Bulldogs, but I was called up a few more times during the season, especially when the Oilers were to meet with particularly physical teams. I played only eleven games in Edmonton that season, and didn't manage to record any goals or assists in my stats book, though I did accumulate fifty-nine penalty minutes. But I did win all of the fights I was involved in while playing with the Albertan team. I had the feeling the wind had changed direction. The future started looking brighter.

The Oilers managed to squeak into the playoffs, thanks notably to the exceptional Curtis Joseph. In the first round they faced the Colorado Avalanche. The latter took a 3–1 lead in the series, but Edmonton managed to come back and win the three next games, again thanks to Joseph. In the next round, though, the Dallas Stars showed no mercy and got rid of us in just five games.

On the Bulldogs side, the team had a better season than the year before. We won 36 games, lost 22, made 17 tie games, and lost 5 times in overtime. I had played 46 games for them during that season, scoring 10 points and accumulating 20 assists and 159 penalty minutes.

In the playoffs, however, after barely managing to defeat the Syracuse Crunch, we got crushed by the Albany River Rats in four straight games.

•

The end of summer 1998 was approaching really fast and so was that crucial training camp I dreaded so much. But this time I felt better than ever, mentally speaking, and my physical condition was top-notch. During the camp, I gave it my all. Still, I was again among the last of the cuts. It didn't get me as mad as the year before, though, because Ron Low had reassured me right before I went back to Hamilton. He took me aside and told me that I'd made great progress and that my stay with the Bulldogs would definitely be temporary. I knew I could trust him, and so I went down to the AHL with a positive attitude.

Low kept his word, and on December 28, 1998, after having played twenty-five games with the Bulldogs, I got the call from the Oilers. The team was about to leave for a five-game road trip against a few pretty tough teams. The thing would be exhausting, the coach warned me. I would be playing with Boyd Devereaux and Mats Lindgren on the fourth line.

During that trip I played only a few minutes a game, but the coach as well as the press agreed that I was playing my part perfectly. I stayed with the team and my reputation started to grow, slowly but surely, throughout the league. My opponents figured out pretty quickly that I could fight, but what really made them keep their heads up was the toughness of my body-checks. There weren't many players on any team that could be expected to fight me, but anyone at all could get hit if they held on to the puck too long. Not that I ever went out to hurt anyone, but in short order I added Vladimir Tsyplakov of the Kings, Jan Vopat of the Predators, and Darren Van Impe of the Bruins to the "injured reserve" list.

Game after game, the press along with the fans began praising the way I was playing. The team was playing better hockey, and more than one person came to the conclusion that my presence in the lineup had something to do with that. I could also feel my power of intimidation growing during that time. The icing on the cake came when I finally scored my first NHL goal against the Phoenix Coyotes on January 7, 1999.

Tough guys have to work twice as hard as other players, and goal scoring is no different. I actually had to score twice before I was credited with my first goal in the league. For my first goal, which no one knew I'd scored—except me—I was crashing the net when a Dean McAmmond shot went in off my shin pad.

Not exactly a highlight-reel goal, but I wanted it. The refs gave it to McAmmond.

I was on fire, though. Later in the game I went hard to the net just as McAmmond was loading up to shoot. This time I got my stick on it and deflected it past Coyotes goalie Jimmy Waite. No one was going to take that goal away from me.

I kept the puck, of course. And how many players can say they have the puck used to score their first *and* second goals?

It wasn't that goal, however, that really established my reputation. Or a hit either. More than anything, it started with something I said. Some people called it a "youthful mistake" at the time. I'm sure some people still think that now. But opening my mouth when there was a bunch of microphones in front of me began the process of turning me into something of a celebrity.

We were facing the Sabres on February 26. That meant I'd be lining up against Rob Ray, the Sabres tough guy. Ray was a first-class fighter, a bona fide NHL heavyweight with a league-wide reputation. Since I was trying to build up my reputation in the league, I gathered my courage and asked him if he wanted to fight. He answered with a no. He wanted only to play his game that night.

That's how it works with tough guys. They respect each other enough that even if one of them invites another one to fight, the bout won't necessarily take place. The one who's invited simply has to say he doesn't feel like it and that he just wants to play his game. If he doesn't mess with the best players of the opposite team, he won't be worried for the rest of the game. If a guy like "Rayzor" didn't feel like fighting me right then, frankly I was more than happy to let it go.

All throughout the game, Ray stayed on a thin line. He played a rough, tough game, but he didn't do anything so out of line that he had to be put in his place. By the time only a few minutes were left in the game, I was beginning to feel relieved that I wouldn't have to fight that huge, powerful player.

That's when Ray jumped Bill Guerin, one of our top skill guys. Maybe he wanted to send a message, since we were winning the game handily. There was certainly all kinds of bad blood between the teams and no shortage of penalties. Doug Weight tried to come to Guerin's rescue, but Weight, another skill guy, was no match for a player like Ray. Ray quickly had my two teammates on their heels.

On the bench, I was mad with rage. I totally forgot my fright and had only one desire: to make Ray pay the price for what he'd just done. But the referees got in the way of my vengeance—they sent Ray to the locker room with a game misconduct.

Right after the game I was so angry I could barely see clearly. Journalists saw that and came up to me to ask what I thought of Ray's behaviour. I didn't even pause to think before answering. You have to remember here that I was a very young player with little or no understanding of how the media machine worked. So when I started talking, all my anger came right out. I said he was a coward, a man with no sense of honour. Moreover, I promised the entire universe that I was going to make him pay for what he'd done and that I certainly wasn't going to ask for his permission next time to punch him in the head.

Recklessness can sometimes put you into trouble. I had no idea whatsoever how those challenges would spread around the hockey world. I was just answering a question as honestly as I could. I simply couldn't imagine that my words would be repeated, ad nauseam, in every single media in Edmonton *and* in Buffalo.

The fans couldn't have been more pleased with what I'd said, and my teammates certainly had no objection. The only person who didn't like it was the head guy of the Oilers' media relations department. And God knows he was right, but at the time I couldn't understand why. He took me aside in the locker room and said, "Georges, I never want to hear such words coming out of your mouth, ever!"

I looked at him, a bit surprised that he wasn't glad I'd gone out to defend my teammates. "I just want that swine to pay for what he's done." He took my hand and told me the following: "You want to break his neck, that's your business, but if you say so publicly and you hurt him badly one day, he'll have everything in hand to sue you—and his lawyers won't have any trouble proving it was no accident but that it was in fact premeditated. If you bear someone a grudge, if you feel like sorting him out, do it, but for God's sake, don't brag about it in front of the whole world."

Suddenly I had one more thing to worry about.

When I woke after an agitated night, I had come back to my senses. I read every newspaper I could get my hands on and realized my blunder. Emotions and anger had blinded me the evening before. In the following days journalists went to see Rob Ray, asking him to respond to my words. Ray is a funny guy, and he had the perfect response to put me in my place: "Georges who?"

We were going up against the Sabres again only a few days later, on March 3. I was still angry, but now I was furious with myself, not Ray. Why couldn't I have kept my mouth shut? Why did I have to provoke one of the most intimidating fighters in the whole league?

Some newspapers started printing countdowns in their pages. Only three days left, two days, one day ...

No one was talking about the actual game.

In the meantime, journalists gave Ray every opportunity to mock me. Asked for his thoughts on my promise to get justice, Ray answered with a confident grin: "What's he going to do? Beat me up?" That made the journalists laugh out loud.

All this back and forth was making me more and more nervous. Reading it, I had the sensation that a boxing match was being promoted, not a hockey game. Or maybe they were talking about my impending death.

The night before the game, I couldn't sleep. I was swimming in sweat. The only thing I was hoping was that a tragedy would happen to me. I even wished I would die. I told myself I was going to pretend to be sick, and I even came up with the perfect ailment: I would be stricken by violent gastroenteritis.

Just to rub more salt in the wound, I had watched and watched again clips of Ray's fights. The guy was a fighting machine, crafty, poised, relentless—not to mention strong. Watching him punch one NHL tough guy after another to the ice, only one conclusion seemed plausible: this guy was going to kill me in the most gruesome way.

The third of March arrived all too soon. The game was in Buffalo, in front of Ray's adoring fans. I perfectly remember not eating a single thing for more than ten hours before the game. I was standing outside the hotel we were staying at, waiting for my teammates to join me. I was looking at all those taxis coming and going and I sincerely thought of throwing myself under one of them, figuring that death by taxi was at least preferable to a public mauling at the hands of Rob Ray.

The whole team left the hotel in the direction of the HSBC Arena, the Sabres temple where my doom awaited. We had our morning training and workout, a pretty light one that day. Right after it, journalists came up to me, looking for one more juicy quote before the brawl.

For obvious reasons I couldn't back off the very day of the game, no matter how I felt. I had set myself on this course, and I had to stick with it. What had been said had been said. I had to live up to it. I tried to temper things a bit, but the journalists knew just what to ask in order to make my answers as provocative as possible. So I said yes, I was ready for him.

And yes, I was still angry about what he'd done to Guerin and Weight a week ago.

And yes, I would accept the challenge if he was up for it.

Back to the hotel for a little pre-game nap, I still couldn't find sleep. When the time came for me to dress in my hotel room, to get ready for the real thing, my shirt and pants stuck to my skin, soaked wet with sweat. The next three hours were to be the longest of my entire life.

I kept thinking about the fights I'd seen involving Rob Ray. Trying to give myself an ounce of confidence, I started remembering some of the fights that had gone well for me in the NHL prior to that day. The only problem was that they were all fought against middleweight guys. I'd never met up with a super heavyweight like Ray before. I truly was scared to death.

The game finally started. Sitting on the bench, I was shaking, sweating like a fountain. And the more I tried to hide my terror, the more it affected me. Right from the outset, Ron Low started teasing me with huge smiles on his face. I'm positive he knew what state of mind I was in, how I was feeling inside. After all, he wasn't born yesterday.

I wanted to die.

The coach grinned at me again, and asked if I was ready. Still faking confidence, I heard myself answer, "Whenever you want!"

Now was the time. My heart was racing. I had the distinct impression that it was going to make my chest explode ... and strangely, I really wanted that to happen before Ray had the time to make my face explode.

Ray jumped on the ice, Low slapped my back, and over the boards I went. My mind was a total blank. I had only one goal. I rushed up to him without even taking the time to figure out where the puck was. I didn't care, and I doubt he did either. He saw me coming, of course. He dropped his gloves so quickly that it was clear he was ready for it. After days of anticipation, I could finally stop thinking. The media, the fans, the worry— none of that mattered once each of us had a fistful of the other's sweater. My punching arm started firing away like a furious machine.

He never got to hit me once.

After so much hype, it was over pretty quickly and very decisively. How I managed to claim that undisputed victory, I really have no clue. I can talk about it today only because I was able to watch replays of it. At the time my mind wasn't nearly as fast as my hands. I do remember, however, how relieved I felt after the fight. All that stress I'd experienced in the week before the game just vanished when the fight was over. Sitting in the penalty box, I felt like I was made of jelly.

The very same evening, all the sport reports on North American television opened with the news. Sports pages in the newspapers did the same the morning after. There wasn't a single hockey analyst who could have predicted what happened. They were amazed to see that an inexperienced, twenty-two-year-old player had not only challenged one of the top fighters in the NHL, but had kept his promise to knock him down. Nobody could remember having seen Rob Ray treated that way.

In less than thirty seconds, on March 3, 1999, I had built myself a solid reputation throughout the league. Nothing would be the same anymore, either for me or for the Oilers.

In the coming games I lined up against some of the most fearsome fighters in the NHL. I'm talking about Donald Brashear, Tony Twist, Stu Grimson, Krzysztof Oliwa—all heavyweight legends. I was still just a kid, but I managed to take care of myself among those giants. But more important, on March 3, 1999, the whole league learned one thing: you don't mess with the Oilers anymore.

●

The job wasn't done yet, as we still had to make it to the playoffs. We'd had a strange season, with some highs and some lows. We had trouble maintaining consistency in our performances. Our new goaltender, Tommy Salo, had joined us on March 20, and frankly, he had to perform miracles to keep us in the playoff hunt.

It wasn't until the eightieth game of an eighty-two-game season that we finally got to know what fate had in store for us. We had to beat the San Jose Sharks on their own ice. If, in the meantime, the Calgary Flames were to lose against the Vancouver Canucks, things would settle up in a good way for us. The games were to be played simultaneously, which added still more drama to the situation.

The night was dramatic all right. With only seventeen seconds remaining in the third period, Todd Marchant picked up a rebound off a Bill Guerin slapshot and managed to swipe it behind Sharks goalie Steve Shields to tie the game at 4–4.

Right before the overtime period was about to begin, we learned that the Canucks had defeated the Flames 2–0. Our destiny was now in our hands—and a tie game wouldn't suffice.

Three minutes and fifty-five seconds had gone by in the five-minute overtime period when Tom Poti gave us victory on a quick shot after receiving a pass from behind the net, courtesy of Bill Guerin. We celebrated as if we had just won the Stanley Cup. And, bolstered by the win, we defeated the Colorado Avalanche and the Flames in our last two games of the regular season.

I'd played 39 games for the Oilers during that 1998–99 season for a total of 5 points, 3 goals, and 59 penalty minutes. Moreover, I was just about to experience the thrill of the post-season for the very first time in my young career.

Let's say it right away: that playoff experience didn't last long. The Dallas Stars swept us in four straight. The most amazing memory I have from those four games is the first one we played at home. When we came out the gate and onto the ice I was blown away by the noise coming from the crowd. The whole arena was shaking. We even had trouble hearing the booming music coming over the sound system.

According to tests made by specialists, finding oneself next to the working turbines of a jet is the only experience that can be compared to what you can hear standing at the centre of the ice in the Oilers arena on a playoff night.

It was almost surreal. It was virtually impossible for us players to speak to each other over the roar of the crowd. The fans were shouting and sweating so much, even the glass at ice level was steaming up.

I often hear people talking about a seventh player when referring to the home crowd. In Edmonton, there might be an eighth. Their cheering gave us so much energy. They made us feel the pride of wearing the Oilers colours and being part of a Canadian team.

The average Edmonton fan had nothing to do with the businessman type who keeps looking more at his smartphone than at what's happening on the ice, a type we'd see often when playing in other rinks. Edmonton fans are average men or women who work hard from nine to five. They know the struggles of real life, and if they decide they want to spend their hard-earned money on a hockey game, it's because they love hockey and they love the Oilers.

They would paint their faces and chests, proudly wearing the Oilers colours. They would shout, chant, and drink. To play hockey in Edmonton was definitely an electrifying experience for anyone who had the opportunity. Even outside the arena, when I'd meet people around town while getting groceries or having dinner in a restaurant, I could feel the love the fans were sending us.

•

The 1998–99 season really made official my status as an NHL player. Since that March 3 game against the Sabres, my confidence had kept on building. My place was in the NHL, I knew that for sure now. I fought most of the major tough guys during that season. Every time, it went pretty well for me.

But I was still scared.

AN ESTABLISHED PLAYER

9

The major event to hit the Oilers during the summer of 1999 was unquestionably the firing of head coach Ron Low. It came to us players as a big surprise, even though the previous season hadn't been one of our best. Low then went to the Houston Aeros for a year before being hired as head coach by the New York Rangers, where he would stay for two years.

His successor was to be Kevin Lowe, who'd been assisting Low during the previous season. Lowe had put an end to his player career at the end of the 1997–98 season, and what a career that had been! As of today, he still holds several records. Among them, he's the one who played the most games in an Oilers uniform. And that's true for games in the regular season (1037) as well as in the playoffs (172). Lowe is also part of the very limited circle of players who never had to play in the minors. And an even smaller circle of guys who have six Stanley Cup rings.

If I had to find one example to prove how much of a hard worker he was on the ice, I'd have to talk about the 1987–88 playoffs. Lowe didn't miss any of the eighteen games the Oilers played to win their fourth Stanley Cup in five years. Yet he'd broken his wrist a few days before the playoffs began, and played the whole series with some broken ribs. After their last victory, Wayne Gretzky said that it was the kind of temper Lowe had showed during the series that one needed to have to win the Stanley Cup.

With Kevin Lowe as the head coach, I was going to go through one of my very best seasons ever. He helped me make progress in every aspect of the game, from my skating to my confidence. The rules were simple with him. It didn't matter whether you were making big money or had a great talent or a great reputation. Maybe some coaches are intimidated by multimillionaire stars on their rosters, but Lowe was a perennial All Star himself, and there was no way any player was going to intimidate him. The only thing that mattered to him was your work ethic. Make the most of your ice time and you'd get more.

The 1999–2000 season began on a sour note off the ice, though. Some sort of media war began between Donald Brashear and me. Maybe my new reputation had stirred up jealousy in some of my competitors. I still don't know if that was Brashear's motivation when he started denigrating me, but I do know that he began to go out of his way to annoy me.

Interviewed by some journalists from the West Coast, he started badmouthing me, calling me a one-dimensional tough guy, incapable of doing anything else on the ice but use my fists. He went on to say that the two of us shouldn't be compared, since he knew how to play the game.

That last comment made me mad with rage. Why was he attacking me like that? I didn't understand what he was trying to do. But the journalists knew what their job was. They came straight to me to get my reaction to his insults. I answered, "Okay, I play seven minutes per game compared to the twelve he's playing. I have four points, he has five. I'm a plus one when on the ice, he's at minus five. Now try to explain his point to me." I was more than ready for a war of words.

I also added that he'd now lost all my respect. Kevin Lowe supported me in that childish war, telling the press that the only reason Brashear had so much ice time with the Canucks was that they had lots of injured players.

If Donald Brashear wanted to run his mouth, that was his problem, not mine. But I didn't appreciate the fact that he denigrated me to pump his own tires. And when I invited him to engage me in the one dimension of the game he conceded I was good at, he refused to drop the gloves with me.

That said, I didn't want to spend my season thinking about Brashear. I really wanted to make progress, and I felt the pressure to do so not only for its own sake but also because I knew I'd have to if I wanted to keep my place in the team lineup. Since the fight against Rob Ray the previous season, only the toughest guys in the league would provoke me.

Now, it's hard to talk about the toughest guys in the league without mentioning Bob Probert. It hadn't been all that long since I was a scared kid back in Montreal, tormented by the possibility that I might one day have to do battle with one of the legends of the game.

As I've already said, tough guys aren't really measured by how hard they punch, or whether they end up on top when a fight ends and the two guys are tangled up on the ice. Real tough guys are the ones that make other people worry about them, and that's one thing Probert could do like almost no one else—anything could happen when Probert was on the ice.

Now that was my job too. And on November 14 that year, Probert and I were doing our jobs on the same shift. A lot of guys wanted to fight him, just to say they'd had the experience of dropping the gloves with the best in the game. But I had too much respect for him to do that.

Instead, he came after me. I'd beaten Mark Janssens in an earlier scrap, and Probert figured he had to get the momentum back for the Blackhawks. He cruised up and said, "Come on, kid," and that was that.

I'll never know what it was like to fight Bob Probert in his prime. By the time he and I went at it, he wasn't the same guy he'd been when he played for the Red Wings. But even an older Probert was a scary guy to tangle with. He was all over me, and had me on my heels a bit. But there I was, toe to toe with a guy who'd figured in my nightmares.

I was now an intimidator more than a fighter. In that sense, I was getting involved in fewer and fewer fights. That was a tendency you could easily spot throughout the league.

Luckily, Kevin Lowe had confidence in me and was giving me quite a lot of ice time, even though I was playing on the fourth line along with Jim Dowd at centre and Boyd Devereaux on the left wing. Halfway through the season, I'd played an average of 7 minutes and 55 seconds per game for only 6 points; Dowd had been used an average of 12 minutes and 20 seconds and had put up 7 points; and Devereaux was the most efficient of the three, with 13 points and an average of 12 minutes and 41 seconds on the ice.

Kevin Lowe had guts and would sometimes make risky decisions, like sending his fourth line out on the ice in the last minutes of a tied game. When asked by the press why he'd done that, his usual answer would be "Because they deserved it."

During the second half of the season, Lowe was going to use me in various situations. He gave me new responsibilities, which made me very happy. A player never plays so well as when he feels he's fully trusted by his coach. Soon I was playing twelve to fifteen minutes per game.

I was also fighting less and less. The Edmonton press started comparing me to ex-Oiler Dave Semenko more and more. In his good years, Semenko didn't have to fight often to be respected by his opponents. And that's exactly what was happening to me then.

Kevin Lowe would even sometimes use me on the first line. In short, he never saw me as only a tough guy. For instance, he really liked the way I was playing along the boards, holding on to the puck and exhausting my opponents.

In the meantime, the childish squabble between Brashear and me was still simmering. It continued throughout the season, as a matter of fact. I tried to provoke him every time we played the Canucks, since he didn't mind taking liberties against some of our top players like Guerin and Weight. But when I tried to sort him out, he would object that he was too good to fight. "I'm beyond that kind of thing!" was his refrain whenever a microphone appeared.

I know I may have been a little immature myself. I started taunting him even more when Lowe decided to use me on the first line with Guerin and Weight after Mike Grier got hurt. How many times had Brashear played on the top line?

Rumours started spreading around the league that this entire verbal war was only smoke and mirrors. Some were even suggesting that it was our way to hide the fact that we were good friends in real life. According to them, we were playing that game only to manufacture an excuse not to drop the gloves.

I quickly set the record straight. I told the press the following: "We have no mutual relationship whatsoever. We hate each other. We're the exact opposite of what a friendship is." That season we did square off twice, but both times it was nothing more than a hugging contest. Brashear never liked to trade heavy punches with big guys. He preferred to hold the big guys close so they couldn't swing. So our fights were pretty boring— just weak little punches that fans probably thought weren't worth watching.

I made quite a lot of progress that year. I knew I'd never become a Wayne Gretzky–type of player, that was for sure, but I gained a lot of confidence in my game. And I owe Kevin Lowe a huge debt of gratitude for that.

Among some of the memorable fights that year, I have to mention a bout against the young Montreal Canadiens tough guy Dave Morissette. And it's not so much the fight I remember today, but more the great sense of humour that Morissette managed to maintain after our fight. It happened in a pre-season game on September 11, 1999.

Dave had provoked me while both teams were skating in the warm-up. Eleven minutes into the first period, we dropped the gloves. Everything went well for me, and the pool of blood that could be seen at centre ice after the fight was over didn't originate from any part of my anatomy.

Asked by a journalist how he felt fighting me, Dave had this witty answer: "I really think I hurt his left fist very badly." Hats off to you, friend, for having been able to maintain your sense of humour despite the stitches. That's one thing about tough guys some fans find surprising—they may be all business on the ice, but they're often the funniest guys in the room.

Some guys only think they're funny, though. Another scrap from that year helped settle accounts for a few jokes I hadn't really laughed at. Dennis Bonvie and I had been a pretty intimidating pair when we suited up for the Bulldogs together the year before, but we weren't exactly buddies in the room. Being an NHL tough guy is an ego job, and maybe he just didn't like having me around, but Bonvie made my life miserable that year.

The worst thing he did was cut my skate laces, which made me late for a game. It sounds like a small thing, but coaches hate late players, and players hate being picked on, so when the Penguins picked up Bonvie, I admit I was looking forward to lining up against him and getting some revenge.

As soon as I got my first chance, I approached him during the play and gave him no choice but to drop his gloves. Everything went well for me.

•

The main event for me during that 1999–2000 season had nothing to do with fighting or the kiddie war between Donald Brashear and me. It had to do with my playing, and it happened on February 21. We were playing a very important game against the Los Angeles Kings. At 7:44 in the first period I scored a goal, assisted by my fourth-line colleagues, Dowd and Devereaux.

At 14:51 in the second, I scored again, assisted this time by Dowd and Roman Hamrlik. Then I started to think about the impossible, something I would never have thought I could achieve in the NHL: a hat trick. I wanted that third goal, and so did my teammates. The crowd started chanting my name.

Here I have to say that I had a very particular way of celebrating when scoring a goal. When I began my career, the local deejay would play a song that's very well known by all wrestling fans. Whenever I scored a goal, the song "Do You Smell What the Rock Is Cooking?" would resound through the whole arena. Then, because of copyright problems, the song couldn't be played anymore. So I found another way to celebrate.

Every time I'd find the back of the net, which wasn't exactly a habit of mine, I would simply skate as fast as possible towards the glass and literally throw myself belly first against it. The first time I did that, fans were kind of surprised and didn't know how to react. After the next goal I scored, I didn't run to the glass. But the fans wanted me to do it, and let me know about it through tons of emails.

It then became a tradition for me to celebrate my rare goals that way. When you're a tough guy, you always celebrate a goal as if it's your last one. Because you never know, it just might *be* your last one.

As I said, that game against the Kings was a really important one. Kevin Lowe was the riskiest head coach I had ever played for, but he wasn't crazy. As the third period was coming to an end, every fan in the house wanted me on the ice so that I could have a shot at scoring that third goal I wanted so much. But we were leading 4–3 and Lowe kept me on the bench, sending his best defensive unit on the ice.

But then the Kings pulled their goalie, Stéphane Fiset, and Janne Niinimaa scored in the empty net. Only twenty-nine seconds were left in the game. No doubt calculating that the Kings couldn't score twice in less than half a minute, Lowe sent my line out. With such little time, and considering my limited skills with the puck, I wasn't dreaming about that hat trick anymore, especially since Fiset was back in his net.

I've always believed in miracles, and one happened that night. Catching a pass from Devereaux with my back to the net, I went around the defenceman trying to block my way to the net in a move I never thought I'd be able to do. I spun around him and beat Fiset with a close backhand shot fifteen seconds before the end of the third period.

I started skating like crazy in every direction, screaming my joy. Fans started throwing their hats to the ice, hundreds of them. I kept quite a few of them, as well as the puck I'd scored the goal with. A few days later, the Oilers made a small trophy with it. That was truly one of the most incredible moments of my career.

I was given the first star of the game, and I heard Glen Sather tell journalists he was expecting a telephone call from my agent the next day to renegotiate my contract. They were also all after me, and the interviews lasted for more than an hour. Even in my wildest dreams I never thought that could be possible to achieve.

The morning after, two events occurred that really warmed my heart. First, an Edmonton radio station asked the fans to come to their studio to sign a huge congratulations poster. It's still hanging on a wall in my house in Edmonton.

The second event, even more personal, was when Wayne Gretzky himself called the arena to congratulate me. Unluckily, I wasn't there when he called. The person in charge of the players' garments, Sparky Kulchisky, got his call and told me in detail what number 99 had told him. I was deeply touched that he'd taken that time to call me, since we didn't know each other at the time. To sum his message up, let's just say he congratulated me and said I had only forty-nine hat tricks left to go to reach his record. (And if I didn't quite make it, at least it wasn't for lack of trying.)

I'd been talking to the press in the locker room for such a long time after that hat trick, still in my soaking-wet uniform, that I wasn't able to attend the morning training. My back was so stiff I could barely move it. My teammates started mocking me, telling me my head had suddenly swollen and that I was starting to act like a superstar.

•

That very same season marked quite an important turning point in the history of the Oilers. After twenty-four years spent in the team's organization, twenty-one in the general manager's seat, Glen Sather decided to resign in mid-May and accept an offer from the New York Rangers to play the same role over there.

"The heart and soul of the Oilers is leaving us," I said to the press the day after. Quickly, Kevin Lowe received an offer he simply couldn't refuse. He was asked to replace Sather. What an incredible route for him. From being a player less than four years earlier, he was now promoted to being the Oilers' general manager.

•

Once again, we managed to make the playoffs with no glory, but in a less dramatic way than the season before. We took seventh place in the Western Conference with a total of eighty-eight points, which was a better number than the seventy-eight we got the previous year.

As for myself, I was very proud of my season, having taken part in 76 of the 82 games. Some minor injuries prevented me from playing all of them. I scored 8 times and had 16 points and 123 penalty minutes, ranking at the 36 spot in that area throughout the league.

We were to meet the Dallas Stars again in the first round of the playoffs. History repeated itself, although we did manage to win a game this time, the first one we played at home. During the game we totally dominated the Stars in all respects, leaving the arena with a 5–2 win. After that match, we were so confident in our chances that we really thought we'd managed to reverse the momentum. No, we hadn't.

I played the five games of that series and was really happy about it. Kevin Lowe really knew how to make his hard-working players get the best out of themselves by proving his confidence in them. My stats weren't great, with only one assist and six minutes spent in the penalty box, but at least I'd played.

I say that because so many tough guys in this league work hard all throughout the regular season to help their team make it to the playoffs, but as soon as the post-season begins, they're left off the team. I had confidence that the next season would be a great one, especially since my fear had disappeared almost completely.

•

I spent that summer in Edmonton. It had become my true home—it still is—and I was so involved in the community that I didn't have time to go back to Montreal for the whole summer.

The only snag was that as of June 30, I was without a contract. The funny thing is that I'd found a totally unlikely ally in the negotiations my agent and the Oilers were about to start. Donald Brashear was also renegotiating with the Canucks. I still hated him, but both of us were tough guys who were able to do something more on the ice than simply use our fists.

One week prior to the training camp opening, there was still no deal between my agent and the Oilers. I certainly wasn't a well-established player like Tie Domi or Bob Probert. The former was going to receive a $1.5 million salary for the next season and the latter had managed to get a $1.8 million deal from the Chicago Blackhawks.

I couldn't expect those kinds of agreements. Still, my reputation was well enough established throughout the league that I sure could think of asking for more than the $360,000 I had earned the year before. My worth in the league was way beyond that amount. The assistant general manager, Scott Howson, was pretty harsh in the way he was negotiating. I told my agent I'd be at day one of the training camp with or without a contract, but he dissuaded me from doing so, telling me it would give him even less latitude in negotiating.

Shortly before midnight on the eve of the camp's beginning, Howson and my agent agreed on the terms of my new contract. He managed to get me a three-year contract worth $2.6 million, an amount that would be divided as follows: $700,000 for the first year, $900,000 the year after, and $1,000,000 the last year. I had just doubled my salary overnight.

The press welcomed the decision, but I understood from the way they did it that I'd have a lot of pressure on my shoulders to prove I could be an even more useful and efficient player. In other words, I had to show that I was worth that amount of money. I could read that between the lines. But I didn't care; I was more than ready.

So I showed up on the very first day of camp with the firm intention to prove in no time that the Oilers had made the best decision in signing that contract with me. I didn't know it yet, but I was at the dawn of the best season of my NHL career.

On that first day we met the new coach, a true hero among the Oilers, Craig MacTavish. We all understood pretty quickly that with him on top of the team, there wouldn't be any comfort zone whatsoever. No one would be allowed to take a shift off. He perfectly knew what every player was capable of doing, and he'd make sure we would give it to the team and more.

That was fine with me. From our very first meeting, I trusted MacTavish. And he trusted me too. He would later become the first coach to trust me enough to let me go on the ice when we were playing four on four.

After a couple of pre-season games, some journalists started to criticize the way I was protecting my teammates. Some even went so far as to say that I should be taking lessons from what Dave Semenko had done during the Gretzky years. I could see that they were questioning the sort of code of honour I had imposed on myself. They didn't like the fact that I was always asking the other team's tough guy if he was ready to fight before dropping the gloves. According to some analysts, there were times when I should have punched first and asked questions later.

Some of the things they were writing were really put in a constructive way and I found them interesting. Media pressure existed (and still exists) in Edmonton. That situation isn't only Montreal's prerogative or Toronto's. But unlike what happens in some other cities, the media pressure is usually pretty useful in Edmonton. Journalists there criticize players without attacking them. Mostly, they're not always trying to question the players' good faith. In other words, they're constructive rather than harmful.

A certain form of dialogue began between some journalists and me. It was critical, of course, but it always remained courteous. I could feel that they asked their questions with the Oilers' well-being in mind. That was pretty different from what I could see happening in Montreal, where the analyst's interests often seemed far more important than the team's.

It's probably the same in Toronto or Vancouver or other cities where hockey is the most important thing in the news each day. I know that for Ontario guys, playing for the Leafs can bring insane levels of scrutiny. I would still say Montreal is probably the worst, though. Why? Because there you get it in two languages rather than just one.

In the meantime, on October 4, 2000, Marty McSorley was convicted by a Vancouver courthouse of assaulting Donald Brashear.

Everyone still remembers that vicious hit. On February 21, 2000, the same day I scored my hat trick, McSorley took a swing at Brashear's head in cold blood and from behind. Brashear fell, already unconscious. His head hit the ice and bounced sickeningly, leaving him with a severe type-3 concussion.

McSorley was sentenced to an eighteen-month probation period. Right after the judgment was delivered, the NHL came under heavy media pressure to ban McSorley from ever playing again in the league. The NHL had previously suspended him until the end of the 1999–2000 season. They then decided to extend the length of that suspension to one full year. McSorley was never to be seen again in the NHL.

Among the players and inside the National Hockey League Players' Association (NHLPA), there was nothing but dismay. Even Brashear didn't want that to happen. No one was forgiving McSorley for what he'd done, but we could really feel that a can of worms had just been opened with his conviction in a civil court. We all knew that the people who'd been crusading for some years now against the violence in hockey would joyfully put one foot in the door that had just been opened, and that they'd never take it out.

The matter here was not to decide whether McSorley's violent assault was acceptable or not. It clearly and undoubtedly was inexcusable. Period. The real questions that affair raised went far beyond that. One proof of this was the difficult situation I was forced into at the time. I wasn't the only one affected by it, of course. Yet I always talk about things I have intimate knowledge of.

On the one hand, I was being asked to hit first and discuss later. On the other, a court had just convicted a player for doing just that. Not that anyone had ever suggested I should club a player with my stick. But public opinion, encouraged by the press, began mixing everything up. My acts on the ice, as well as those of other tough guys like Probert, Grimson, Domi, Twist and company, were now associated with McSorley's. For most observers from outside the hockey world we became the equivalent of bloodthirsty beasts, incapable of handling a puck, pursuing only one goal in life: hurt people! We kept hearing the same thing: the game didn't need that kind of player anymore.

Luckily, some people who knew what they were talking about came to our defence. Leading the way was the sparkling figure of Don Cherry. They started to explain the difference between what a tough guy does and what McSorley had done. They also tried to explain how tough guys like me were there to keep the sport clean—to *prevent* exactly that kind of stickwork.

●

Since that last assertion of mine might have upset some readers, I'll allow myself to open a pretty long parenthesis that will cover three related subjects: 1) the real role of a tough guy in the NHL; 2) that fear I had for a long time; and 3) how difficult it is to be a tough guy.

Winning the Memorial Cup with the Granby Prédateurs in junior marked the end of a period for me. I was now definitely leaving a little kingdom where I was the king. No one had scared me during those junior years.

When I got to the American league and again when I joined the Oilers for good, the deal had changed radically. I was now facing the "killers" I'd seen on my television screen. I just had to think about Probert, Grimson, Twist—not to mention Brown—to feel my blood freeze in my veins. As I imagine I've already made pretty clear, those guys scared me to death.

Players in the NHL usually take a small nap in the afternoon before a game. For more than three years, I wasn't able to sleep a wink during those naps. It was even worse if I had the feeling I would have to fight the same evening. Every time the same question would pop up in my head: "How will I manage to survive?"

The games themselves were even worse, mentally speaking. During those games I had only one wish: for the fight to be behind me as soon as possible. That's why I would usually provoke it as early in the game as I could. It wasn't that I couldn't control my rage; it was that I wanted that unpleasant event out of the way.

Days off weren't much more relaxing for me. I'd be trying and trying to think about something else, to clear my mind of the fights to come. It haunted my mind everywhere and all the time. I'd watch a movie to unwind, but it wouldn't work. There was no escape from the reality of a fighter's life.

When I was with friends, I was always the life of the party. What nobody could have known was that I was consumed with anxiety. My jokes and clowning around were often no more than a way of hiding what I was really thinking about. That was the state of mind I was in during my first three years as a pro.

The other tough guys, at least the more established ones, knew that I had everything to prove, that I was trying to build my reputation. They were always ready for me, and most important, they seemed to have no fear of me. Even after my first fight against Rob Ray and the way it helped build my credibility as a tough guy in the NHL, I was still afraid. That state of permanent anxiety even had consequences for my blood pressure. It was abnormally high for a young athlete like me.

Talking with some of my brothers-in-arms, I would later learn that I wasn't the only one suffering from these symptoms of anxiety and fear. They all had the same ones, at least in their first career years. I firmly believe that anxiety is the worst enemy possible, and it's probably one of the reasons why so many tough guys have experienced and are still experiencing alcohol and/or drug problems.

It can be lonely, and it's always hard. I don't want to pretend to be a psychologist, or to mention any names disrespectfully, but a number of guys who once dropped their gloves for a living have been in the headlines lately for the tragic way their lives came to an end. These guys had to call on their courage in ways other players don't, and I know that takes a huge toll.

You have to understand that every time a tough guy drops his gloves on the ice, he's afraid of an amazing number of things. First of all, it's an ego thing. Tough guys know that thousands, maybe millions, of people are watching them when they fight. Hockey stops being a team sport and becomes an individual one. All eyes turn to those two players, and nobody wants to be humiliated in front of such a huge crowd.

Plus, there are the teammates. A tough guy has to prove to them that he's there to protect them and that they can count on him to do so. He's there to bring confidence, and the second you start losing a fight, that confidence starts to leak away. If you're losing, you're not doing your job.

And then there's the simplest kind of fear—the fighter is afraid he'll get hurt. Your bones can break, your face can get cut, your brain can be severely concussed. Any fighter who's given a moment's thought to what he does for a living is even scared of dying—imagine the consequences that a six-foot-five, 260-pound guy's punch can have if it lands square on a guy's temple. Some of these guys can crack a helmet with a punch. Anyone who doesn't worry about putting his face in front of a punch like that hasn't thought very hard about his job description.

It took me about five years, not to make that fear disappear, but to be able to master it. It never vanished for good; same thing with the anxiety. The main reason I managed to control my fears was that I'd become one of the toughest and most dangerous among my peers. The others would try all kinds of ways to avoid fighting me. They'd come up to me and ask me how I'd been, congratulating me for past games or fights. Pretty hard after that to jump on them with no obvious reason.

They also began bodychecking my teammates, if not lightly, at least without putting all their energy and strength into it. Some would even miss them on purpose. Why? Because they knew that a heavy hit would bring consequences they would prefer to avoid. I began perceiving this change in their attitudes during that 2000–01 season I was talking about right before opening this parenthesis.

From that moment on, not only did I start winning more and more fights, but I was truly dominating them. Which led other tough guys to be more and more cautious when facing my team. They would show a lot of prudence even when I was sitting on the bench.

In my eyes, what I've just said proves undoubtedly why tough guys are not only useful but a necessity when it comes to keeping the game clean. We don't just punish dirty hits—we prevent them. And we keep each other in check, too. When a tough guy knew that I'd be on the bench and sometimes on the ice during a game, he would start it in a different state of mind. He'd think twice before taking liberties against one of my teammates. Referees can't see everything happening on the ice. I could.

I remember something Craig MacTavish once said to the whole team. It was the morning after a game we'd won against the Minnesota Wild. During a video session, right before our practice, he showed the guys images of my fight against Wild's tough guy Derek Boogaard. He asked my teammates to notice how calm I looked before a fight, and then he added, "Guys, it looks like Georges's heart rate has barely moved." Only after six or seven seasons in the NHL could I really envisage fighting with serenity, and to such an extent that I actually started smiling at my opponent before the fighting was on. That grin on my face would make him nervous. I was basically telling him he'd lost the fight even before it started.

Some would get mad when I did that, and would rush towards me with their heads down. I simply had to get a grip of their shirt with my right hand, putting all my weight on that grip so they couldn't really move anymore, and then start punching them with the left one. I used that technique so many times that I still wonder today why no one ever tried to counter it in some way.

That appearance of calm, added to my smile, inevitably had one of two effects on my direct opponent: anger or fear. And when a tough guy let one of those two feelings take possession of his mind, he immediately became easy prey. Then, to add to the smile, I had another somewhat crazy idea. I started wishing my opponent good luck before the fight. That would finish disorienting him mentally and give me an almost unfair advantage over him.

As well, the more my career progressed, the more I started analyzing everything, from my opponent's footwork to his balance on the ice. I would also watch videos of his fights just to figure out his tactics. I wanted to challenge my opponent not only with my confidence but also with a precise knowledge of the kind of fighter he was.

In the last years of my career, only a handful of players would still make me a bit nervous before a fight: Donald Brashear, Brian McGrattan, and mostly Derek Boogaard—may he rest in peace. And the reason why those two latter players would frighten me was obvious when you looked at the way they fought. These guys were fearless punchers. But it was more than that. Those guys simply loved fighting.

Lots of hockey fans think that every tough guy loves the fighting part of his job. Nothing could be more wrong. I know them all, and throughout my career I've met only four guys who really loved to fight. To McGrattan and Boogaard I would have to add the names Jody Shelley and Steve MacIntyre. I can't think of anything more intense than to start a fight with a tough guy who loves it. Not only are these guys ready to hurt you, but that's also their goal. The only reason Brashear isn't on this list is that he turned down a lot of fights if he didn't feel like getting into it or didn't like the matchup. But these other guys never turned down an invitation.

Every other tough guy in the league would rather do anything but fight on the ice. They would love to score tons of goals, become more and more talented, and earn bigger salaries, all the things hockey players dream of the moment they become hockey players. And I was one of those. I never enjoyed fighting. I did it because it was my job and the only way for me to keep playing in the NHL. Period.

Some sociologists who study sports have come to the conclusion that being a tough guy in the NHL may well be the hardest job in the world of sports. I can truly believe that, when one analyzes what that job demands, mentally as well as physically, on the ones doing it.

I could be injured, hurting everywhere—it didn't matter. If I had to go, I simply had to. When my team was being dominated, I had to go. If my team was running up the score, I had to be ready to be jumped at any moment. In hockey, a lopsided score means there's going to be trouble, and if there's trouble, guys like me have to go to work. I remember a few times when I hoped the score would remain tight between the two teams just so that I could catch my breath. Even then, if one of the top players on my side was being harassed by an opponent, same thing, I had to go.

For every moment in the sixty minutes of a game, I had to remain alert and vigilant, ready to go nose to nose with another guy who was probably only in the lineup because his coach figured he was strong enough and mean enough to tangle with me. The state of stress it put me into was sometimes unbearable. Especially on nights when I didn't feel in top shape. I really believe that those permanent feelings of anxiety and stress, when you add them to the constant fear, are pretty rare in professional sports. That's one of the reasons I've always said that this job is 10 percent muscle, 90 percent mental.

And when a fight occurred, even though it almost never lasted more than a minute, I needed a lot more than the five minutes spent in the penalty box to recover from the stress and the massive dose of energy needed for it.

Quite early in my career I started asking the NHLPA to take action against all the performance-enhancing drugs some players would use to become bigger in order to stop feeling the pain. The job was hard and harsh enough not to have to compete against "killers" swollen with steroids.

The NHLPA listened to me, but refused to take any action on that front, for obvious political reasons. They wanted to keep drug testing as a card in their negotiations with the league. Plus, since their main goal was to protect the players, to take action against drugs would have harmed some of those players. I understood that, but in the meantime I didn't want to stop fighting against those drugs.

I have to say here that tough guys weren't the only players using steroids in the NHL. It was true that quite a lot of them did use this drug, but other, more talented players did too. Most of us knew who they were, but not a single player, not even me, would ever think of raising his hand to break the silence and accuse a fellow player. I don't like snitches and will never be one.

That said, I can give you some clues here that will help you identify the ones using steroids, if you really feel like it. First, you just have to notice how some talented players will experience an efficiency loss as well as a weight loss every four years, those years being the ones where the Winter Olympics are held.

In the following season they make a strong comeback; they manage a mysterious return to form.

As for the tough guys, a statistics maniac can easily identify who's taking drugs and who's not. You just have to compare their last junior league's weight to the one they had arriving with the pros. Nobody, and I really mean nobody, can gain forty to seventy pounds in just one summer without taking anything suspicious. When you're in close contact with them, it's even easier to tell: the change in their voice, the swelling neck, the appearance of acne—they're not fooling anyone.

The use of steroids by tough guys makes it unfair for the ones who decide to remain clean. But even more than steroids, some other drugs would really make fighting even more danger-ous for the clean ones like me. Substances like Ephedrine, for instance, totally desensitize the player who takes them. Before a game, as I would warm up on the ice, I would always look at the tough guy on the other side. If his arms were trembling, if his eyes were bulging, I knew for sure he wasn't going to feel any of the punches I would give him. Totally anaesthetized, his face sweating despite the thick film of Vaseline he'd covered his face with, I knew the guy would be able to take a lot more hits than his fair share.

In my final years in the NHL, the league finally decided to set clear and precise rules against the use of any performance-enhancing drugs. I was relieved, and found it funny how much weight some players had lost in just one year.

Nowadays, the fight has moved to another level. Hockey, as well as any other sport in the world, has to take action against the human growth hormone that players have been using for a couple of years now.

Before ending this parenthesis, I really want to dispel a myth here. Too many hockey fans still think tough guys hate each other. There might be some exceptions, but for the vast majority of them, there's absolutely no bad feelings directed towards the other tough guys. On the contrary, I would say.

During my career, I only hated one player, Donald Brashear, because he'd been denigrating me for absolutely no reason I could see. And even in his case, that hate slowly vanished to transform itself into some sort of *entente cordiale.*

We fight each other, that's for sure, but a great complicity keeps us united. After every fight, for instance, I would always talk to my opponent from one penalty box to the other. I'd always ask him if he was okay. Sometimes I'd even congratulate him for the fight. After all, there was going to be a life after hockey. And though I *always* wanted to win, I was never motivated by a desire to hurt anyone. They're not the same thing at all.

I certainly had my rivalries with some players, but we would always put respect in first place. We did the same job, and so we had to pull together. The McSorley affair even strengthened the links between us. We wanted to stand united and prove to the league and the public that tough guys are there to make sure the dirty stuff is kept out of the game. After all, when Bob Probert and I would fight, no one was attacking anyone from behind.

Now to conclude that parenthesis: I really want the families of the three tough guys who died dramatically while this book was being written to accept my deepest and sincerest condolences.

Those guys did a tough job, a job they probably didn't want to do most nights. No matter what anyone says about that job, it takes a lot of courage to always be accountable and to always stand up for your teammates, whether you feel like it or not. It is one thing to hold your head high only when you're the toughest guy around—any bully can do that. But to be willing to stand up when you know there is a guy just as tough as you on the other team—that takes courage. A lot of things have been said about the guys we have lost, but one thing they had in common was that they must have been made of something special to do the job they did.

The deaths of Derek Boogaard, Wade Belak, and Rick Rypien brought back under the media spotlight the subject of violence in hockey. There's one point I'd like to add to everything that has been said regarding their tragic loss.

Don't get me wrong, but I'd like to make a somewhat shaky comparison here between the tough guys' experience and what soldiers and former soldiers go through.

When our soldiers come back from a dangerous mission abroad, more often than not they are left out in the cold. They experience psychological problems that often prevent them from being able to fully reintegrate into society and to find jobs. The stress they went through when they were doing their jobs often leads them to fall into drug and alcohol abuse.

Well, the same goes for some of the NHL tough guys after their careers—with a couple of huge differences, though. First, soldiers are national heroes defending and protecting their countries. And, second, they don't get paid nearly as much as hockey players do.

So, yes, it is urgent we take some action to protect the NHL tough guys during and after their careers, but it is even more urgent we do the same for our true heroes.

•

Let's return to that 2000–01 season. As I said earlier, our new head coach, Craig MacTavish, and I were on the same wavelength. I perfectly understood what he expected from a player in terms of his behaviour on the ice and what role he wanted me to play.

Often, especially when Ethan Moreau was out of the lineup due to injury, MacTavish would put me on the first line with Bill Guerin and Doug Weight. And right at the beginning of the season, people started saying good things about me.

I remember, for instance, what the head coach of the Phoenix Coyotes, Bob Francis, said about me after a hard-fought game against his team on October 22 when I'd scored the equalizing goal: "Every time the Oilers want to change the pace of a game, they simply send Georges Laraque in. What happens then? One of two things: either they get a scoring chance or he'll give a solid bodycheck." That night I'd spent sixteen minutes on the ice, a career record for me.

On November 15, we were dealt an unpleasant surprise. One of our top players, Bill Guerin, was traded to the Bruins. In return, though, we were welcoming Anson Carter. That day the Oilers became the very first team in NHL history to have five black players on its roster. Besides Carter and me, we could count on Mike Grier, Sean Brown, and Joaquin Gage. In the entire NHL there were only fourteen black players—and more than a third were on my team.

My joke to the press was that the Oilers were looking more and more like a football team. But I knew that Anson's arrival had a serious and beneficial implication. I added, "This situation has many positive aspects to it. I'm sure the Oilers will become the favourite team of a lot of young black kids. This will make us an example, and mostly it will be great publicity for our sport among the black community."

•

I had great offensive statistics during that season. Okay, I admit it, for a player like Sidney Crosby or Evgeni Malkin, it would have been a disastrous season, but for a tough guy it was really unexpected. And this led me to start being really superstitious. In fact, it had all started after my previous season's hat trick and went from there.

Hockey players are a superstitious bunch, but I'm pretty much the opposite most of the time, especially in everyday life. I'm quite obsessed with order and cleanliness, but that's another problem. When the puck started going in for me, though, I shoved reason aside and became the most superstitious guy on the team. Every game day I started repeating the same ritual without ever missing one part of it. And parts kept growing in number.

I know in advance that by describing this routine, some of you, dear readers, will truly think I'm crazy, but I promised I'd say everything in this book and so I will. And in my defence, I'm not the only hockey player or sportsman in the world to have his pre-game ritual.

For instance, I had to arrive at the arena at least three hours prior to the game start; I would take a shower and pray in it. I also had rituals involving some of my teammates. This included a mandatory game of ping-pong with one of them and a special handshake with another. The oddest of my rituals had to be the one I shared with Shawn Horcoff. Just before jumping on the ice for the warm-up, I'd go up to him and he had to say "Hello,

Clarice" to me, imitating the voice of Hannibal Lecter in *The Silence of the Lambs*. Bizarre, I know.

I had a ritual for almost every single one of my teammates. They all had to be carried out so that I could feel good beginning the game. As Anson Carter once said to journalist Joanne Ireland, "He has something for everyone. And don't even try to escape it, he will hunt you and hunt you and hunt you ..." I don't know if that was exaggerated, but I would drive some of my teammates insane, although they'd still play the game with a smile. Some of them even started developing their own rituals involving other teammates, too. A locker room populated by a bunch of madmen, that's what it was!

But we were a very united team, with an even greater team spirit than before. We ended the year with 93 points. I myself scored 13 goals for a total of 29 points, which was going to be, although I didn't know it back then, the very best offensive season of my whole career. Moreover, I played all 82 games of the regular season. I also spent 148 minutes in the penalty box.

I would always compare my offensive statistics to those of the other tough guys. Season after season, I always ended up being in the leading pack.

●

The road to the playoffs that year had been the easiest one since I arrived with the Oilers. Rotten luck was there again, though. Yes, you got it. We were to meet up with the Dallas Stars for the third time in a row. The Stars had a clear psychological advantage over us due to their two consecutive and pretty easy previous wins. We were, however, truly ready for the struggle.

The Stars won the first game in overtime. Despite that painful loss, we believed in our chances this time. It had been a tight game. My ice time had been very limited, but even so, I felt I could have an interesting impact on the way the series would go.

As soon as we got back in the locker room, I started haranguing my teammates with an improvised, impassioned motivation speech. I promised them and the press that we were going to win the next game in Dallas, and that I'd be a great contributor to that victory.

We did win that second game. I didn't play much, to say the least, but I'd like to think my presence on the ice had an impact. I also scored our second goal in that 4–3 win. Right after the game, Craig MacTavish told the press that even though I'd only played 3:15, I could have been given one of the three stars.

The next two games both went into overtime—a win and a loss for us. We went back to Dallas with the series tied, but lost 4–3 in overtime again. That one hurt. We knew we should have won it. The sixth one, back in Edmonton, was an emotional one. We lost again, 3–1.

The Stars' greater collective experience and maturity had made the difference in a very close series. To lose a series in four straight games doesn't generally leave a bitter taste in one's mouth. It's a totally different story, though, when you have the feeling that the slightest alteration in the bounce of the puck could have resulted in another outcome. It leads to a summer filled with frustration.

•

On September 12, 2001, the Oilers training camp got off to a flying start. Our loss against the Stars had brought us down mentally at the end of the previous season. Three months later, though, it seemed as if it had become a huge source of motivation. We were all convinced that we had what it took to go a lot further in the season to come. We were wrong ...

In spite of a pretty good regular season, which saw us end it with ninety-two points, we weren't able to get into the playoffs. It was a great disappointment for all of us. I had slowed down offensively and wasn't happy about it at all: I'd scored only five goals for nineteen points. And I missed two games during the regular season, not because I was injured but because MacTavish wanted to test a few young players before the playoffs started. Frankly, it was a season to forget because we'd had such big collective expectations when it started.

•

The 2002–03 campaign began on a sad note for me. While I was about to earn a seven-figure salary for the first time in my career, three events of a totally different nature were just about to spoil the party.

First, after 448 games in the Oilers uniform, the guy I thought of as my brother and my mentor, Mike Grier, was traded to the Washington Capitals in return for a few draft choices. He'd had a difficult year the season before, but I must admit his leaving left me in a state of shock. Grier had taken me under his wing as soon as I began playing with the Oilers. He went on to help me in so many ways that it's impossible to list them all here. He taught me how to be and act as a pro. He really gave me the keys to that job, and he did it with so much generosity. Most of all, he was a great guy. Never complaining, always in a good mood, he knew how to cheer me up when I was down, and he was the first to congratulate me when I deserved it.

I was sure to get some more ice time with him leaving the team, though. The fans were asking for that, and MacTavish had promised it to me. But that wasn't enough to cheer me up.

The day after we learned Grier was leaving the team would prove to be one of the worst days of my life, as well as one of the luckiest ones.

I was driving my car, a BMW X5, to the nearest courier's office. I had a parcel to send. Just before I got there, I had an intersection to cross. What I didn't know was that an illegally parked truck was hiding a stop sign. The cars coming from the left and right had no stop signs. So when I blew through the invisible stop sign and into the intersection, the traffic was coming at me full speed.

I never saw the car that hit me.

A deafening smash almost made my eardrums explode while I felt a great shock within my whole body. I lifted my eyes up just in time to see a Jeep Cherokee whirling about twenty feet in the air. It crashed to the ground and started turning over and over and over ...

My neck totally jammed under the impact. I remember being surprised my airbag didn't open under such a jolt. I was in a deep state of shock. I was looking at the Jeep that was now standing still about ninety feet away from my car. Whoever was in that car was dead, I was sure of it.

After about ten seconds of silent eternity during which I couldn't move, people started to arrive from everywhere, running towards my car. Some recognized me. I yelled at them, ordering them to go see to the other car.

Inside the Jeep was a woman in her mid-forties and her mother. An ambulance took me to the hospital. All through the ride and then during tests at the hospital I kept asking everyone around what had happened to the women in the other car. A nurse finally told me that they had suffered nothing but minor bruises. I couldn't believe my ears.

As soon as I got out of the hospital, I tried to contact them, in vain. They didn't want to talk to me until the police inquiry results were known. Those results would determine who was responsible for the accident. The problem was that nobody seemed to be able to understand what had really happened.

My car's on-board computer indicated that I was driving at thirty kilometres an hour at the moment of impact. (Incidentally, I learned that day that planes weren't the only means of transportation to carry black boxes.) Moreover, there were no braking marks on either road.

I tried many times to contact them in the days after the accident. I wanted to apologize, get some news, make sure they really were all right. At one point I learned that they had hired a lawyer. Once I knew a lawsuit was in the works, I stopped trying to reach them.

The inquiry showed that no one was to blame in the accident. I was simply given a fine for not obeying a stop sign. The story ended like that. Almost.

A few months later, while I was in a mall for an autograph session, I saw a woman storming towards me. She was obviously angry. When she got near, she threw a pile of photos at my face and on the table I was sitting at.

A bit stunned, I looked at a few of the photographs and immediately recognized the Jeep. She started screaming at me, calling me names, telling me that I had smashed her car and that all her insurance company had given her in compensation was a small cheque.

I let her go through her diatribe against me and then said I'd tried several times to discuss the problem with her, but in vain. With rage and fury, she started asking me for money. Calmly, I told her, "Miss, if back when it happened you had talked to me instead of trying to get more and more money from your insurance company and threatening to sue everyone, maybe I would have been generous. That said, miss, I have a job to do." She turned around and disappeared for good.

The day after that terrible accident the Oilers were playing against the Colorado Avalanche. At one point during the game, one of our defencemen simply swept the puck out of our zone to release some of the pressure our opponents were putting on us. In a desperate attempt to catch the puck and avoid an icing, I skated as fast as I could with a Colorado player by my side. Unfortunately, I accidentally stumbled on his stick and fell on the ice. I crashed violently into the board and smashed one of my elbows against it. It exploded. Thirty stitches, a minor operation, and a one-week antibiotics prescription later, I thought about the accident again. Life is sometimes strange ...

I was back on the ice pretty quickly, though. On December 8 we were playing a game against the Nashville Predators, the team of Stu Grimson. The third distressing event of that season was about to unfold.

At one point during the game, Grimson came out of the penalty box and jumped on me fiercely. I punched him on the head several times with my left fist. After the referees had interceded, I could see he was pretty unsteady. He then tried to hit me twice with his right fist. That was not his style. Grimson was a tough fighter, but he'd always been a decent guy. I remember asking myself what could possibly have made him do it. It unsettled me that a guy I thought of as someone I could respect would do something like that. He was a veteran of fourteen seasons in the NHL, and I'd never seen him do such a thing. My questions would be answered just a few days later.

Among the punches I'd given Grimson that night was the punch too many. He'd made a courageous comeback some years earlier after a violent fight against Dave Brown that left him disfigured. He had then kept playing his role, and now there he was, ending his career against my fist. The one concussion too many ...

I knew, and he sure knew too, that what had happened was part of the job. I talked earlier about the risks we took doing this job. Still, I felt miserable when I first heard the news. I remembered that Grimson had once accepted my challenge to drop the gloves against me back when I was a young tough guy trying to build my reputation. He didn't have to do it at the time, but he did.

Strange to think that it hadn't been all that long ago that I'd been terrified of guys like Grimson. But now that he was gone, I felt grateful to him for dropping the gloves with me.

After that December 8 incident, the press wanted to talk to me a lot. The only thing I felt like doing was to profusely apologize to him. A pure gentleman, Grimson told me not to worry about it. There seemed to be no bounds to his praise for me and he wished me good luck for the rest of my career. I admired him then, and I still do.

Needless to say, the beginning of the 2002–03 season wasn't the favourite of my career. Add to that the fact that I kept accumulating small injuries that would slow me down. Even though I was experiencing a so-so season, rumours started spreading around the league and in the press regarding my future with the Oilers. Were they going to trade me before the March 11 trade deadline?

To counter those rumours, I started multiplying my statements to the Alberta as well as to the Quebec press. Most of the rumours were sending me to the Montreal Canadiens, and so I'd repeat and repeat again how much I wanted to stay with the Oilers until the end of my career. Edmonton was now called home for me. Journalist Simon Drouin of Montreal's *La Presse* even wrote an article entitled "Georges Laraque: The Oil Drop Tattooed on His Heart."

The trade deadline came and I stayed with the Oilers. I breathed a huge sigh of relief. I was so involved in the Edmonton community that I couldn't see myself starting all over somewhere else. I was and still am deeply in love with that city, its people, and of course the Oilers fans.

About ten days after that date, I wrote a column in the pages of the weekly paper *Montréal Métropolitain* and on the Réseau des Sports website entitled "Why I Wouldn't Want to Play in Montreal." In it, I described everything I didn't like about the Montreal hockey planet: the media pressure, the easy booing, the unremitting complaints … I even went so far as to declare that if my agent were to tell me I'd been traded to the Montreal Canadiens, I thought I would simply retire immediately. Needless to say, this article came as a blow in Montreal. Following its publication, I received thousands of emails seething with hate. Just a few days before the trade deadline the Montreal press had described me as a saviour; two weeks later, I was no longer worth my weight in pucks. That simply confirmed for me that I was right not to want to play there.

I had a good end of the season, even though I wasn't that efficient from an offensive point of view. I was getting quite a lot of ice time and was able to have a favourable impact on the team. Just a few days before the playoffs were to begin, Craig MacTavish told the press that I was playing very well and that I was certainly going to be a major factor in the playoffs.

The Oilers closed out their regular season with the same amount of points as the year before, but it was enough to make the playoffs this time. I had missed eighteen games that year due to the minor injuries I talked about earlier. I got thirteen points with six goals.

•

"Not them again!!!"

That sentence pretty well sums up the feeling shared by the whole team when we learned we would again be facing the Dallas Stars in the first round of the playoffs. And just as it had happened in the previous two years, the series was tied after four games. We collapsed in the fifth game and lost once again on our ice in the sixth.

Dallas really had become the Oilers' nemesis.

ON THE ROAD TO THE LOCKOUT AND THE MOST BEAUTIFUL SEASON OF MY LIFE

10

I know it's pretty unusual to give such a long title to a chapter, but since I've never done things the way they're supposed to be done, I'll go for it anyway. There were some real highs and lows for me in 2003, as I'm sure there were for a lot of guys who play hockey for a living, but I remember that year less for its disappointments than for one of the most exhilarating moments of my career.

As soon as training camp opened in Edmonton that summer, there was really only one thing the guys wanted to talk about in the locker room. In less than a year, the collective bargaining agreement (CBA) between the NHLPA and the NHL would come to an end. A lockout was already a very likely possibility. As a matter of fact, and without mentioning any names, some players, mostly Europeans, had already started looking for an exit door for the next September.

And while I'm talking about the European players, I'd like to clarify something here that most North American observers still don't seem to understand. Canadian and American players go through their careers with a unique goal in mind: the Stanley Cup. From the second any of us picks up a hockey stick, that's what we think about. But European players think differently.

The highest emotional moments they have as hockey players are the ones they experience while playing for their respective countries internationally. And for them, the biggest international tournament is the Olympics. I'm not saying there's anything wrong with that. If they grow up dreaming of Olympic gold, who am I to suggest they should have some other dream? But the fact is, their reality is different from ours.

Even though we had the CBA in mind, we still had to concentrate on the upcoming season. The first Oilers game of the regular season was at home against the San Jose Sharks.

That night, MacTavish had the strange idea of having me play with centre Shawn Horcoff and left-winger Raffi Torres. Not that it was such a bizarre line combination, but still, we'd never played together before, not even in pre-season games. We asked ourselves what had gone through MacTavish's mind when he dreamed up that line.

In any case, he must have known what he was doing. Sometimes even elite players can't seem to find each other on the ice, and other times three guys who may not be perennial All Stars can be a threat in every shift if they're reading the game the same way. I guess MacTavish had seen in this combination something we hadn't, because we had a great game, harvesting five points. We even executed some power-play shifts. That marked a great start to the season for me—but my early euphoria wouldn't last long.

The puck just stopped going in for me. And after only a few games off the score sheet, the press began grumbling about my slow start. Journalists began to say they couldn't even find me out there on the ice. And if a guy like me was becoming invisible, I really must not have been playing well.

We were to meet up with the Canadiens twice that season, which didn't happen often in the two teams' histories. One of those games was the scene of one of the biggest events I'd ever participated in as far as hockey is concerned: on November 22, the Canadiens and the Oilers played a fabulous outdoor game at the Commonwealth Stadium in Edmonton—the first Heritage Classic.

We were so impatient to play that game. We knew it would be an extraordinary experience and that we were lucky to be part of it. In the days preceding the game, the Oilers' players looked like a bunch of kids on the eve of a trip to Walt Disney World.

Well, as high as our expectations were, reality was even better. When the players skated out onto the ice in front of more than 57,000 fans, the roaring we heard was absolutely incredible. I understood how soccer players must feel when they run out into a crowded stadium.

Two flaws would, however, prevent an unforgettable experience from being a perfect one. First, the ice was pretty mediocre, which made the puck hard to control. (I guess when the NHL decided to stage a game outdoors, they wanted the authentically bumpy ice of a backyard rink or a farmer's field.) Players waiting for a pass kept having the puck bounce away or veer off without warning.

The second problem was the freezing-cold temperature. Throughout the day the thermometer wouldn't budge over minus 20 Celsius. We had wrapped ourselves up warmly—it had been a long time since any of us had played hockey wearing scarves, caps, and gloves—but nothing was enough to prevent us from feeling the cold. It was almost unbearable. Our faces would freeze as soon as we started skating. The organizers had installed huge electric radiators next to each of the team's benches, so the water in our bottles was almost boiling, but not us—we were chilled to the bone.

It was pond hockey in the purest sense: there was no hitting, no intensity. And that suited me just fine. I was suffering enough as it was without getting punched in the face. And I knew the Habs' Darren Langdon felt the same way. At one point we caught each other's eye, and the look we exchanged left nothing to doubt. There was no *way* we were going to fight.

At least we got to move every time we jumped on the ice. It was a whole different story for the fans: they were singing, cheering, dancing, but nothing was enough to warm them up, and hypothermia cases were numerous. And before the Oilers vs. Canadiens game was held, the two teams' old-timers had faced off against each other. Some spectators had been out there in the cold for six hours. To be truthful, nobody really wanted that game to go to overtime. We lost it 4–3. Hard to believe that the day after was a beautiful sunny one, with temperatures rising to a comfortable zero degrees.

Still, bad ice and cold toes couldn't do much to take away from the joy of that game. It was truly a highlight of that season.

Apart from that, though, 2003–04 wasn't a season I would gladly remember. Neither the team nor I played up to expectations. We called it the Heritage Hangover. It was as though we had looked forward to that game so much that we forgot to play once it was over. We fell into a depressing losing streak. Once again, as the trade deadline approached rumours sending me away from Edmonton started spreading; and once again I began telling the press that I didn't want to move. I even went so far as to say that I wouldn't be dropping my gloves anymore if I were to be traded. There was only one team I was ready to break my bones for and it was the Oilers. Period.

Still, even while I was declaring my commitment, the press didn't see things the same way. Sportswriters didn't think I was as involved or as effective as I'd been the season before. MacTavish was saying the same thing to me. I really was scared that time, and with a lockout looking more and more plausible, I knew anything could happen. Once again, I stayed with the Oilers; and once again, yes, you know it, I breathed an even deeper sigh of relief than in the past.

We missed the playoffs by one point that year. (Suddenly the Heritage Hangover looked even worse for us—if we had just won one more game, we would have been in the playoffs.) I'd played 66 games, scoring only 6 times for 17 points. The 99 penalty minutes I had in the bank made me the seventieth most punished player that season. Not that I wanted to be number one in that book. It really had never been a goal of mine. But I wanted to create a good balance between the points I put up and the time I spent in the penalty box. In other words, if I wasn't putting the puck in the net, I had to contribute in other ways, and my stats that year suggested I hadn't managed to do that. I wasn't really surprised that others weren't satisfied by the overall results, because I wasn't either.

I found a bit of healing in a poll that Edmonton newspapers organized just before Christmas, 2003. They had asked forty-two journalists from across North America who they thought was the best tough guy in the NHL. I came in first place, far ahead of my four closest competitors, Peter Worrell, Tie Domi, Donald Brashear, and Jody Shelley. I guess the reason why I wasn't fighting as much as the press expected me to was probably that no one really wanted to fight me.

•

I had been totally naive that season. Or should I say, I'd been quite the usual me, a hopeless optimist whose faith in the good-will of human beings wasn't always warranted by the real world. Like everybody else, I saw the labour war coming. But I thought, a bit stupidly I must admit, that both sides had too much to lose not to find some kind of agreement. Poor little Georges.

The summer before what would finally be a lockout, while every other player was shopping around for a team, I was speaking highly of the NHL. Some players, physically or mentally, had already left North America. Meanwhile, I was explaining to anyone who would listen why we had to stay there and fight to prevent the lockout from happening.

I guess I was still a kid as far as business was concerned. For several months the NHL, led by Gary Bettman, and the NHLPA were scrapping it out like street fighters. Our leader, Bob Goodenow, had been repeating to us for years that we should be far-sighted, that we should put some money aside in the eventuality of a lockout or a strike. Some did, others didn't. The NHLPA had an emergency fund ready to be used if such a thing as a lockout was to occur, but it would allow each player only a $5000 monthly compensation. A professional hockey player's standard of living is hard to maintain with such a small compensation.

Don't get me wrong here. I know perfectly well that such a salary would be more than enough for the vast majority of people. That said, just like everybody else, professional hockey players have recurring expenses to meet, and $5000 simply wouldn't allow them to cover those, whether it be their housing loans, their car payments, or the insurance they had to subscribe to.

We knew the NHL was trying to break the players' union. According to Bettman, it was pure nonsense to see players earning those kinds of salaries while most of the teams were deeply in debt with no hope of climbing out. He claimed that the NHL teams had collectively lost more than $270 million during the previous season alone. Moreover, salaries represented 75 percent of all teams' expenses, a percentage that wasn't seen in any other professional league. Why, he asked, should the players get such an unfair share of the revenues?

Negotiations were extremely tense and tight right up until the end. Bob Goodenow did try everything he could, but all his efforts couldn't prevent the talks from bogging down. The main problem for Goodenow was that the players weren't united behind him. They were in fact divided into two completely opposite sides, and the ditch between the two kept growing as time went by.

On the one hand, there were the ones who became the advocates of finding an agreement by any means, first because they wanted to play but also because the prospect of a year without a salary wasn't something they could or wanted to experience. The players who chose this side of the ditch started criticizing Goodenow's inflexibility more and more openly. On the other hand, there were those, the majority, who weren't scared by the possibility of a lockout. According to them, it was more important to protect future players with a long-term agreement than to lose one year.

The summer of 2004 saw those two sides move further away from each other, weakening Goodenow's ability to negotiate. Bettman knew that and took advantage of the ever-growing schism between the players. He was becoming more and more intransigent about every point on the negotiation table.

The summer was coming to an end, and it was becoming pretty obvious to everyone that the eighty-eighth season of the NHL would be cancelled. Some of us players even stopped training hard, even though the lockout or the strike hadn't been announced yet. Actually, that was the only question that still needed an answer: lockout or strike?

Since the players' side was deeply divided into two camps, the NHL finally had the last word, and on September 16, 2004, Gary Bettman took the lead and cancelled the season. The lockout was on.

Weeks before that announcement, quite a lot of players, mostly European ones, had already moved to Europe to join the ranks of teams that had been hoping for months for this to happen. The European teams were waiting for their long-lost stars with open arms. After September 16 a load of other players followed them, a situation that saddened me and even made me furious at times.

I totally understood the European players who wanted to go back to their initial fans for a year. Russians went to Russia, Swedes to Sweden, Finns to Finland. Who could possibly object to that? The European fans, just like the players from that continent, live only for their national teams. For the fans in Europe, it was a real blessing to see all those expat players coming back. And those players really gave everything they had to help the teams that had hired them for the lockout—sometimes even more than they'd helped the teams they played for in the NHL.

Then there were the North American players. With their emergency funds in their pockets, they simply sold themselves to the highest bidder. In acting like that they totally forgot, or worse, absolutely didn't care, about all the regular European players who would lose their jobs as a result. Guys who had been devoted to their teams for years were simply fired in order to allow room for the Mister Smith who was coming to town simply to stretch his legs and play tourist.

My agent had told me that some European teams may be interested in hiring me. I simply didn't want to go. I was so ashamed by the blatant opportunism of some of my North American colleagues that I couldn't see myself being part of a mercenary contingent that in some cases was driving honest European players to ruin.

So I kept on training during the fall and early winter, but a bit more lightly than I used to do. It was the first time in decades that hockey wasn't part of my life during those seasons. I was sitting home with nothing to do and it sure felt strange.

After Christmas, more than four hundred NHL players had already crossed the Atlantic while I was shovelling snow from my driveway. I began feeling kind of rusty and started wondering if I could really be out of the hockey world for a complete season and still be competitive at an NHL level. I also have to mention that twelve of my Oilers teammates were playing in European leagues by now.

•

An unexpected solution to my problem came to me out of the blue in February. The regular season was coming to an end in Sweden and the playoffs were soon to begin. The rules over there are the same as in the NHL: players are paid for the regular season but play "voluntarily" all through the post-season series. In other words, if I was going as a volunteer, I wouldn't be a mercenary. I wouldn't be taking another player's job, since no one was getting paid anyway. I had no ethical reason not to go.

I received the offer from the Stockholm Allmänna Idrottsklubben Ishockeyförening (AIK). They wanted to bring depth to their team on the eve of the playoffs. Founded in 1891, that team is as prestigious in Sweden as the Montreal Canadiens are in Canada.

They had experienced deep financial problems a few years earlier, and these had affected the team on the ice. In order to understand how these problems affected them, one has to understand how the European leagues work.

In North America, the NHL teams are in the league to stay, whatever their results are. Even if a team finishes last for a couple of consecutive seasons, its place in the NHL isn't threatened. But in Europe it's a totally different story. When a team finishes at the bottom of the league standings, it immediately goes down one division. It's as if the team finishing last in the NHL has to play the next season in the American league, while the team who wins the championship in the minors gets to be promoted into the NHL.

The AIK had left the Eliteserien (the Swedish Elite League) some years earlier and were now playing in the third division, trying hard to get back to where they belonged. They absolutely had to win that year's series in order to jump up one division for the next season. That was the context in which I accepted the Swedish-team offer. I learned at the same time that the Los Angeles Kings' Swedish player, Mattias Norström, had also accepted an offer to help the AIK in the playoffs.

Only one thing was making me nervous about playing in Sweden. In Europe, they play on Olympic-size rinks that are quite a bit larger than the ones you find in the NHL. I sure wasn't the most skilful skater, and I knew that on the bigger ice surface you had to be fast to make a play. A bodycheck, especially in open ice, is a challenging athletic feat. Add to that the fact that most Swedish players are small and extremely fleet—and that I'd be rusty after being away from the game—and you can see why suiting up in Europe made me a bit anxious.

That wasn't enough to make me back off, though. I'd wanted to discover that country for a long time, and especially its capital, Stockholm. So, Olympic-size ice or not, I was pumped to make my first trip to Europe.

As soon as I accepted their offer, the Swedish press started to attack the AIK and myself. They simply couldn't understand how a *goon* could possibly be of any help to the AIK. Journalists said that the AIK had had multiple choices and that they just couldn't understand why they'd chosen me. On television, programs devoted to sports began showing some of my most violent fights. I was starting to feel pretty uncomfortable, and I wasn't even in Sweden yet.

Needless to say, I had a knot in my stomach when I first arrived at the Hovet Arena, home of the AIK. Right after my sixteen-hour trip from Edmonton to Sweden I had to attend my first practice with the team. Everything was new to me. I was looking at my new teammates and they sure were looking back at me. They were all small, blond, and skated like the wind! What the heck was I doing there?

I was intimidated. My legs were like marshmallows. I was totally jetlagged and out of shape. Add to that the fact that I couldn't understand a thing the head coach was saying to me, and you had the perfect example of what the expression "bull in a china shop" means. I had to watch my teammates first just so I could stagger my way through the on-ice drills.

I could feel the disappointment in the way the head coach and some of my teammates were looking at me. When the workout ended I had only one idea in mind: take a plane back to Canada! And yet, it was only the beginning of one of the most tremendous experiences of my entire life.

Going back to the little apartment the team was lending me for the length of my stay in Stockholm, I sat on the bed, thought for a minute, and decided to get a hold of myself. That morning's practice didn't mean a thing after all. I was tired, stiff, and jetlagged.

I also thought about what had been written about me in the Swedish press. I'd been overly criticized before I played even one game in the AIK uniform. A new challenge had offered itself to me. Just as I had won over racism to become an NHL player, I was going to prove those Swedish critics wrong. I was going to help the AIK win those playoffs with all my strength and all my skills. That was the resolution I made at the end of that first afternoon in Stockholm.

I knew for sure that lots of North American players in Europe were there for money, to keep in shape, and to play tourist as long as it suited them. Some even left their adopted teams right in the middle of the season, and sometimes for trivial reasons, such as they didn't like the food. I had decided I wasn't going to be one of them.

•

In just a few games, I managed to shut the critics up. It wasn't long before the positive impact I had on the team became obvious to everyone. The bodychecks I was giving would allow the most talented of my teammates to play without being bugged. Best of all, I was scoring.

The press were suddenly praising me. Some journalists even profusely apologized to the team and to me. Gradually, I fell in love with the team, the fans, and the city. And all of them were sending me back the love a hundredfold most times.

The European fans, at least some of them, are quite different from the ones you find in North America. They form into organized groups. They can sometimes be really violent, not unlike what you see on the European soccer scene. The main fan group for the AIK is called the Black Army. They spend the whole game standing up, singing, yelling, dancing and, of course, drinking. Not only do they come to every single home game, but they also follow their team on the road.

I soon became the Black Army's and the entire crowd's favourite player. They created lots of songs just for me—a specific one for every occasion. They were pretty mischievous, but in a good way. I particularly liked one of the things they did for me: every time I was getting ready to bodycheck an opponent, the fans' screams would rise up into some sort of a crescendo that would culminate when I'd hit the player.

The other players could of course hear that crescendo and began knowing what it meant. Hearing those screams, some players would simply leave the puck there and escape. In short, I'd gone from being *persona non grata* to hero almost overnight.

Moreover, it was the first time in all my professional years— and the only one, I must say!—that I felt like a complete player. I certainly wasn't there to fight, since there is simply no fighting in the Swedish game. I wasn't put on the ice only to disturb the opponents, but mostly to score goals. I was mainly used on the first line.

I loved it. Playing in a European league is like getting paid to play pond hockey. Everything is faster, guys are making ambitious, high-risk, high-skill plays—and there is almost no contact. At least not much a Canadian player would think of as contact. There's more hitting in an NHL practice than in a Swedish game.

Still, as much as I enjoyed hanging on to the puck longer and playing more minutes, I didn't forget that I had a pretty unique skill set in that league. After I played the body a bit, I could slow the other team down, since they would stop skating, or would be thinking about getting rid of the puck rather than wheeling and dealing the way they liked to do. After a few shifts, it started to look a bit more like an NHL game. Guys were certainly skating with their heads up.

My AIK teammates didn't mind at all. In fact, they'd start chirping at the other teams and taunting players who'd given them a hard time in the past. Of course, they were taunting them in Swedish, so I didn't always know exactly what they were saying. But hockey is hockey, no matter where you play it, and it's not very hard to figure out what two guys are talking about when they're trying to get under each other's skin.

So I guess the experience was a bit of a cultural exchange. I got to play the part of a slick playmaking European, and my teammates got to try on the role of hard-nosed Canadian for a while.

After six weeks, the AIK won the playoffs and gained the right to move up to the second division, the one just under the Eliteserien. I had ended my campaign with 11 goals and 16 points in 16 games, and I served only 24 minutes in the penalty box. (I didn't come close to the team record for penalty minutes, set by Maple Leaf legend Börje Salming—a guy not exactly known for his rough play. Salming spent 100 minutes in the box as a member of the AIK.) And considering how strict the referees are in Sweden, 24 minutes was a very low total for me.

When I wasn't playing or training with the team, I would simply go out and walk around the marvellous city of Stockholm. I would visit every museum, every sight, every attraction I came across while wandering around.

And I didn't really have any problems communicating with the Swedes, as the vast majority of them spoke English and about half of them were able to talk to me in French. Quickly, people started recognizing me in the streets of Stockholm. True, I'm probably not difficult to pick out on a sidewalk full of Swedes ...

I was living in an apartment located in downtown Stockholm, and the team had lent me a small car to drive around. That Nissan Micra was so small I could have lifted it over my head. Every time I had to climb in or get out of it, I had to tie myself in knots that would make everyone around laugh out loud. It was truly a show.

It's also in Sweden that I first became aware of some ecological and environmental issues. Not enough that it would make me change my behaviour, but the seeds of what I would become in the future had been planted. The strictness of their laws regarding the environment, even when it came to food, stunned me. I couldn't believe my eyes when I saw that their milk was good for only three days since it was neither pasteurized nor homogenized, nor did it contain any preservatives.

Another thing that struck me when walking in the streets of Stockholm was that obesity didn't seem to exist over there. The Swedes eat a lot, but only healthy food. Cleanliness was a way of life, and people would dress up with a real sense of fashion.

After the six weeks of my stay had gone by, no one wanted me to go back to North America anymore. The team, the fans, and the press were all over me, begging me to stay with the team for at least another year so that I could be there to help them get back to the Eliteserien.

What I'd seen in Sweden and in the Swedish people for those six weeks, plus the amazing hockey experience I'd had, were things that made me question myself about my future. I really hesitated. And yet, I had to remain rational. I also really loved Edmonton, the Oilers, and their fans, and, let's face it, European salaries are nothing compared to the ones prevailing in the NHL. I declined their offer, promising them that I'd be back one day.

•

I kept up some great relationships with the people I met in Sweden, with the AIK and its fans. I still receive quite a lot of emails from Sweden on an everyday basis. They kept on following my career after I'd gone back to North America, and every time I ended up in the press box in an NHL rink, they would beg me to come back, telling me I would never be out of the lineup with the AIK.

Needless to say, when the Montreal Canadiens released me in 2010, I was overwhelmed with emails telling me that it was now time for me to return to Sweden. At that time, it wasn't only the fans that wanted me back but also the AIK's general manager. For various contractual reasons I couldn't accept their offer. The disappointment it caused among the AIK fans was huge and widely covered by the press.

A promise is a promise, though. Right from the month of September 2010, AIK fans started writing me to mention that February 15, 2011, would mark the 120th anniversary of the team. They began insisting I be there.

Overwhelmed by all my professional activities as well as by my social and community involvements, I once again declined their offer. That was when the team's officials called and told me that my presence was deeply wanted during the ceremonies and that both the fans and the team were to honour me. I was receiving loads of emails from AIK fans, and so were they!

I finally accepted, with great pleasure. On my website and on my Facebook page, I posted a note telling the news: yes, I would be there to celebrate with the team and the fans the 120th anniversary of the AIK. Reactions weren't long in coming, and my email inbox almost exploded. Hundreds of fans wrote me, saying they wanted to take pictures with me. Some even said it would be the most beautiful day of their lives. Others left messages on my Facebook page referring to me as a living God. Although I know exaggeration when I read it, I was sincerely touched by these marks of affection.

Just a few days after I'd committed to making the trip to Stockholm, my agent received a phone call from the AIK officials. They told him they were thrilled I could make it for the 120th anniversary celebrations, but, unfortunately, since they had just hired Richard Zednik, the cupboard was bare, and they couldn't pay for my airplane ticket.

Sincerely sorry about that news, I wrote another note on my Facebook page saying that, even though I really wanted to go, I wouldn't be able to make it to the celebrations. I also wrote that my stay in Stockholm wouldn't even last twenty-four hours. The cost of the airplane ticket was about $7000 and I even offered to split that amount in half, but the team was so broke they couldn't even accept that deal.

Once again, my email inbox got saturated. Fans were disappointed, broken-hearted. And of all the messages I received, one made me change my mind. An AIK fan, instead of joining his voice to the thousands of others who were telling me they were really sad I wasn't coming, had the crafty idea of sending me a newspaper article.

Really, I had set myself up. That article told the story of how I'd offered $100,000 to the Edmonton zoo so that one of its residents, an elephant named Lucy, could be moved to a sanctuary in the United States to end its days quietly. Under the article, the fan had written, "So you're ready to pay $100,000 for an elephant but you won't spend a thin $7000 to come and meet the thousands of fans you have in Sweden?" When I finished reading his email, I burst into laughter. That little rascal had me!

I left Montreal on February 14 so that I could arrive in Stockholm on the fifteenth, the day the commemorative game was to be held. And even though I left the next day and ended up spending more time in the air than on the ground in Sweden, I never ever regretted making that trip.

As soon as I set foot in the Stockholm airport, I was welcomed by a crowd of fans, a lot of them emotional. I had the sensation that I was the Pope. The team's officials came to pick me up and drove me to a beautiful hotel close to the rink, where they had booked me a room. If I hadn't known the room was sponsored I would have thought they were mocking me when they told me they were broke.

I took a quick shower and got ready to go to the celebrations that were to be held at the Ericsson Globe, a bigger arena the AIK was using for important games. Rest assured, I wasn't playing that night.

Since I had announced I was coming I'd repeatedly written on my Facebook page that I would watch the games with the crowd, right in the middle of the Black Army fans. Another car came and picked me up at my hotel, and as soon as I got to the arena, the team's officials told me I had the best seat in the whole arena waiting for me.

They didn't want me to watch the game with the Black Army. That would be far too dangerous, since fights often occurred there. I smiled at them and said it was out of the question for me to be seated anywhere else but among the rawest and most devoted AIK fans. They had been directly responsible for my experience in Sweden and for bringing me back that night, and I wanted to thank them.

After giving several interviews to the local press and television stations, I went up into the stands to join the members of the Black Army. They simply couldn't believe their eyes that I was actually going to spend the whole time among them. Their welcome was so warm and joyful that I had tears in my eyes half the night. I danced, sang, and jumped the whole game long.

Many times during the match the fans would sing my name. At some moments they weren't even following what was happening on the ice, but simply looking at me and chanting my name. Rarely had I lived through something as intensely emotional. Never had I been that much appreciated as a player.

That night, I experienced something I never thought I would—something that few hockey players ever will: I really knew what it feels like to be Wayne Gretzky. For a day, I was Sweden's 250-pound, black Wayne Gretzky.

AIK, *i mitt hjärta för evigt.*

BACK TO THE NHL

11

Throughout the lockout months, the NHL and the NHLPA had kept on negotiating but no real progress was made. And the more time went by, the more Bob Goodenow was coming under pressure from an ever-growing number of players. Even if Europe had been a great experience for some of us, we all had the feeling that now was the time to go back home. We wanted to play.

Goodenow managed to hold his ground even as the stakes got higher. Summer arrived and there was still no agreement between the two parties. Suddenly, even though no one wanted to believe it, a second cancelled season seemed like a real possibility. It wasn't to happen, though.

The NHLPA and the NHL finally managed to agree on a new CBA on July 3, 2005. A few weeks later, even though he'd fought hard to get what I thought wasn't such a bad compromise between what the players wanted and what the NHL was demanding, Bob Goodenow had to resign and was immediately replaced by Ted Saskin, who was then the commercial affairs director of the NHLPA.

One more reason for me to be happy about the settlement was that I was starting the last year of my contract with the Oilers.

In one year I would become a free agent. Since my heart and soul was with the Oilers and the city of Edmonton, I wanted to take the opportunity the 2005–06 season offered to prove to everyone that I should stay in Edmonton. I was all pumped up and ready to rumble.

•

Unfortunately, and even though we were to have an excellent end to the season, things began in a chaotic way for the team as well as for me. First, there was the Sean Avery incident. During a game against the LA Kings, on October 11, he took a run at one of our top players, Ales Hemsky.

As soon as I got back on the ice, I lined up against him at the faceoff. I asked him to settle this up right away. Not only did he refuse my invitation, he used a word that I won't repeat here. It was the first time I had ever experienced racism in the NHL. I was stunned.

My teammates jumped on him. I couldn't do it myself, and this for only one reason: I would have killed him. Fights are the tough guys' work. But in this context, it wouldn't have been a job, it would have been pure pleasure.

In the locker room after the game, journalists questioned me about what had really happened on the ice. I told them what I'd heard coming out of Avery's mouth and that the NHL would have to pronounce on the incident.

After having showered, the whole team made its way to the Staples Center's parking lot where our bus was waiting for us. Coincidentally, Avery came out into the parking lot at the same time. He was with his girlfriend of the moment, just a few metres away from us.

Craig MacTavish saw red. Although he was already seated on the bus, he jumped out of his seat and made a straight line towards the Kings player. He was shouting, jabbing his finger in Avery's face, asking him how he dared insult me on the colour of my skin. Suddenly all my teammates were off the bus and closing in on Avery, giving him an earful I'm sure he'll remember. Avery's girlfriend was holding him to prevent a fight from erupting. I hope he thanked her on his way back home. A fight that night would have had major consequences for his health.

In the following days, I had a meeting with chief NHL disciplinarian Colin Campbell to discuss the incident, which he took very seriously. After all the bad publicity the league had suffered because of the lockout, he didn't want a racism scandal right at the beginning of the new season to tarnish its reputation even more.

He truly believed my version, but since no one but me had heard the insult, there was nothing he could do against Avery. In other words, no witness, no case. Avery was once again going to run his mouth and then hide from the consequences, exactly as he had done a couple of years earlier when players Denis Gauthier and Ian Laperrière had tried to confront him on his anti-francophone discrimination. Next time we played the Kings, I was wearing a microphone. Was he going to repeat his word? He didn't.

The guy is not stupid enough to make that mistake twice. But that's about the best thing I can say about Avery. To this day he hasn't been man enough to apologize for what he said. And for that reason alone, I don't mind saying that of all the guys I've played against over the course of my career—and I was never a Lady Byng candidate—Avery is the only guy I don't respect.

The incident had a good side to it: despite a not-so-good beginning of the season, the Oilers bonded again as a team and were still as united as they'd been before the lockout.

That said, the more the season wore on, the less I was playing. With the new CBA came new rules, and stricter enforcement by the refs, which made the role of the tough guys almost obsolete. All kinds of little things that might not have been called before were suddenly penalties. There was a lot less stickwork around the league. Scoring was way up, and fighting started to become rare. Almost three-quarters of the NHL games that season were fight-free. This didn't go unnoticed by Craig MacTavish, either. He was keeping me on the bench more than ever. I was still in uniform, but I do remember a series of games in which my ice time would average three minutes per game.

The situation was frustrating after what I'd known in Sweden, of course, but also in the previous season with the Oilers. In an interview I gave to Montreal journalist Marc-Antoine Godin, I even said that ballet dancers would soon be invited to play in the NHL and that they wouldn't have to be afraid of getting hit.

In that same interview I also said something a lot of people were surprised by. When Godin asked me if my position towards the Montreal Canadiens had stayed the same even after the lockout, I told him the following: "I could be interested in coming to Montreal. I'll be a free agent at the end of the present season and I'll consider every offer I receive. Only fools never change their minds." Deep inside me, though, my only wish was to remain an Oiler.

Christmas arrived and MacTavish still had me nailed to the bench. I certainly couldn't blame him. During my rare presences on the ice I was trying hard to make things happen offensively, but nothing seemed to work anymore. No matter what line a guy is on, he wants to play. Not playing eats at you. You get angry. Even as a fan, you can probably read the body language of the guy who's missed a few shifts. He's pissed off. If he's an established, well-paid player, he might give in to temptation and get in his coach's face and demand more ice time. Some guys can win confrontations with coaches.

Not many tough guys can do that, though. If you complain about your ice time, and you're expendable, you're gone. Other players don't want to hear a guy complaining either. Sometimes not complaining is the best thing you can do for your team.

So there I was, warming the bench, still looking for my first goal of the season. I kept telling myself my lethargy wouldn't last forever. But I was getting angrier all the time.

Coaches are coaches for a reason, though—they should know what players are thinking. They sit their stars to send them a message. And they know that sitting on the bench makes guys like me angry. So why do they do it? They want us to play angry. In this case, MacTavish's mind games and shrewd coaching paid off on January 21, during a game in Phoenix against the Coyotes. I'd played only a frustrating 1:52 minutes in the first period. I watched the second one entirely from the bench. In the beginning of the third, the Coyotes were leading 2–1.

Looking to shake things up, MacTavish decided to send his fourth line out. My job was pretty simple. When we got the puck deep in the Coyotes' zone, I went straight to the crease to create some havoc. Soon our forecheck had the Coyotes running around a bit and we got a shot on net. Picking up a rebound off former Oiler goaltender Curtis Joseph in front of the Coyotes' net, I took a backhand shot that he partially blocked. Not knowing if the puck was going to enter the net or not, defender Dennis Seidenberg tried to shovel it into the corner, but ended up banging it into his own net. That was probably the ugliest goal I ever scored, but at least it ended the scoring drought that dated back to March 2004.

I wouldn't go so far as to say that after this goal things started going well for me, but it sure brought back some confidence. MacTavish noticed it and began giving me a bit more ice time, an average of eight to nine minutes per game. I was now on a trio with Fernando Pisani and Marty Reasoner, and we were doing a good offensive job.

Even though I was spending a lot less time on the ice than I had during the pre-lockout season, I was still among the lucky ones. A lot of tough guys—good guys I had always respected—had simply lost their jobs since the new rules had come in. The list of tough guys whose careers ended along with the 2003–04 season reads like a who's who of the toughest guys in the league when the lockout started. Reed Low, Andrei Nazarov, Jim Cummins, Sandy McCarthy, Krystof Oliwa—these guys together played a total of eight games after that season. This is just a partial list, and of course not every guy left the game for the same reason (and some guys didn't leave at all), but there is one guy in particular I should add: Matt Johnson.

I fought Johnson eleven times, dating back to my rookie season, usually twice a season. He wasn't the biggest guy I ever fought, and probably not the meanest, but I'll never forget that he's the only guy to have ever legitimately knocked me down with a punch. He put me on the ice in a game against Minnesota—so my hat is off to Mr. Johnson.

In any case, for all the tough guys who were gone that year, there was a new name that started coming up when people talked about NHL heavyweights: Derek Boogaard. The guy was dominating the league. At six-foot-seven, 270 pounds, Boogaard was a guy anyone in his right mind would be wary of.

At that point, I was one of the biggest guys in the league, but Boogaard was bigger. Naturally, people wanted to see what would happen if we met up, and I'm sure he did too. That's how a rookie makes his name.

So when we went to Minnesota in November, there was more than a little anticipation. The Minnesota media couldn't get enough of the story, and they hounded me for comments in order to hype what looked like an inevitable confrontation. But I wasn't eager to do anything stupid.

Plus, I figured I had half the battle won already when I saw Boogaard watching the pre-game skate. Sometimes tough guys will watch their opponents in practice to observe their balance and skating styles. They also hang around at the end of the skate to see who's still on the ice. If a guy is still skating when most of his teammates have left, that means he's probably not in the lineup that night—so if he's the guy you'd probably have to fight, you know you may have less to worry about.

There was Boogaard at the end of our skate. I knew I was already inside his head.

That may have been half the battle, but unfortunately it was the easy half. Every time I was on the ice I waited to see if his coach would send him over the boards. Then, at the end of the first period, there we were, shoulder to shoulder at a faceoff at the offside dot in front of his bench.

Anyway, it went fine for me, but I have to admit that I approached the fight very cautiously—I may have been arguably the toughest guy in the league, but there was no point pissing off Derek Boogaard.

Fortunately, MacTavish had always seen me as more than just a policeman. He knew I was able to accomplish good things on the ice even if I wasn't the most skilful or fastest of players.

And despite the new rules, and the drop in the number of fights, it's not as though fighting had disappeared altogether. Referees weren't able to see all the vicious hits and stickwork going on on the ice. Some players had figured out how to get their shots in when the refs were looking the other way. And one of the best at getting away with the dirty stuff had to be the Flames' Chris Simon.

On April 1 we were playing Calgary. They'd managed to build a 3–0 lead, and we knew that with Miikka Kiprusoff in their net it was an almost impossible task to even think about levelling the score. Knowing the game was getting out of reach for us, Simon started to figure he had a bit more leeway. He was having fun messing with players like Ryan Smyth and Ales Hemsky without the referees seeing anything.

Pretty fed up with his liberties, and looking for a way to change the momentum of the game, I got in Simon's face and provoked him. Things went very well for me in that fight and I was given a one-minute-long ovation for it. Fans from both teams started fights here and there in the stands. The rivalry between the two Alberta teams was at its peak, except that if the Flames were already in the playoffs, that sure wasn't the case for us.

Yet we managed to finish eighth in the Western Conference and secure our spot in the playoffs. I'd missed about a dozen games during the regular season due to a minor but really painful hip injury. With a harvest of only two goals for a ten-point total, I had just gotten through my worst offensive season since my full-time debut in the NHL. Not really ideal statistics for a player who was to be a free agent by June 30.

•

We were to meet up with the Detroit Red Wings in the first round of the playoffs. They'd had a brilliant season and were going to be a big challenge to overcome. I don't think anyone would square off with a team that featured guys like Brendan Shanahan, Steve Yzerman, Pavel Datsyuk, Henrik Zetterberg, and Niklas Lidstrom and take them lightly, especially if they'd just won the President's Trophy and had 124 points in the regular season. But at least we wouldn't be playing the Dallas Stars.

I only played the first game against the Wings. Since that team was counting a lot more on its speed than on its roughness, MacTavish decided to leave me off the roster. The Wings took us a bit lightly, though, and we surprised them in six hard-fought games.

I would have loved to face the Flames in the second round. First, I'm sure the series would have been amazingly entertaining because of the natural rivalry between both teams; and second, on a more egocentric note, the Flames being a really physical team, I'm sure MacTavish would have used me quite a lot. But fate decided otherwise, Calgary being evicted from the playoffs by the surprising Mighty Ducks in seven games. We were then to face the San Jose Sharks.

Despite being the underdog once again, our victory against the Red Wings gave us a lot of confidence, maybe a little bit too much. We didn't play well in the first game and San Jose won quite easily. I wasn't in uniform that night, and I saw the Sharks players running our guys repeatedly throughout the game. Those kinds of moments would make me furious. Nothing is more frustrating for a tough guy than to watch from the stands as his teammates get pushed around.

After seeing that, MacTavish decided to dress me for the second game. Before the game he jokingly told the press that I would make a difference in the series in my first two shifts. Thank you, Coach, for putting such pressure on my shoulders!

I had to be really cautious returning to the game. I knew I had to walk a fine line. It was no mystery that MacTavish wanted me to play physically. My job was to make sure my teammates wouldn't get harassed as they had been during the previous game.

On the other hand, I knew that if I took useless penalties, MacTavish would surely leave me on the bench for the rest of the game. I succeeded at playing my part the way I was expected to, which led to an increase in my ice time period after period. So, even though we lost that one again, I had gained the right to remain with the team for the rest of the series.

The third game was a must-win. It was our first home game of the series and we were trailing 2–0. We simply *had* to win.

The building was electric, and we were playing more like it was game seven than game three. Then, at 13:38 in the second period, I saw I had a good angle on Jonathan Cheechoo, the best scorer of the league during the regular season. I caught him with a solid but legal bodycheck. Unfortunately, the Sharks player hit the glass awkwardly and came away with a cut on his face. Not only did I receive a major penalty for what I'd thought was a clean hit, but the referee added a game misconduct on top of it all. I was furious.

Yes, the bodycheck was a rough one; yes, I weighed about sixty pounds more than Cheechoo, but I knew he'd seen me coming. I was punished so severely only because he was a star. The NHL didn't suspend me for that gesture, judging that it had been performed according to the rules of the game.

The rest of the game gave the Edmonton fans reason to be tense. At the end of regulation time, the score was tied at two. The noise in the arena was unbearable. Things could swing to one side or the other in no time, as is always the case during overtime.

We had to wait until the second minute of the third overtime before Shawn Horcoff found a loose puck in the San Jose crease and buried it to give us the win, liberating the 16,839 fans in the house from unbelievable stress. The way they let it all out will always remain in my head as the most deafening roar I've ever heard.

The San Jose Sharks had just played the longest game in their history, and they had lost. They weren't going to recover from it. Totally pumped up, our confidence at its pinnacle, we dominated the three following games in every respect. And there we were, in the Conference finals for the first time since the 1991–92 season.

Facing us in that next series were the Anaheim Mighty Ducks. They had struggled quite a bit to defeat the Calgary Flames, but they'd had no problems getting rid of the Avalanche in four straight games. Because of that easy win against Colorado, the Ducks were the favourite among the analysts, even though we'd been quite impressive in the last three games of our series against the Sharks.

As is often the case when a team is seen as the favourite to win a series, the Mighty Ducks went out on their home ice with too much confidence and not enough concentration for the first two games. We, meanwhile, had nothing to lose. After such an average season, not a single serious hockey analyst had predicted we would end up in the Conference finals.

We won those first two games with the same 3–1 score. They weren't easy wins at all, but still, we felt comfortable. Our team spirit was now invulnerable. Or so we thought.

The reality check was to come soon.

With those two wins on the road, MacTavish tried to motivate us, to keep us focused. Yes, we'd won, but we still had to pay close attention to the game plan. He really wanted us to close that series as fast as possible so that we could get some rest before the *real* finals. We began the game ready for war, ready to win it.

There were only fifteen minutes left in the third period and we were leading 4–0. It was in the bag and we started to ease up. Foolishly. Within a four-minute span the Ducks scored three fast goals. Our confidence vanished. Suddenly we were skating around, afraid of making a fatal mistake.

Fortunately, Fernando Pisani scored to give us a two-goal advantage. Teemu Selanne managed to score one more for the Ducks at 18:15 in the third, but it was too late. We had squeaked through on Pisani's goal.

Even though we had a 3–0 lead in the series, we had the feeling the Ducks wouldn't let it go that easily. They won the fourth game on our ice with a convincing 6–3. We knew it was almost impossible for a team to catch up a 3–0 deficit in a series, but we got anxious anyway.

That was when MacTavish's long and deep experience in the playoffs paid off. He prepared us so well for that fifth game, using the right words to make sure we'd stay focused. Looking back, it was mostly things we already knew on some level, or things we'd already heard before. We knew that the fourth game is the toughest to win, that the playoffs only get harder the deeper you go. We knew that it would have been a terrible mistake to show mercy now, and that the Ducks were going to come out desperate. But if we'd heard those things from a taxi driver or a well-meaning uncle, they wouldn't have meant as much. Hearing them from a playoff warrior sent chills down my spine.

Even when the Ducks took a quick 1–0 lead in the first we didn't panic. We responded with two goals in the second. And from that point on, the two teams went at it with everything we had. I had never been part of a faster, fiercer game. It's amazing to see how much more you can do when you want something that badly. We all thought we'd been playing at 100 percent all along, but we found something more when there was more on the line. The Ducks had it too. Every play, every faceoff, every backcheck, every line change was performed with an exhilarating focus and intensity.

But the score remained the same until the end. I couldn't believe it. I was going to play in the Stanley Cup finals.

●

The feelings I had that evening and in the days that followed remain indescribable. To come that close to something you've dreamed of your whole life is something bigger than words.

For the first time in the history of modern hockey, the team that had accumulated the fewest points during the regular season was reaching the finals. We were making history, and we had no intention of stopping.

Our opponents were to be the veteran-laden Carolina Hurricanes. They would start the finals tired, having had to play seven very tough games against the Buffalo Sabres to reach that final. We figured our youth was going to work in our favour. And not only were we thinking that, but the press was too. For the first time in the playoffs, we were the team favoured to win a series. And it was the one I'd spent my life dreaming of winning.

The first game was on June 5 in Raleigh. It started at a relatively slow pace, the two teams testing each other, afraid of making the first mistake. In these kinds of games, the first goal is huge. And we got it off the stick of Pisani. Then Chris Pronger scored.

At 16:23 of the second period, Ethan Moreau scored. We were now leading 3–0. We tried to stay focused, tried to keep it simple. But we were riding on a cloud, and our youth might have played against us.

Rod Brind'Amour scored quickly to get the Hurricanes back in it. Then Ray Whitney scored a couple of quick ones to tie it up. Suddenly the veterans weren't looking like liabilities anymore.

At 10:02 in the third, Justin Williams scored a short-handed goal for the Hurricanes to give them the lead. We didn't panic, but we were definitely shaken by that sudden and unexpected turnaround. Thank God for us, Ales Hemsky evened the score three minutes later. A new game had just started.

But one minute after Hemsky's goal a terrible thing happened, something that would change the series. The Carolina left-winger, Andrew Ladd, entered our zone on the wing and cut to the centre of the ice, heading for our goalie Dwayne Roloson's crease. Marc-André Bergeron tried to keep Ladd from going to the net, but ended up directing him right into Roloson. Our goalie looked as though he'd been hit by a freight train, and remained lying on the ice for an agonizingly long time.

He then staggered off the ice, supported by our medical staff.

He never came back.

Roloson had stolen game after game for us. We'd been out-shot again and again during the first three rounds, and Roloson had shut the door. Now we had to do it without him. There was only about thirty seconds left in the third period. Our fate depended on the outcome of sudden-death overtime.

That was when Roloson's substitute, Ty Conklin, made one big mistake. Not that I want to point the finger at Conklin. The young goalie had played only eighteen games during the regular season and hadn't touched a puck in the playoffs. And now he was in the spotlight in a sudden death in the biggest game of his life. When the puck went behind the net, he left his crease to play it. Looking to move it to Jason Smith, he handcuffed the defenceman with an unexpected pass. The puck bounced off Smith's stick and found its way to Rod Brind'Amour, who tapped it calmly into our open net.

We had just lost a game we should have won. And we had just lost our spine in the person of Roloson.

However, we were so pumped up that it would take more than that to discourage us. We were ready to take our revenge. We were ready to start game two immediately. Those Carolina old-timers, we would wear them down.

Glen Wesley, Rod Brind'Amour, Bret Hedican, Doug Weight, and Ray Whitney were great players, but together they had accu-mulated seventy-eight years of experience in the NHL without getting to touch the Cup once. And we were ready to do every-thing to keep them from touching it for at least another year.

That was the dominant feeling among the whole Oilers orga-nization. Every one of us was sharing it, from the bottom to the top of the staff. But the Hurricanes had thoughts of their own.

They also had a kid named Eric Staal among those veterans. He was only twenty-one, but he was the one who would bring us to reality in the second game. He didn't score, but he seemed to be everywhere on the ice, making things happen, keeping us on our toes, controlling the play for his old-timer teammates.

That chemistry, made from a perfect mix of great experience and dexterity-filled youth, simply dazzled us during the game. The score, 5–0, reflected what had happened. We couldn't blame Jussi Markkanen, who'd replaced Conklin in net. We were all responsible for our failure. We had simply been outclassed.

On June 10 we were back in Edmonton for game three. We were all a bit disconcerted by how things had turned out in Carolina. Yet we kept reminding ourselves that the Stanley Cup finals is a unique experience. Lots of players have played years in the NHL without ever getting a taste of it. It wasn't time to quit. We were there now and it might just be the only chance we'd ever get in our career to win that trophy.

MacTavish let his experience talk once again and insisted on that point himself. He'd been part of the last Oilers' team to win the Cup back in 1990. He knew what it took to get there. And he also knew that it had gotten harder since he played. The new CBA signed the summer before and the way revenues would now be shared throughout the NHL were making it almost impossible to ever see dynasties like the 1980s Oilers again. We had to take our chance while we had it.

Fully focused and really united, we began the third game just as if nothing had happened. We had to come out as if it were game one, not game three. We had to come out like the team that had won the Western Conference, not the team that had just dropped two games. There was a reason we were there, and we had to play that way.

The energy in the rink was insane. The fans had the place absolutely vibrating. And we came out flying. It's as though the fans can make you do what they're all hoping for—make you skate faster, or haul in a pass that's in your skates, or deliver a crushing check to choke off the opponent's breakout. Sometimes the fans' energy seems to be making things happen on the ice.

We were all energy, all focus. When Shawn Horcoff opened the score at 2:31 in the first, we didn't act as we had in the first game when we'd taken a 3–0 lead halfway into the game. We played by the book and kept in mind the game plan set for us by MacTavish. I guess we were starting to learn.

Rod Brind'Amour evened the score in the tenth minute of the third. We started to play a little tight, but instead of panicking, we all started concentrating on simple plays. Both teams were now walking on thin ice, no one wanting to commit the fatal mistake.

There were about two minutes left in the third and everything seemed to be leading us straight into overtime. That was when Ryan Smith bulled his way into the crease and got the puck behind Cam Ward. The referees asked for the video goal judge in order to see whether the goal would count. The following seconds seemed like an eternity. The fans were holding their breath in the stands. We needed that goal; we needed that victory.

The verdict finally came. The referee pointed to the centre of the ice. The goal was valid. The crowd roared. We felt liberated. Confidence could now come back. We were going to win that Cup!

When Sergei Samsonov scored for us at 8:40 in the first period of the fourth game, we felt galvanized. Nothing could stop us now. That feeling lasted exactly twenty-nine seconds. Cory Stillman evened the score at 9:09. And veteran Mark Recchi sealed the game at the end of the second. The Hurricanes had now taken a 3–1 lead in the series.

Thirty-three minutes and forty-six seconds. That was the time spent on the ice by Chris Pronger in the fifth game. Hockey is surely a team sport, but that night, even though he didn't score, he was our undisputed leader and led us to victory. Pronger was virtually everywhere. He would block a shot and then in the next second lead the counter-offensive; he would deliver a tough bodycheck and then be bodychecked in turn; he would provoke our best power-play moments and lead the team when short-handed. It was a Pronger shot that Pisani redirected for the opening goal. It was Pronger who laid the bodycheck on Doug Weight and put him out of the series.

Chris Pronger had risen up and everyone in the team had gained one foot. His leadership had set the example in our 4–3 overtime win, and put some swagger back in our step heading back to Edmonton for game six.

With the Edmonton fans loudly and unconditionally behind us, we dominated the sixth game 4–0, both physically and on the score sheet. The Hurricanes hardly got a shot on net, and the goaltending problem that arose when Roloson went down seemed to have been solved with Jussi Markkanen's first play-off shutout. We were feeling confident. And the press? They announced that we were invincible going into the seventh game.

The Oilers officials were so optimistic that they decided to charter a second plane for our last trip to Carolina. Close friends, players' wives, family members, and lots of champagne bottles would be boarding that plane. Everything was set for the celebrations!

Craig MacTavish made the decision not to have me play that night, but I felt not a single ounce of frustration about it. He was the head coach, he knew what was best for the team, and all I wanted was for the Oilers to win. I'd played fifteen games throughout the playoffs, and I knew I had contributed. Victory would be mine whether or not I took a shift in the final game.

But that doesn't mean I was calm. At least guys in the lineup can focus on what they have to do. They can prepare. They have their destiny in their own hands. At that moment, though, all I could do was count on the guys I had battled with all year.

The hours before a game seven are agony. You're fuelled by an intoxicating blend of desire and anxiety, of aggression and fear of making a mistake. You do everything you can to focus on the challenge in front of you, but you see the sixty minutes of hockey ahead not just as a sport but as the pinnacle of years of hard work.

There's a reason why teams that are serious about taking a run at the Stanley Cup load up on veterans at the trade deadline. Veterans know how to win. They know how to keep their head when it counts. The Hurricanes had gone out and got Recchi and Weight. They already had guys like Brind'Amour and Stillman. The team had been to the finals in 2002.

The Hurricanes' experience spoke out loud during that last game. The confidence and energy of youth was no match. Veteran Aaron Ward nailed us in the very first minutes of the opening period. Then František Kaberle scored again at the beginning of the second. Pisani scored for us early in the third, but the Hurricanes managed to shut us down for the rest of the period, winning it with a last goal in an empty net. The Carolina Hurricanes became the 2005–06 Stanley Cup champions.

After the game, in the Oilers locker room, all you could hear were the sounds of total despair. The guys started drinking that champagne the organization had brought to Raleigh to celebrate our supposedly inevitable victory. Back at the hotel, some guys got drunk and started throwing bottles against the conference room walls. Proud and loyal men, strong and competitive men were falling apart and in tears in front of me. All that stress they'd lived on for the past ten weeks was suddenly vanishing, leaving them exhausted and with nothing to soothe away the pain. I had never witnessed or felt anything worse in my entire career.

Imagine working on a project for nearly a year—a year of injuries and disappointment and stress—only to find at the end that it had amounted to nothing. Imagine how crushing that would be. Now imagine that you'd dreamed of that project your whole life and fallen short. Now imagine you may never get another chance.

That's how we felt. Given the choice between not making the playoffs and losing the seventh game of the Stanley Cup finals, I'd pick the first option any time. Any player who's gone through both will doubtlessly share my opinion.

And it was even worse for me, since that seventh game I hadn't played was to be my last one as an Oiler.

FROM THE DESERT
TO THE PENGUINS

12

All summer long after that heart-rending loss, every person I met wanted to talk about the Oilers' playoff run, and how magnificently we had played. I was grateful for all those congratulations, of course, but it was difficult to accept them—they really just rubbed in the bitterness of how close we'd come to what we wanted so badly. I would change the subject as quickly as I could.

Edmonton's mayor and city council wanted to organize a ceremony in our honour at City Hall. After consulting the players, the Oilers' management simply declined the offer. Sure, we'd had a good run, but we hadn't won the only game we wanted to. There was no way we could stand in front of our fans with our heads held high, as if we were champions of some kind—there is no silver medal in the NHL playoffs.

The other subject everyone wanted to talk about wasn't any more pleasant to my ears. They all wanted to know what the future held in store for me. The last game of the finals had been in the middle of June, not even two weeks before July 1—the first day of my free agency. I was still stinging from the worst defeat in my career, and there I was, a player without a team.

Je voulais me prouver que j'étais capable de survivre au racisme »

— Georges Laraque

"I wanted to prove to myself that I could succeed in hockey despite racism"

With Don Cherry, a man who ows what tough guys are there for

The famous fight against
Rob Ray, on March 3, 1999
(AP) →

Celebrating the third goal of my only hat trick in the NHL, February 21, 2000 (Perry Mah)

I kept the three pucks and many of the hats the fans threw on the ice (Perry Mah)

The Laraque Leap—there was no other way for me to celebrate a goal (Perry Mah)

↑→   My first goal in the AIK uniform in Stockholm

↓   Yes, I managed to fit into the Nissan Micra that the AIK provided for me

www.georgeslaraque.com

Georges Laraque

Pourquoi je n'aimerais pas jouer à Montréal

Why I would not want to play in Montreal

If I am traded ... I will no longer drop the gloves

Si je suis échangé... je ne laisserai plus tomber les gants

KING GEORGES!

By PIERRE LEBRUN
The Canadian Press

Fighting is down 42% in the new NHL, where you don't dress if you can't keep up.

There were 858 fighting majors handed down this season through Monday night, down from 1,471 through the same number of games in 2003-04.

"The thing about the new NHL is that we've had our ice time reduced," says Edmonton's Georges Laraque. And the dean of the NHL tough guys doesn't like it.

"The NHL is almost becoming like a European league," continued Laraque.

"There's not enough hitting or fighting. A team will win the Stanley Cup without any bumps or bruises. Whoever has the best power play will win the Stanley Cup."

But fellow tough guy George Parros of Los Angeles is OK with the new NHL.

"I love the new rules, I think the game is more exciting, and at the same time it got rid of the guys that were just there to beat each other's brains in," said Parros, one of the league's busiest fighters.

Fedoruk had 23 points (4-19) in 69 games before the Mighty Ducks took on Los Angeles last night.

The busiest tough guys this season have been the rookies, led by Ottawa's Brian McGrattan, who has an NHL-high 18 fighting majors.

Parros, also a rookie, is next at 17 followed by Minnesota first-year tough guy Derek Boogaard at 16.

Here's a subjective top-10 ranking of the NHL's tough guys ...

1. Georges Laraque
Team: Edmonton
Age: 29
Size: 6-3, 243 pounds.
Skinny: He's only 16th in the league with nine fighting majors this season and has slowed down the number of times he drops the gloves over the last few years, but every single tough guy interviewed for this piece mentioned him as the most feared fighter in the league. Has two goals and nine assists in 70 games.

"Georges has ... constantly overpowered guys in fights over the years," said Todd Fedoruk.

(Sun Media Corporation)

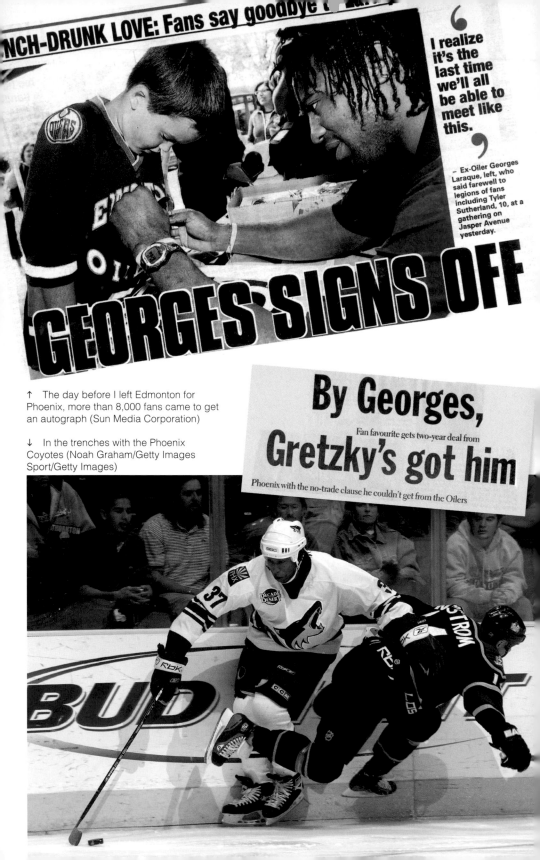

I realize it's the last time we'll all be able to meet like this.

– Ex-Oiler Georges Laraque, left, who said farewell to legions of fans including Tyler Sutherland, 10, at a gathering on Jasper Avenue yesterday.

GEORGES SIGNS OFF

↑ The day before I left Edmonton for Phoenix, more than 8,000 fans came to get an autograph (Sun Media Corporation)

↓ In the trenches with the Phoenix Coyotes (Noah Graham/Getty Images Sport/Getty Images)

By Georges, Gretzky's got him

Fan favourite gets two-year deal from Phoenix with the no-trade clause he couldn't get from the Oilers

↑ After the first goal I scored with the Penguins (Christian Petersen/ Getty Images Sport/ Getty Images)

↑ The Penguins faced off against the Sabres in the 2008 Winter Classic at the Ralph Wilson Stadium in front of more than 71,000 spectators (Harry How/Getty Images Sport/Getty Images)

Le CH ne se fera plus brasse

– Georges Laraque

The Habs won't be pushed around anymore

↑ (The Montreal Canadiens)

← The Montreal Canadiens' official hundredth-anniversary card (The Montreal Canadiens)

Even though about fifteen teams had made me an offer or at least shown an interest, in my heart and soul I was still an Oiler.

I had slowly but surely built a great life in Edmonton. I had a beautiful house and good friends, and I was deeply involved in the community. I was going back to Montreal for only a few days every summer to see my family. In short, my life was now in Alberta and I didn't want to leave it for anything in the world.

Add to that the fact that night after night I'd been fighting for the Oilers in a very real sense for as long as I'd been in professional hockey, and you can see why I didn't want to go anywhere else.

That was my message that summer, and I found myself repeating it everywhere I went. The Edmonton fans were making it pretty clear to me that they wanted that too. I received hundreds of emails that all said the same thing. In fact, the whole city of Edmonton seemed to want me to stay. All of Edmonton except the Oilers, that is. They were the only ones who didn't seem too excited about the idea. Even though my agent was pressing them to negotiate, they didn't seem to be in a hurry to make me an offer. I even told the press that I was ready to accept a lower salary if the Oilers could guarantee me a contract that would allow me to play in Edmonton until the end of my career.

I did finally get an offer from them. It was a three-year contract for a million dollars a year. That was $100,000 less than what I'd earned the season before. No one likes a pay cut—it seems to say you've been overpaid all along. And a pay cut is even less attractive when other teams are offering you a raise. A pretty decent raise.

Still, I was ready to sign with the Oilers if they were ready to include a no-trade clause in the contract. They refused. I then understood that the only reason they'd made me an offer was that I had good value on the market, and that they'd trade me as soon as another team was ready to give them something they wanted in exchange.

The thing was, I had the feeling that, because of the new rules, Craig MacTavish wasn't convinced he needed a tough guy on his team anymore. A year later, though, he figured out the mistake he'd made. Without a decent tough guy in his ranks to protect his skilled players, the Oilers would be one of the most injured teams in all the NHL. Rule changes only work when they're enforced, and sometimes the guy who enforces them is already on your roster.

But I wasn't going to be that guy anymore.

Broken-hearted, I finally came to the conclusion that I had no choice but to leave Edmonton. I'd probably have to move to the United States, which wasn't something I was looking forward to. Don't get me wrong here, I had nothing against the States. It's just that I was used to the Canadian lifestyle and didn't feel like changing it for anything else.

Among all the teams that were interested in hiring me, the Phoenix Coyotes had made the best offer. I wasn't convinced I wanted to play with the Coyotes, but Mike Comrie, my ex-teammate assured me it was a great place to play hockey.

The person who finally persuaded me to accept the contract was actually the most glorious of the ex-Oilers. The Coyotes' co-owner and head coach, Wayne Gretzky, gave me a call. He told me how much he wanted me on his team, and that he had an important role for me to play. He also flattered me a bit, telling me that I reminded him of Dave Semenko, but with more talent. When the best player of all time talks to you like that and offers you the best contract on the table, it becomes pretty impossible to say no.

So I accepted the Coyotes' offer, a two-year contract for $2.5 million that included the no-movement clause I had been fighting for. Even better, though NHL rules stipulate that a player must have been in the league ten years to get his own room on the road, the Coyotes were offering me that privilege in my ninth.

I have to make a confession here, a little lie I made at the beginning of my career that allowed me to be one of the only NHL players who never had to share his room with anyone while on the road.

On the very first trip I made with the Oilers, Kevin Lowe was my roommate. All through the night I snored so heavily that Lowe didn't sleep at all. Even the players in the room next to us had trouble sleeping. Lowe spent the night shouting at me, hitting me, trying in vain to wake me up. But I guess that if I could sleep through my own snoring, I could sleep through his complaints.

On the next three trips, Andreï Kovalenko, Josef Beránek, and Ryan Smyth were the ones who endured a sleepless night thanks to the deafening roar of my snoring. The team then decided to give me my own room, but made me promise I would get operated on during the summer to settle up that snoring problem. It was a minor operation, but the results weren't guaranteed.

So that summer, I went under the knife—not for a knee or shoulder surgery, but to have my tonsils and uvula taken out. The uvula was the organ responsible for that unbearable rattle I would make in my sleep. The operation was a success—but I told the team it hadn't worked.

The next season, Kevin Lowe was now the head coach. During our first road trip, he sent a spy to room with me, the newcomer Marc-André Bergeron. He was to share my room for the first night and then report to Lowe.

I'd seen it coming, so, just before going to bed, I made Bergeron promise he would tell Lowe that I'd snored all night and kept him awake. Bergeron accepted and went back to Lowe as a double agent. Lowe believed Bergeron, and so in the years to come I never had to share my room with any other players.

•

It was time to get ready to leave my adopted city.

A few days before leaving Edmonton, a local radio station had the idea of inviting Oilers fans to come and say a last good-bye to me. The station set up a small table just outside their studios on Jasper Street in downtown Edmonton so that I could meet the fans who wanted to see me one last time.

On July 13, 2006, around 7:45 A.M., I went down to their studios for that last meeting with the fans. The autograph session was to begin at 8:00. When I arrived, I had a shock. Hundreds of people were already standing in line waiting to meet me. I knew I had a place in some Oilers fans' hearts, but I would never have expected to see so many of them standing there that early in the morning. I was so deeply moved.

From 8 A.M. to 6 P.M., I signed over eight thousand autographs and posed for hundreds of photographs with the fans. I didn't eat anything all day long and only had time to go to the bathroom twice. People were crying, and some were telling me that this transaction was the worst one the Oilers had made since the day Gretzky was sent to Los Angeles. A lot of them had brought Oilers shirts, pucks, and sticks they wanted me to sign.

Around 4 P.M. I asked the radio deejays to stop publicizing the event, since my hand was starting to shake from all that writing and I knew I wouldn't be able to go on for too much longer. That was really a very touching moment I will never ever forget. Thank you, Oilers fans!

•

Arriving in Phoenix, I was like a fish out of water. First, I'd never played for a U.S. team; and second, it was so hot that I could hardly imagine playing hockey here. Even during winter months they average 20 degrees Celsius.

The guy who welcomed me to the team most warmly was Jeremy Roenick, and he quickly became my best friend on the team. He showed me around the city and helped me find the best places to shop and eat. Right from the beginning I started spending a lot of time with him and his family. I ended up eating at his house half the time, and spent more than a few evenings babysitting his kids, Brett and Brandy. J.R. is one of the most open, generous guys in the league, and for me, the best thing about going to Phoenix was getting to know him.

I didn't know it right away, but only a few days after my arrival, I had the feeling I would really enjoy my new city.

But that was before I laced up my skates as a Coyote. When the season started I was brutally brought down to earth. The stands were half-empty and the people sitting in them seemed to enjoy the show about as much as they might enjoy a funeral. Every night, I missed the roar of the Oilers' fans—fans who were passionate about the game, who understood the flow of what was happening on the ice and could read every play as it unfolded. And life is even harder for a tough guy playing in the desert than it is for a skills guy—there's nothing worse than dropping your gloves in a rink so quiet you can hear them hit the ice.

To make things even worse, the team was already out of the playoffs before Christmas. We were losing so many games that I started thinking the guys didn't care at all.

And what about the Great One? I find it strange to say, but Wayne Gretzky is the worst coach I've ever played for. Never would he shout at his players, or tear into them to motivate them. I've heard that he yelled at his teammates when he was a player, but he never yelled at us. The only people he would shout at were the referees. We could lose five or six games in a row and it didn't seem to matter to him.

Maybe he was too kind-hearted to insult us. Maybe he saw something we didn't. But he sure didn't have any special system he wanted us to play. He wasn't a strategist. He wasn't a tactician. He would sometimes just throw the first three players closest to the door on the ice even if there was no centre among them.

As players, we quickly figured out that if we stayed near the middle of the bench, he would just forget about us. So we ended up more or less running the bench ourselves. We would take turns getting closer to the door, and eventually Wayne would just send us out there.

It's impossible to say anything bad about Wayne Gretzky as a player. As a coach, though? He could hardly have been worse. When we were on the road he was almost never there for practice; he'd have to be at an autograph session or a press conference or an endorsement or whatever. He would leave the hotel in a limousine while his assistants would try to implement a game plan he'd never told them about. It was frankly ridiculous.

Rumours spread that the other co-owners had thought of relieving him of his coaching duties. But with the five-year contract he'd signed and the fact that as co-owner of the franchise he was pretty much his own boss, he was a tough guy to fire. So there he was, game after game, sending guys over the boards in a state of confusion and indifference.

In Phoenix, I had the sensation that every day was a day off. Right after what was typically a light practice, most of the players would head out to play golf. I truly had the impression that I'd joined the ranks of a country club for millionaires, not an NHL team. It was so effortless to play in Phoenix that in only a few months I gained thirty pounds.

I don't want to blame the guys in the room. Shane Doan was one of the best captains I ever played with. He and Roenick gave everything they had every night. And despite what the media sometimes suggests, every player wants to win. But nothing was working properly there.

Well, not quite nothing. I was about to experience the best offensive season of my career. After 56 games in the Coyotes uniform, I had already put up 22 points.

I had mixed feelings about the fact that my first goal as a Coyote came against the Oilers, but then, my first goal as an Oiler had come against the Coyotes. I missed Edmonton, of course. I really missed the fans, and I was delighted to find out they missed me too. The Coyotes' first regular-season game was in Edmonton, and the fans gave me an ovation every time I touched the puck. If I'd been an Alexei Kovalev, I would have ragged the puck all night to hear the applause. As it was, I held on to it as long as I could. I'm sure Wayne must have been scratching his head behind the bench, wondering why I suddenly wanted to stickhandle all night. Too bad we lost 6–0.

But despite my sudden offensive outburst, everything else from my past hockey life was missing. As I've said before, I hate to lose. I'd rather win than pad my stats with meaningless goals. I only play to win.

In Edmonton the team thought alike. Every year we fought like crazy to make the playoffs. I fit in with a team like that, and I was in desperate need of finding that kind of environment again. I just couldn't stand the apathy that surrounded me in Phoenix anymore.

So a few weeks before the trade deadline, I called my agent and begged him to find me a team that deserved to be called a team and had a shot at making the playoffs.

I then informed Wayne about that phone call. It wasn't a habit of his to get angry, but he sure did that day. The way he saw it, I had nothing to complain about in Phoenix—all he saw was that I was embarrassing him in front of the press and the other co-owners.

I answered him that it was absolutely not my intention to do so, that I simply needed to play in an environment where guys play to win, not with a team where half the players thought they were on holiday. The Great One was furious. By this point he was yelling at the top of his lungs, promising me I would never play a game for him anymore. That was exactly what I wanted.

My contract did contain a no-trade clause. So the general manager, Mike Barnett, and I sat down to figure out a solution. He asked me what teams I would agree to play for. Since I didn't have one in mind, he told me that there were two who were interested in me: the Calgary Flames and the Pittsburgh Penguins.

My first instinct was to choose Calgary, simply because I still owned a house in Edmonton and playing with the Flames would practically put me back in the neighbourhood. On the other hand, I couldn't help but think about what would be the Oilers fans' reaction if I were to go back to Alberta and play for the rivals.

As for the Penguins, I knew they had a great young and talented team. Moreover, if I were to choose the Penguins, I'd be playing for my former head coach with the Granby Prédateurs, Michel Therrien.

I hesitated for quite a while. The decision was almost impossible to make. Both teams would be a great fit. I would wake up in the morning and feel certain that I wanted to join the Flames, then, a couple of hours later, feel convinced that I should be a Penguin.

I finally decided it would be the Flames. Edmonton fans were probably going to be mad at me, but, after all, it wasn't as though I'd chosen to leave Edmonton. The Oilers had only to give me a no-trade clause and I would have stayed with them until the end of my career. I agreed to the terms of the contract with the Flames' general manager, Daryl Sutter, and the case was closed.

Or so I thought. Right at the deadline, I received a phone call from Mike Barnett, who begged me to accept the Penguins' offer instead of the Flames'. I told him it was impossible, since I had already accepted Sutter's offer. He insisted and insisted, telling me the Penguins were ready to give the Coyotes a talented young tough guy with pretty good hands in return.

Since he'd done me a favour by agreeing to trade me even though he didn't have to, I decided to give in. That's how Daniel Carcillo became a Coyote and I became a Penguin. My time in the desert had turned out to be a disappointment, but at least I'd leave the Coyotes on good terms.

The only question that nagged at me concerned the owner of my new team, Mario Lemieux. After my Gretzky experience, I wondered how Mario would act with his players. If the problem with Gretzky was that he'd had too much talent as a player, then I might not be any better off playing for the one guy in history who could out-score the Great One. I had nothing to worry about, though. The Magnificent One knew exactly how to communicate with his players.

The only problem I had wasn't related to my new team—I had to worry about myself. I'd played myself out of shape and was far from the lean specimen I'd been less than a year before. But I knew I could count on my coach. Michel Therrien sure hadn't changed a bit since my junior days. He was still that bulldog, knowing exactly how to get the best out of his players.

My role was pretty clear. I had to protect a couple of pretty talented young guys named Sidney Crosby and Evgeni Malkin—not to mention a kid named Jordan Staal.

Anyway, other teams had figured out that they couldn't counter the Pens' talent by outskating them; even pushing Sid, Malkin, and Staal off the puck was no easy thing. What they could do, though, was shove them around, get sticks on them, face-wash them, and yap at them all night until they lost their focus. My job was to let other teams know there was a price to pay for that.

People have a lot of opinions about Crosby—one thing you hear a lot is that he's a whiner. As the guy who had the job of protecting him, I can say a couple of things about Crosby. First, the guy wants to win. I've never seen a guy who wants to win more passionately than Sidney Crosby. Sid is like a winning machine. Any other result, and he feels like the machine is broken. I think that what some people think is his whining is really just an expression of his will to win. Second, the guy has a lot to whine about. No one in the league takes more hacks and slashes and other dirty stuff than Sid. Other teams would love nothing more than to get him off his game. And if you were playing against a guy everyone is calling the best player in the world, you might be tempted to give him a little slash too. But the fact is, he has to fight through things that other players don't.

Still, he faced less and less of that as the season went on. Gary Roberts also joined the Penguins at the deadline, and even if Roberts wasn't exactly a heavyweight, he could definitely handle himself, and other teams would think twice about annoying him, especially after one particular game against the Flyers.

We were up for the game, and so were they. Ben Eager wanted to set the tone, and caught me with a high elbow. I picked myself up, and went right after him. There was no way I was going to take something like that. But when I got hold of him, Eager turtled.

He may have wished later that he'd fought me. Because the next Penguin he had to talk to was Gary Roberts.

Now remember, Eager is about twenty years younger than Roberts, and about forty pounds heavier. Also, Eager's job is to intimidate other players, and Roberts' job has always been to provide leadership and big goals.

So Eager thought he'd be safe to accept an invitation from Gary right after he'd refused one from me.

Big mistake. Roberts has earned himself the nickname "Scary Gary" over the years, and if Ben Eager had ever seen him in the dressing room, he would have known that scrapping with our alternate captain would be a dangerous proposition. Gary is pure muscle. You could teach an anatomy class by showing students the muscle groups under his T-shirt.

Eager grabbed Gary and tried to overpower him. Gary calmly got position, and started feeding Eager a series of lefts. He absolutely ragdolled the younger man. Eager took a couple of wild swings, but never touched Gary. When it was over, Eager was crumpled on the ice, and Gary looked as though he'd hardly got started.

That just shows how a fight can change a team. Suddenly, Pittsburgh was in love with Gary Roberts. Songs were written about him. Bracelets were made asking "What Would Gary Roberts Do?" And Chuck Norris–style jokes started going around the dressing room—things like, When Gary Roberts goes for a swim, he doesn't get wet; the water gets Gary Roberts.

The media got in on the humour too. The usual joke went something like, The Pens brought in Laraque to take care of the stars, then they brought in Roberts to take care of Laraque.

I have to say, though, that Roberts was embarrassed by all this. He's a down-to-earth, humble guy, who'd probably be just as happy without all the praise he usually gets. Along with Colby Armstrong, he was one of my best friends on the team.

•

Suddenly, the Pens were a lot less fun to play against. I played seventeen games that year with the Penguins, and although I managed to get only two assists, other guys on the team had a lot more room to skate. (Crosby ended up with 120 points, which covered the shortfall in my offensive output.)

We made the playoffs, but the team was so young and inexperienced that we failed to qualify for the second round. We lost in five against the Ottawa Senators, a series in which I played only two games, with no points and not a single penalty minute.

Summer came along, and I promised myself as well as Michel Therrien that I'd get back into my Olympic shape before training camp opened. I really wanted to honour the last year of my contract with the Penguins by playing the best hockey of my life. The good thing was that I knew Therrien would put his confidence in me, since he'd learned how stubborn and determined a player I'd been during my junior years.

I started the 2007–08 season feeling great and ready to protect the skilled Penguins from all comers. Everyone in the league knew we were loaded with elite talent, and that meant no one would be taking a night off against us. Therrien was really happy that I'd taken the summer not only to get back into great shape but also to build my confidence and motivation for the season to come. I was going to make sure that all that talent could express itself without being bugged by anyone.

I must have been doing something right, because our best players were lighting up the league. Every season has its ups and downs—it's not like we won every game—but we were a team that could win every time we stepped onto the ice that season. I'm not saying I can take the credit for that. It was Therrien who managed to create the amazing chemistry between our best players, a chemistry that made them so dangerous. I just helped make sure no one managed to spoil the magic.

As for me, I remembered how pleasurable it was to be on the ice, to be back competing fiercely. The guys I was now playing with were the types who would have banned the word "defeat" from the dictionary if they could. Defeat was just not acceptable. I was back with my kind of players and enjoying myself a lot.

Moreover, the fans were great—they reminded me of the ones in Edmonton. The rink was sold out night after night. I felt I was back in a real hockey town, with the small difference that Pittsburgh was a more cosmopolitan city than Edmonton. Rapidly I became one of the favourites among the fans. In short, I was breathing again.

That season I also had the opportunity to do something many players don't get to do even once—I played another outdoor game. The first time was absolutely amazing, and the second time was even better.

For one thing, it wasn't played in arctic cold and the fans and players weren't suffering. For another, it was an even bigger rink—more than 71,000 fans watched that game in Buffalo. Unbelievable. Also, it was snowing so hard you sometimes couldn't see the puck, just like when you're a kid playing outside. Add the fact that we won in a shootout, and the whole thing was unreal.

We ended the season in second place in the Eastern Conference, just two points behind the first-place Montreal Canadiens. We were ready for war, a bit more experienced than the year before. We had everything a team needs to go far in the play-offs, and we knew it. And adding Marián Hossa at the deadline just made us more dangerous.

Even so, we got a bit nervous when we learned that we'd be facing the Senators for the second year in a row. Like us, the Sens were loaded with talent—in fact, in Dany Heatley, Daniel Alfredsson, Jason Spezza, Ray Emery, Chris Phillips, and Wade Redden, they had more players than any other team in that year's All-Star game. They'd been to the finals the year before and lost—and I knew what that felt like. So I knew the Sens had been waiting all year for their chance to get back to the finals.

I didn't talk about that to anyone, but in my mind I sure was hoping Ottawa wouldn't become what the Stars had been for Edmonton in my first years there.

Well, we'd been waiting all year too. You always want revenge against the team that knocks you out of the playoffs, and we were ready to get ours against Ottawa. I played on a line with Roberts and Maxime Talbot, and we had the Sens on their heels every time we were on the ice. Which was a lot. We set the tone for a very physical series, and Ottawa had no answer for us.

We swept them in four. They were hardly in the series. When you get out the brooms to move past one of the teams favoured to challenge for the Cup, your confidence gets a real boost.

Our opponents in the next round, the New York Rangers, had been pretty impressive themselves in getting rid of the powerful New Jersey Devils in five games. But we weren't the Devils. We put New York out of their misery in five, losing only the fourth game on their ice.

We were on a collision course with our rivals, the Philadelphia Flyers, in the Conference finals. Some teams just hate each other: Montreal and Toronto (all right, a lot of teams hate Toronto), Calgary and Edmonton, the Rangers and Islanders. But the Flyers–Penguins rivalry is right up there, and the fact that the Flyers always dress a team stacked with guys who don't mind throwing their weight around suggested to me that I'd have a big role to play.

The thing about the Flyers is that if they can't intimidate you, they're not going to win. And absolutely no one intimidated us that year. Although I did play my game, our players were so fast the Flyers couldn't even manage to slow them down long enough to bully them. The Flyers didn't last any longer than the Rangers. We lost only one game, the fourth, on their ice. Maybe we were getting a little ahead of ourselves—when we won game three we became the first team since Gretzky's Oilers in 1993 to go 11–3 to open the playoffs. The Flyers caught us in game four, but that just gave us the wake-up call we needed. We came back to crush them 6–0 in game five.

It began to smell very good in Pittsburgh, where we hadn't lost a single game in the playoffs. Around the league as well as in the press, everyone favoured us to beat Detroit to win it all.

In the locker room, the young, talented players were all excited and were already talking as if they'd won the supreme trophy. I didn't want to be the grumpy old guy in the room, but I tried to calm them down. I reminded them of what I'd gone through with the Oilers two years before, when everyone was seeing us with the Cup in our hands. I insisted on the importance of staying focused on what we had to do and, most important, I warned them against the dangers of overconfidence. We had the talent in the room to win it all, but that didn't mean we were destined to win.

I suddenly realized that I'd become a veteran.

But kids never listen, do they?

Detroit spanked us 4–0 in game one.

Then they spanked us 3–0 in game two.

Suddenly the scariest offensive team in the league couldn't find the net. We managed to squeak out a 3–2 win in game three, then lost again in game four. Facing elimination back in Detroit, we forced overtime with goalie Marc-André Fleury out of the net, and Petr Sýkora managed to score to keep us in the series.

But in game six we ran out of magic. With Fleury out of the net again, we very nearly managed to force a second overtime, but fell short.

We had lost the series in six. I felt bad about our loss, although the disappointment wasn't as demoralizing as it had been two years before. Detroit had an extraordinary team, absolutely unbeatable on its own ice. In 2006 the Oilers had lost a series we could and should have won, but in 2008 the Penguins lost to a better team. It's no fun losing to a better team, believe me. But it doesn't hurt as much as squandering one of the most precious opportunities of your life.

After that sixth game, Sidney Crosby came up to me in the locker room and said, "Georges, I promise you, here and now, that we'll win that Cup in less than three years." He was more than right, since the Penguins won it the year after.

The trouble is, I wouldn't be there to enjoy it.

BACK TO WHERE
I COME FROM

13

The fact that we'd lost to a better team wasn't the only reason this defeat didn't affect me as much as the one with the Oilers two years before. First, I was more mature; and second, the Penguins had a far better team to build on than the one the Oilers had two years earlier. And even though I was once again a free agent, I wasn't really nervous, since everyone in the Penguins organization had said they wanted to keep me. I was pretty sure that, with a team like ours, I would get my chance again at winning the Stanley Cup.

During that past season my market value had increased again, but I was realistic. Tough guys weren't as much in demand as they'd been before the lockout. I wanted a raise, but I wasn't going to be too greedy. Plus, I really wanted to stay with Pittsburgh.

The Penguins' general manager, Ray Shero, called a meeting to say he had an offer to present to me. I sat in his office, pretty confident that we would come to an agreement. I received a cold shower instead. The contract he had on the table was for three years, which was good, but when he started talking about salary, I couldn't believe my ears.

He was offering me $750,000 for each year of the contract, a net loss of $650,000 compared to what I'd earned the previous season. I thought he was joking, but he was dead serious. The reason for the pay cut, he told me, had nothing to do with my performance on the ice, but with the fact that he had to renegotiate the contracts of three of his star players: Sidney Crosby, Evgeni Malkin, and Marc-André Fleury. There just wasn't enough money to go around in the new world of the NHL-imposed salary cap. He couldn't offer me money he didn't have; his hands were tied. But I was flabbergasted.

Shero's offer was nonsense, and he knew that perfectly well. It would have been pointless for me to try to explain what my worth was on the free-agent market, as he knew that too. I asked him to reconsider his offer just a bit, to give me at least a million a year, although I could probably get half a million more somewhere else. He refused, and asked me to consider it for another twenty-four hours before giving him my final answer. It was *all* I thought about.

When he called me the day after, I repeated that even though I wanted to stay with the Penguins, I really couldn't accept such an offer. I told him that I understood his decision and respected it. But what I'd decided while I was thinking it over was that I couldn't base my decision on the possibility that the Pens might go on to win the Cup the next season. Even if I had known for sure they would, I still couldn't have stayed under those conditions. I knew I could get twice what he'd offered me, which means I would have lost $2.25 million to get a Stanley Cup ring around my finger.

I like to win, and a Stanley Cup will always be a cherished dream. But I'm not such a dreamer that I thought I could justify spending more than $2 million to buy a shot at a dream. If I'd made $5 million a year, my thoughts might have been different. But in my situation it was too high a price.

The next day Shero hired Eric Godard, the tough guy the Flames had hired when I decided to go to Pittsburgh. He gave him the exact same contract he had offered me just a day before. Maybe he just scratched out my name and wrote Eric's instead. Godard was quite a different player from me, but I knew he could do the job he'd be paid for. He was the one who would win the Stanley Cup. Life is strange sometimes. Congratulations to him. And to Shero too.

I went back to spend the summer in Edmonton not knowing at all what the future held for me. I didn't have to wait for long, though. A dozen teams contacted me within two weeks. Three teams were leading the pack: Nashville, Edmonton, and Montreal.

The Predators were the most generous. They were offering me a three-year contract at $1.7 million a year. Taking into account the fact that the taxes in Tennessee were among the lowest ones in all the U.S., Nashville was way ahead of the other two as far as the money was concerned.

I spoke for a long time with Jean-Pierre Dumont, who had just completed his second season with the Predators. I wanted his honest opinion about the team, the hockey environment, and the city. Even though he was enthusiastic, he didn't manage to really convince me. I also spoke to the head coach, Barry Trotz, who insisted he had a real need for a player like me.

I remained skeptical, mostly because I was afraid of another experience like my time with the Coyotes. Could hockey in Tennessee really be as intense as the game in Edmonton or Pittsburgh? Add the fact that the team was going through enormous financial difficulties, which were even threatening its survival, and the Nashville case was closed for good. Edmonton and Montreal were the only two teams left. The good thing was that I knew I'd be back in Canada.

In Edmonton, Craig MacTavish had changed his mind about the usefulness of tough guys. After watching his best players being intimidated and injured by the other teams' tough guys, he really wanted me back. In fact, since I was spending the summer in Edmonton, it seemed the whole city wanted me back with the Oilers.

But that started to give me a strange feeling.

The eight years I spent with the Oilers organization hadn't been forgotten, that was obvious. But more than that, the two seasons I'd played in Phoenix and Pittsburgh, far away from Edmonton, had conferred a bit of an aura to my years spent in Alberta. Maybe Edmonton fans were remembering me as something better than I actually was when I was suiting up as an Oiler. Without scaring me, it troubled me a bit.

To be desired by a whole city is a great thing when you've never played there. But reading emails sent by Oilers fans, looking at what was said about me in the press, and listening to what people were telling me in the streets made me realize that I had everything to lose if I signed in Edmonton. I could only go down in the esteem of Oilers fans.

In the meantime, the Oilers were offering me a watertight contract that made me think a lot. Not only was it a four-year agreement with a salary of $1.5 million a year, but they were also promising me a job for life inside the Oilers organization. When I played in Edmonton, I used to say—and I was sincere in saying it—that I would love to play my whole career there. And now there they were, saying that I could be with them for the rest of my life. Boy, was I tempted!

And then there was Montreal. They were offering me the same salary as the Oilers but for three years. And nothing was offered to me for when my playing days were over. But what the Montreal offer lacked in promises, it made up for with a massive challenge. Now that I was a veteran, I didn't mind the press anymore. Plus, I was so used to them after my years in Edmonton and Pittsburgh that I knew how to handle them.

Moreover, Montreal had the big advantage of being the place where I was born. My family was still there and the prospect of playing in front of them, in their hometown and for their home team, had something emotional to it that not much else could compete with.

Both head coaches—Craig MacTavish and Guy Carbonneau—promised me that I'd have an important role to play and would get quite a lot of ice time. Both reassured me that they saw me as much more than just a tough guy.

In short, I was facing an almost unsolvable dilemma. I had to choose between going back home and going back home.

One morning in July, I called my agent and told him to call Bob Gainey. My decision had been made—I was going to play for the Montreal Canadiens for the next three years. He asked me if I was sure, and I told him to call now because I might change my mind in just a few hours.

What had happened on that specific morning? What was the deep reason animating me when I decided it would be Montreal over Edmonton? Let's just say that the reason had nothing to do with hockey. It didn't even have anything to do with either of the two teams I was hesitating between.

I had woken up that morning with something in my head, something from my deep past. God knows why, but I remembered that day from my youth when I was thirteen and a judge asked me to choose between my mom and my dad as to where I wanted to live after their divorce.

I still felt guilty about the sorrows I'd caused my mom with my answer. That's what made me choose the Canadiens. Nothing else. I was going back to where I was born for my dear Évelyne.

●

My decision to go with the Canadiens had a deep impact both in Montreal and Edmonton. I received hundreds of phone calls and emails all summer long. Those coming from Edmonton would express some disappointment and sadness. But they were all understanding and generous. Even under those circumstances, Edmonton fans were pure class. Some guys don't know how lucky they are to play for the Oilers. From Montreal, I got a lot of messages welcoming me back to my hometown. Others asked me about how I'd handle the media pressure.

In the Edmonton press, one could read things similar to what was in the fans' emails. Disappointment and a bit of grief. On the Montreal side, some journalists were already crowing about the effect I would have on the team, and others were already complaining.

Curiously, the enthusiastic articles were the ones worrying me. As had become a habit in Montreal, some journalists and analysts tended to see me as the saviour of the team, the man who would radically change the way the Canadiens were behaving on the ice. Sometimes, as I was reading them, I'd ask myself if they were really talking about me or about some superstar the Canadiens had signed without me noticing.

Two and a half weeks before leaving Edmonton for training camp in Montreal, a cousin of mine called me. He told me that right then, as we were speaking, radio anchorman Jean-Charles Lajoie was talking about captain Saku Koivu and me on the air, asking his listeners if they thought we really cared about the team since we weren't there for the annual Montreal Canadiens golf tournament. I remember thinking, "I'm not even in Montreal and they're already complaining about my attitude."

I was at home, in Edmonton, training as hard as I could to be in top condition when I joined the Canadiens. Saku was doing the exact same, surrounded by his family in Finland.

Impulsively, I called the radio station where Lajoie was criticizing me on the air. When the receptionist answered the phone, I introduced myself and asked to speak to Lajoie. A few seconds later I was live on radio.

I immediately jumped to Saku's defence—as well as my own. I told Lajoie that neither Saku's family nor my kids were living in Montreal and that there were no rules that said we had to be part of the golf tournament. He remained almost speechless, not knowing how he could respond to what I'd just told him. The vast majority of listeners who called in after my intervention would agree with me.

Anyway, Laraque, 1; Montreal media, 0.

Obviously, since we were in Quebec, the news of the phone call I'd just given Lajoie went around the little Montreal hockey planet in no time. Every journalist wanted to interview me on the subject. Of those who commented on the "affair," most were saying I had done the right thing. I personally believed they were happy to see someone as frank as me coming to Montreal.

In Montreal, silence is the law when you're a player; every media appearance or interview has to be approved by the team's public relations department. The more they refuse interview requests, the more comfortable they are. But now, with me arriving, the attitude was totally different. Interviews? Give me some!

Other observers, while commenting on the affair, would mock me a bit, saying that I was naive, that I still hadn't understood how the team was handling public relations, that I would rapidly fall into line as soon as I got to Montreal. That was when I truly realized what ship I had boarded. I was too frank. I never spoke to the media just to be provocative, but I wasn't going to hide anything, either. I've always thought that the media is a way for players to communicate with the people who pay their salaries—the fans. And there was no way I was going to lie to the fans.

•

I was in splendid shape when I arrived in Montreal for my very first Canadiens training camp.

I can't lie—I can't say here that it was a dream come true to walk into the Montreal Canadiens' dressing room as a player (especially after saying again and again that I would never play there). But it was definitely an honour to wear a sweater that so many legends had worn. No matter what my thoughts had been up to that point about the Quebec media, there was no question about it—it was awesome to play for the Habs.

It is no exaggeration or cliché to say I was coming home. I had always heard from my mother and other family members that people kept harassing them at work because they'd cheered for my team rather than the Canadiens. But now they could be down at the arena, cheering for me *and* the Habs.

I knew what I was getting myself into, though. Every tough guy leaves Montreal chased by the media. Just look at the time Brashear spent with the Habs. Tough guys there have targets on their backs, no doubt about it. But to be honest, that was part of the appeal.

And anyway, my new teammates welcomed me with big smiles and lots of encouraging words, visibly happy to see me among them. The Habs were loaded with French Canadian players that year: Patrice Brisebois, Matthieu Dandenault, Steve Begin, Maxim Lapierre, Alex Tanguay, Guillaume Latendresse—and me, of course. I was also delighted to see Francis Bouillon, with whom I hadn't played since my Hamilton years. Those seemed like decades ago.

But that homecoming was not destined to be joyous for me. I had barely shaken hands with my new teammates and the Habs staff before everything started to go wrong. During my first skate, my back, my groin, and my knee began to make me suffer as if someone was sticking thousand of needles in them at the same time. I couldn't even make it through the first practice.

I went to see the team doctor right away. He tried a few things to treat me, in vain. I had to wait a few days to undergo a magnetic resonance imaging (MRI) test to finally know what was going on. The doctor told me I was suffering from a slipped disc that seemed to be pinching my sciatic nerve.

One solution was an operation. That was fine with me. It wouldn't be the first one I'd had, or the last. I then asked him how long the physiotherapy treatment would be before I could get back on the ice. That was when the roof fell in on me.

He told me that it usually took patients about a year and a half to fully recover from that kind of operation; one year if everything went fine. I nearly collapsed.

I immediately refused the surgical option and started talking about my options with both an osteopath and the Montreal Canadiens' doctor. I wanted to know everything about the existing alternatives, if there were any. They told me they would try the impossible, but they weren't able to tell me if it was going to work or not.

The physical trainers started working on my back on a daily basis, having me do exercises in order to make my back more supple. I was doing yoga and acupuncture sessions two to three times a week. And, of course, I started taking anti-inflammatory medicine like crazy.

I missed the beginning of the season, to the great disappointment of my family, for whom I had bought season tickets. I was even more disappointed. After all, they were the reason I was in Montreal. After relentlessly working on my back, the doctors finally gave their consent and told the team I was ready to return to the ice. It was going to be a home game against the Boston Bruins on October 15.

I was so excited to make my official debut with the Montreal Canadiens in the Bell Centre with my family watching me from the stands. And my first shift was to be pretty spectacular, since I invited the Bruins' tough guy Shawn Thornton to dance right away and he managed to get me off balance. I lost my footing before the fight had really even started, but there was no way anyone was going to hold me down on my first shift in front of my family and the Habs fans. Soon I was back on my feet and back in control. It went well, very well for me. The crowd gave me a standing ovation, and my teammates were all smiles.

I had just given the whole league a clear message. Nobody would be able to mess with the Montreal Canadiens players anymore—at least not without having to settle things with me.

In the season before, the team had ranked first in the Eastern Conference without the presence of a tough guy. But when they met up with the Philadelphia Flyers in the Conference finals, they were given a lesson in how a tough guy could have helped them. The Flyers prevented the team from playing its game, and played the body against the talented Habs. Montreal was eliminated from the series in five.

That situation would never repeat itself now that I was with the team. If only my injury would heal ...

In the next three games, I had to fight again. Todd Fedoruk from my old team, the Coyotes, didn't like a hit and challenged me. Then the truly gigantic Mitch Fritz of the Islanders challenged me for his first NHL fight, and later the Flyers' Josh Gratton took exception to another of my bodychecks and came to have a word with me about it. I had a heavy workload to start the season.

The average number of fights I'd have during a complete season was about ten, a number shared by the most respected heavyweights in the league. If a tough guy has to fight more than that, it simply means he's not respected and doesn't scare anyone. There shouldn't be a lot of guys out there who *want* to fight you.

Having guys refuse your invitation means you're doing your job. The best example of that came that November, when the Bruins were in Montreal. The season before, Milan Lucic would run around, playing the body on our guys. Lucic is a big, strong kid. He knows that part of his job is to scare the guys he plays against. And part of my job is to scare guys like Lucic.

So when I lined up against him at the faceoff I gave him a friendly invitation to drop the gloves with me. We talked for quite a while as the linesman waited. Finally Marc Savard skated over to chirp a bit too. But there was no way Lucic was going to dance. Lucic is a great guy. We share an agent, and I really like and respect him. But I had a job to do.

Still, a tough guy can do his job even if the other guy won't fight. The more he skates away, the more I intimidate his whole bench and the less he plays his own physical game. A tough guy can make it even worse by roughing up the opponents' skill guys after an encounter like that. When they complain, you say, "Go thank so-and-so"—whoever their tough guy is. The best way to play the enforcer is to embarrass guys, not punch them out. Any professional hockey player has a lot of pride. Now that fight that didn't happen is one Lucic will never win.

A couple of years before, Donald Brashear had fallen into a trap I'm glad I never found myself in. He had to square off with Brendan Shanahan. Shanahan was a lot like Lucic. He knew how to handle himself, but he was also an elite player. When those two went at it, Shanahan had almost nothing to lose. As long as he did a decent job, he would lift his bench and look like a fearless leader. He didn't even have to win the fight to win the confrontation. It was the opposite for Brashear. If he lost the fight, he would look weak. But if he won, he would look like a bully. And the more decisively he won, the worse he would look.

In the end, fighting is about maintaining respect in the game. If you go out and act like a bully, you're only defeating yourself. To do your job right, you have to know when *not* to fight.

However, the main problem with the way I started with the Canadiens was not that I fought a lot. It was that every single fight was simply ruining my back a bit more. Add to that all the other pushing and shoving and bodychecks, and I was downing anti-inflammatory pills like candy.

I didn't want an operation. That's how much I wanted to play for the Canadiens. I was giving everything I had, but I knew for certain inside me that I wasn't the same player anymore. Although Guy Carbonneau knew my situation, he couldn't do anything else but give me less and less ice time. I was really frustrated, but in the meantime I perfectly understood that he really had no choice.

•

Even though I had trouble on the ice, my tongue was still in great shape in the presence of journalists. During that season the young goalie Jonathan Roy, son of Patrick, severely punched his opponent Bobby Nadeau during the QMJHL playoffs. The minister of sports then started a crusade to ban all fights from the junior leagues.

Interviewed about this by journalist Pierre Durocher of the *Journal de Montréal*, I said, "If she was to win her cause, the QMJHL would have to change its name and be called the Quebec national ballet dancer league." I added: "I think we should think about banning blades from hockey skates. Players can get hurt with them, you know."

But let's get back to my ice time, which was melting away alarmingly. The press wanted to know how I felt about it. I have to tell you here that I was totally forbidden to talk about my back problems. But that didn't mean I wasn't going to talk at all. So, in a moment of frustration, I said that if I'd known I wasn't going to play more, I never would have signed with the

Canadiens. It started a shock wave, and trade rumours began to spread.

But that's just the way I talk. I say what I mean. Never in my career had I been the kind of guy who would say things like "We gave it 110 percent" or "We've just got to move our feet and keep it simple and get bodies to the net and the puck will start going in for us." And I wasn't going to start now just because I was in Montreal. Fans aren't idiots. They know perfectly well that when a player isn't playing, he gets frustrated.

Since the team's officials didn't want me to talk about the injury preventing me from playing as I used to, the rumour machine got crazy and terrible things were being said about me. Some said I was on drugs, others that I was in rehab.

But the worst thing was when analysts or journalists started pretending I wasn't a hundred-percent proud to be a Montreal Canadiens player and that I wasn't ready to really involve myself for the team. That situation was so frustrating because I knew the truth about my condition but wasn't allowed to reveal it to the fans.

Faced with all those things being said about me, things that were starting to hurt the team itself, the Canadiens' officials had no choice but to say something to the press to calm everyone down. They issued a press release that said I was suffering from a minor injury in the upper body. What a stupid expression, stupid because it opened the doors to all sorts of new rumours.

●

As I said earlier, those first four consecutive fights totally ruined my back. Guy Carbonneau started to rotate players in and out of his fourth line—four guys for three spots. Since he rarely or never talked to his players, he'd found a way to inform us of who would and wouldn't be playing without having to actually talk to us.

During the pre-game warm-up, he would write the line combinations on a blackboard. And yet, he would have announced them to the media right after morning practice. So rather than waiting for the evening, all we had to do was check the internet to find out whether we were playing or not. This non-communication process frustrated me, and I wasn't the only one, starting with my teammates on the fourth line. We were living with the situation, but we sure didn't like it.

After Christmas, my back was worse than ever. It was bearable only when I was at home, sitting on a couch doing nothing. The problem was that my life was not about doing nothing. The games, the training sessions, the plane and bus trips, the hotel beds were all contributing efficiently to the business of killing my back. Still, I couldn't understand why the pain was getting heavier, since I was keeping up with my treatments.

The doctors decided to give me a new MRI. The results were clear: I was suffering from a second herniated disc. I was devastated. The playoffs were approaching and it was getting obvious that our first opponent would be the Boston Bruins. I knew I would have a big role to play against them.

That was when I started taking tons of cortisone pills. I had no choice: it was either that or the end of my career. I was suffering agony, and the team's officials were telling everyone I was in perfect shape and that my upper-body injury was completely healed. Carbonneau even said that I now had my fate in my hands. I couldn't believe it. He knew exactly what my condition was. My relationship with him was deteriorating, and his relationship with the rest of the team wasn't getting any better either.

I played on a line mostly with Maxim Lapierre and Steve Begin, and ended up joking around with them a lot off the ice as well. (Like my friend Colby Armstrong from the Pens, agitators like Lapierre make their share of enemies the way they play, so it's not uncommon for agitators and tough guys to share common cause.) But Begin was traded to Dallas in February, so that was one less guy to have a laugh with, and a sign of the way the wind was blowing.

All kinds of controversy swirled around the team that year. Bob Gainey raised a lot of eyebrows by sending superstar Alexei Kovalev home to take a break. Then more eyebrows were raised when allegations surfaced that the Kostitsyn brothers were somehow implicated in organized crime. It was one headline after another for us.

But Gainey wasn't done. The day after we had a big on-the-road win against Dallas, Bob Gainey made the courageous decision to fire Carbonneau. It was on March 9, 2009, and the general manager was going to replace him for the balance of the season.

The following day the press said that Carbonneau had been the victim of an organized putsch, which was totally false. Carbonneau had been the victim of his own lack of communication with his players. Yes, players went to see Bob Gainey, but they did so individually, not as a group. Gainey had to act, and he did.

I have to admit, I felt a bit better with Carbonneau out of the picture. But the weight of all my other critics still felt pretty heavy on my shoulders. Even when the team was on a winning streak, the press seemed interested only in my problems. Only in Montreal will you hear and read journalists talking about the negative aspects of a victory. But luckily, I had the fans behind me. I could read it every day in my email inbox.

I still couldn't believe what was written and said about me in the press, though. Some writers were suggesting I had hidden my injury from the Canadiens until after I'd signed to Montreal. The people writing those stupidities were not only insulting me but the whole Canadiens organization. As if a great team like the Canadiens would hire a player without testing him from head to toe. Ridiculous.

Others hinted that my struggles came down to a lack of heart. They thought I wasn't trying hard enough, that I didn't care enough. I kept reading that I didn't have the Habs logo tattooed on my heart. Maybe those fools thought I'd chosen Montreal and bought season tickets for all my family members so that they could come and see me lazying around on the ice. What those people didn't know was that I could have chosen to get operated on and simply stay home with my full salary being deposited into my bank account every two weeks.

I was always the first one to arrive at the arena in the morning so that I could get my treatments from the medical team. And I was the last one out at night because I still had to receive some treatments before going back home. Usually the guy who shows up first and leaves last is called the heart-and-soul leader of the team. Not in Montreal.

When Gainey took over the team, my ice time went up. He also reassured me, telling me he'd need my help in the playoffs against the Bruins. And despite everything, I was pumped for that first round. I hadn't had a season worth rejoicing about: I'd played only thirty-three games for two assists. But I'd been brought in for the playoffs, and a series against a physical team like Boston was my chance to shine.

I was stuffed with cortisone pills when we faced the Bruins. But even though we lost in four games straight, the way I played compensated in a way for my mediocre season. Gainey had me skating on a line with Saku Koivu and Alexei Kovalev. Not exactly the fourth line. I was there to protect them against the Bruins' Zdeno Chara, of course—even a guy the size of Chara would hear footsteps when I was out there. But it was also because I knew how to control the puck along the boards. As long as I had the puck, I had two Bruins on my back, which meant more room on the ice for Saku and Alex. It wasn't enough to push us past Boston, but it was a real show of confidence from Gainey to put me on the top line. It was a pretty clear message that my skills were what the Habs needed.

Right before I left for Edmonton for the summer, Gainey and I sat down to talk about the next season. He told me he'd take the summer to find a new head coach, and added that whoever was behind the bench, the team needed me to be in the best shape possible for the next season. He also congratulated me for the series I'd had and wished me good luck. That mark of confidence warmed my heart. The 2009–10 season would be the good one, and I would play the role people wanted me to.

If only my back would cooperate.

•

My summer was divided in two. On the one hand, I trained and worked out a lot to get back in shape. On the other, I followed a whole regimen of treatments to try to fix my back. While others were playing golf and hanging out at their cottages, yoga, acupuncture, and massage were on the agenda for me.

On June 1, I learned from an Edmonton newspaper that the Montreal Canadiens had just hired Jacques Martin as their new head coach. People seemed to think that was excellent news. But I wasn't so sure.

The first person to call me after I learned the news was André Roy. We'd played in the junior leagues during the same years and I'd met him a couple of times off the ice while in the NHL. Roy was a bona fide heavyweight and a good guy. He'd played under Jacques Martin with the Senators, and a bit later with the Lightning.

He wasn't calling to chat. He was calling with a friendly warning. Our conversation went something like this: "Georges, I want to tell you you're not lucky at all. I know you had health problems last season, but even if you manage to fix them this summer, the worst is yet to come. Your new head coach, Jacques Martin, simply hates tough guys. You'll see—he'll cope with your presence in the first months because Gainey seems to like you. But as soon as he feels he has the freedom to do it, he'll start denigrating you and will do everything he can to get rid of you."

As I hung up the phone, I thought at first that this call had been a dream. Then I asked myself—why did André call to tell me such things? I started rationalizing, telling myself the Canadiens had a talented team, that was obvious, but that the best players weren't the tallest guys. Montreal needed a tough guy to protect them, and I was the best one for the job. Nothing Roy had said made sense. I decided to forget everything about his call and keep concentrating on what I had to do: fix my back and make sure I showed up at camp in shape.

During that summer, I popped into Montreal for a quick visit to attend an event organized by the Canadiens (only a year after going on the radio to scoff at the idea of trekking across the country in the middle of summer, there I was ...). That's where I met Jacques Martin for the first time. We had a very courteous talk, and to conclude it, he simply told me to be back in top shape when the camp opened because he had great plans for me and the team would greatly be counting on me. When he left and went to talk to other players I thought about what André Roy had told me—and I pitied him. I figured that whatever had gone on between Martin and him must have been more personal than professional.

Having worked a lot on my back and my physical condition during the summer, I felt very good when arriving at the camp in September. I had also made a decision while I was on vacation and let the press know about it right away: that season I was going to stay away from microphones. I saw disappointment in a lot of journalists' eyes. I'd been candy for their microphones the past season, but that wouldn't be the case for the next one.

Not all of them, but a lot of sport journalists are lazy. Plus, they're often rushed by tight deadlines. Those are probably the two main reasons why they'd always come up to me: they could be certain I would give them the quote they needed for their articles or newscasts. But for the next season, they'd have to go somewhere else to get it. The media was over for me. From now on, I would express myself on the ice and nowhere else. It was time to focus on hockey.

But the pain started again as soon as I got back on the ice. Training camp was the same agony it had been the year before.

Still, I began the season with the team and I wanted to do my part. There was no way I was going to complain. And the team doctors were happy I'd given them my confidence rather than accepting the operation. I will never thank them enough for everything they did, and the least I can do to show them my respect is to name them: Graham Rynbend, Nick Addey-Jibb, osteopath Dave Campbell, physiotherapist Donald Balmforth, doctor-in-chief David Mulder, my "guru" Fernand Morneau, yoga trainer Dina Tsouluhas, and all the people who gave me acupuncture treatments.

And since I would always get to the Bell Centre four hours before the game would start, I ended up spending lots of time with the Canadiens' technical team, so thank you Scott Livingston, Pierre Ouellette, Patrick Langlois, and my very best friend, Pierre Gervais.

I had to show the fans, the only important critics in my view, that Georges Laraque was ready to suffer to help their team win. And that's exactly what I was planning to do.

But Jacques Martin had other plans.

Despite my efforts and the overwhelming support I was getting from both my teammates and the fans, Martin would leave me on the bench more and more. It got to the point where I was getting only three or four shifts a game. And because of my back, I was barely playing in practice either. I had never experienced anything like it. Not even as a rookie.

Yet, we had our fair share of physical games. The Flyers and the Bruins, for instance, were running our guys all over the ice while I sat on the bench. I had no idea what Martin was doing.

No one has ever questioned the size of Brian Gionta's heart. And Scott Gomez and Mike Cammalleri play like much bigger men. I have no problem with the way those guys play the game. But they're not the biggest guys in the NHL, and they have targets on their back for that reason. No doubt about it, they'd be able to put their skills to better use if they had more ice to work with, and it's a tough guy's job to open up the ice for them.

In the meantime, my teammates were getting bullied all over the ice. You can't dress the smallest roster in the NHL and not expect other teams to take advantage. If you're slow, a team will beat you with speed. If you're too offensively oriented, a team will beat you with good defence and a counterattack. And if you're small, they'll play the body all night to the point where your skill guys don't want to touch the puck. That doesn't make skill guys cowards—if Zdeno Chara or Milan Lucic stuffed your face into the glass every time you tried to make a play, you might start getting rid of the puck in a hurry too. That's why teams dress guys like me. To intimidate the intimidators. I just felt that our guys couldn't play their game, and I wanted to change that.

But there they were, getting hit from behind right in front of my eyes. I would beg Jacques Martin to put me on the ice so that I could restore the balance a bit. No one would dare behave like that if I had played just a little more. That's what I'd been hired to do, and I just wanted to do my job. I wouldn't even have to take any penalties—I could intimidate the opponents just by skating out onto the ice. I didn't need to fight, but simply to play. But it was no use talking to Martin, I realized, so I turned my attention to the assistant coach, Kirk Muller, who was a former player himself, a gritty guy who loved to win. But all he could do was shrug me off, telling me he wasn't the head coach.

When I used to ask Michel Therrien or Craig MacTavish to put me on the ice so that I could sort out some guy who'd been taking liberties with our players, not only would they send me out, they would do it with pleasure. I remembered their smiles years later when I was stuck there on the Canadiens' bench.

Jacques Martin always answered vaguely when I begged him to let me go out and protect my teammates. According to him, there was really no need. He thought everything would be fine without my intervention. And my teammates and the staff on the bench were the only ones to see that Jacques Martin didn't want me on the ice. The fans and journalists were pointing their fingers at me instead: "Georges has softened, he doesn't want to do the job anymore." That was the kind of thing I heard and read about me. Worst of all, when journalists were interviewing Martin after a game, he never contradicted their criticisms of me.

I went to see Martin many times, simply to ask him what I had done to deserve this disgrace; and what I was supposed to do in order to play more. I never got a straight answer. All he had for me was that classic of coaching clichés: he told me to remain positive. He told me I had to understand that he had to shorten the bench from time to time. In short, to his mind, there was nothing to worry about.

That guy was going to drive me crazy.

Things were going badly for me, but they would get even worse on November 21, 2009. During one of my rare shifts in a game against the Red Wings, I lined up defenceman Niklas Kronwall for what I thought was going to be a clean hit when my knee connected with his. He was seriously injured on the play. I got two minutes.

Back in the locker room, I told the press that I was sorry he got hurt but that I didn't feel responsible for it since there was nothing wrong with the hit. But when I saw the play on video, I knew I'd been wrong. I decided to make an apology and to acknowledge that I deserved a suspension.

After a short conference call with NHL official Colin Campbell, I was sentenced to a five-game suspension. I was feeling
really down now, but I decided I'd try to benefit from that
suspension and heal my back as much as I could.

When I came back I was feeling a lot better, but the situation on the team remained the same. I was nailed on the bench
most of the time. On December 7, on my thirty-third birthday,
I managed to get my career's hundredth assist. But what I was
really looking for was to score my very first goal wearing the
Montreal Canadiens uniform.

But I also had my pride. The straw that broke the camel's
back happened on December 17. We were playing the Minnesota Wild, and that meant Derek Boogaard. Once again, may
he rest in peace.

The game marked Guillaume Latendresse's first game in
Montreal after being traded to the Wild for Benoit Pouliot. I
knew the atmosphere in the Bell Centre would be electric, and
I wanted to add to that. I figured that wouldn't be too hard to
do with Boogaard in the lineup for the Wild. He was easily one
of the toughest guys in the league, and I knew the fans would
want to see us go at it.

I invited him to go on the first shift. He declined. I was jawing
with him the whole shift, but he wouldn't go. I couldn't believe
it. He told me he didn't feel like it, which is fair enough. But he
also said I wasn't playing enough to be a factor in the game. It's
not like Boogaard was a guy who played ten minutes a game—
and it wasn't all that long ago that I used to log the most minutes
of any tough guy in the league. When a dedicated tough guy like
Boogaard tells you you're not worth fighting, that's a bad sign.

It's even worse when your coach tells you pretty much the
same thing. I wanted to get back out there, if not to fight then at

least to play hockey. But my coach wasn't going to play along. By the end of the game, Boogaard had played about twice as much as I had.

That's the way things had been going. When I asked Martin what was going on, he always had an answer. He wanted to get his top line out against the other team's fourth line. He wanted to try out new line combinations. He wanted to shorten his bench. It all amounted to the same thing: I wasn't playing, and I wasn't contributing, because it seemed there was always a reason to have someone on the ice other than me.

Wherever I had played in my career, I had always had an impact. It was in my job description to go out and change games. Now Martin was telling me that I wouldn't make a difference out there. I *knew* that couldn't be true.

The sheer stupidity of what he'd said made everything clear. That night I understood that nothing could be done to solve the situation.

At that precise moment I remembered André Roy's phone call. Boy, was he right! I also started thinking—yes, I had a lot of time to think on the Canadiens' bench at that time—about the teams Martin had coached in the past. Under his iron rule, both the Lightning and the Senators used to get great results during their regular seasons. And then they would choke in the playoffs, as the analysts would say. I know for sure now that the players from the Lightning and the Senators never choked during the playoffs. They were simply badly coached.

The man was repeating the same mistakes with the Montreal Canadiens. Despite all his great coaching skills, I will be surprised if Martin ever wins a Stanley Cup as head coach of a team because he would have to accept a reality he just can't see: a tough guy is indispensable in a team to protect and let the most talented players express themselves freely.

Maybe Martin's coaching style would work if every guy in the NHL played like Mark Messier or Jarome Iginla. But they don't. It's only skill guys like that—guys who have the hands to play on the first line, but know how to take care of themselves—who can create enough open ice for themselves without the help of a guy like me. They're a rare breed, though, and when guys like that come along the fans adore them. Brendan Shanahan, Wendel Clark, and let's not forget Gary Roberts—the list of guys who can play the game without fear is also a list of players the fans will never forget.

The reason I mention Messier is that he's one of the players I respected the most throughout my career. He made sure guys respected him. You just never knew what he was going to do out there. His retaliations could be so disproportionate that other players figured that even a little jostle or tap of the stick could result in a mouth full of Messier's Sherwood, so people just left him alone. I know I did. I remember one evening in New York when I had him lined up in my bomb sights for a big hit. He was flatfooted, and there was no way he could avoid me. Maybe I was already congratulating myself on running over one of the game's legendary warriors. If so, it was too soon for self-congratulation. At the very last moment, he welcomed me with the famous Messier elbow. That was the last time I tried to hit him.

That's the thing, though. If you don't want a tough guy in the lineup, you need a lineup full of guys who can convince tough guys not to hit them. It's hard enough to find one guy like that, never mind twenty-three.

•

Just before Christmas, Martin called me to his office. He started by talking about trivial things, and then suddenly asked me what I thought about the possibility of the Canadiens putting me on the waiver list. I had a simple answer: according to my contract, the team couldn't do that.

He insisted, asking me whether I thought another team would be interested if they were to waive me. I told him that I thought so, but that again, his question was absolutely irrelevant since I had a no-trade clause in my contract.

I left his office. He hadn't looked at me once during our discussion. The man was like that. Martin would never look you in the eye. He would drone on emotionlessly, shuffling papers and glancing at his computer, trying to make you feel as if you're wasting his time, even though he called the meeting.

From that day on and with no further explanations, I started watching the games from the press box. Even though I was frustrated as never before, I tried to keep a positive and joyful attitude. In the locker room I still was a real live wire, and I kept on being the players' representative while managing the funds we would collect for our team activities. My good mood was still contagious.

Lots of my teammates suggested that I go to Bob Gainey and talk about the situation. They were probably right, but back then I wasn't sure it was a good thing to do. Once again, I was too optimistic about the situation. I kept trying to convince myself that Jacques Martin wasn't a moron, that one day he'd realize that I could really help the team, especially when the Bruins or the Flyers were in town.

•

Tuesday, January 12, 2010. On that day, the Montreal Canadiens players were visiting the Montreal Children's Hospital, as we used to do as often as we could. That's when we learned about the terrible earthquake that had just ravaged Haiti. The first news reports were horrible. The country had been totally devastated and thousands of people had been killed in the disaster. I couldn't believe it. I told myself the press was once again exaggerating.

When I got back home, I turned on my television to see that the catastrophe was even worse than what the first news had reported. It was like the apocalypse happening right in front of my eyes. I started calling all my close relatives. Most of them were crying over the phone, and we all had the same question in mind: what had happened to the members of our family who'd stayed in Haiti? The question was impossible to answer since all the communications with the island were cut.

Two days after the tragedy, the Canadiens were playing Dallas at the Bell Centre. If I had prayed a lot for the Haitian people since I learned about the earthquake, I was also praying to God to let me score a goal that night. I wanted to dedicate my first goal with the Canadiens to the Haitian people and to the 100,000 Quebecers of Haitian origin.

Right before the game, everybody in the Bell Centre observed one minute of silence. The silence was total. I wasn't the only player of Haitian origin on the ice. The Stars had called the young Maxime Fortunus up from the minors for the occasion. We were all deeply moved.

Even though I desperately wanted to score a goal that night, I had no illusions. Jacques Martin wouldn't be modifying his game plan to suit me. And that plan, as you may have noticed, rarely included me. And yet I was still praying for the thing to happen. And it happened.

Right at the start of the second period, I made a pass from behind the net towards my teammate Patrice Bergeron, who got off a quick shot. Marty Turco stopped it but couldn't control the puck. I took the rebound and scored that goal I'd prayed so much for. I let my joy explode and threw myself at the glass the way I used to do in Edmonton.

In the locker room after the game, talking to the press, I gladly dedicated that goal to Haitian people all over the world. I also said that a goal wasn't much, that I wanted to do more, that I almost felt guilty playing hockey while people were still dying on the island. Then I promised that I would invest a lot of my efforts towards Haiti when the season came to an end.

But my joy didn't last long. When I got back home, I turned on the television to watch Jacques Martin's post-game press conference. Journalists asked him what he thought of the goal I'd scored. He simply told them that my line hadn't played that well and that I had ended the game with a minus one.

"What!" I heard myself screaming in my living room. Not only didn't he congratulate me when he knew perfectly how important that goal was for me, but he lied about my statistics. I'd ended the game even. I was totally stunned!

If I'd been naive to the point of no return up till then, that night I knew for sure there was definitely something wrong with that man. And when rethinking it a month later, I realized that the Canadiens would probably have released me before they did if the Haitian tragedy hadn't happened.

A few days later in New York, we were playing against the Rangers. We were losing by three and the Rangers were having fun giving my teammates a taste of the boards. Once again Martin said no when I begged him to let me help my team.

The post-game press conference was kind of surreal. Journalists were bombarding Martin with questions about me. They simply couldn't understand why, with the toughest guy in the league on his bench, Martin had let such a massacre unfold. Everybody thought I was hiding an injury or something like that.

Martin shamelessly answered that I'd had my chance, but I didn't take it. That was an absolute lie, since I was on the ice only three times that night and never had the chance to sort things out. My job wasn't to go out and take stupid penalties or jump the first Ranger to cross my path. To suggest that I should have laid down the law in three shifts is like saying the police should be able to prevent crime during a quick drive around the block. He was deliberately lying, and I knew for sure now that he was doing it simply to denigrate me in the eyes of the press.

It would be my last game with the Montreal Canadiens.

•

On January 19, Bob Gainey called me into his office. He told me how sad he was about what was going on in Haiti, and that he knew what it was to go through tough times since he had lost his daughter a few years before. He really seemed to be moved by the tragedy.

Just before finishing our discussion, he asked me if I needed time to pause from hockey to do something for Haiti or even to go there. I answered that even if I was deeply touched by what was happening over there, I was a professional, and I was paid to help his team win games. If I was to do something for Haiti, I would do it once the season was over.

What a strange conversation that was. Since when does a general manager offer a lengthy pause to one of his players under contract?

The next day we were to meet up with the Blues at the Bell Centre. That team could count on one of the most impressive tough guys in the league, Cam Janssen. It was to be our only game against the Blues that season. But despite that fact, Martin chose to let me watch the game from the press box. Jensen was going to be free to do whatever he wanted on the ice, and he sure took the opportunity to do so.

At one point during the game, he ran over Carey Price—about as serious a provocation as there is in hockey. If a team can't stand up for their goalie, it's pretty much defenceless. The press went berserk. Journalist Pierre McGuire was commentating the game, standing right between the two benches. He started blasting Jacques Martin on the air, saying he had made the worst possible decision by not dressing me for that game. Martin was standing right beside McGuire—too close not to have heard what the journalist said.

The day after, we were leaving for New Jersey to get ready for the Devils. As usual, I was the first to arrive at the practice arena that morning. Somebody told me Bob Gainey wanted to see me in his office.

As I entered the room, I noticed that his assistant, Julien Brisebois, was also present. I knew then that something serious was going to happen. Without any further notice, Gainey told me that the Montreal Canadiens were sending me home—I had been released. He added that the team would honour its obligations and would pay me full salary until the end of the season. He then asked me to go back down to the locker room, get my things, and go home.

Although I should have seen it coming for a long time, I was in total disbelief. I asked him if it was a joke, adding that if it was, I really didn't think it was a funny one. He confirmed the seriousness of what he'd just said. I wanted reasons for what was happening, but he answered that he didn't have to give me any and ordered me once again to go get my things.

I unsteadily went down the stairs towards the locker room. Some of my teammates had started to arrive. BriseBois had followed me all the way down, probably to make sure I wasn't going to do something wrong. I asked him if, at least, I could say goodbye to the guys. He nodded.

I approached the guys who'd been my teammates for a year and a half now. I was staggering. I told them what was happening, said goodbye, and wished them good luck for the rest of the season. Everyone thought I'd been traded. I had to repeat the story several times for them to understand it.

Even then they thought I was joking, but when they saw Julien Brisebois waiting by the door they knew for sure I was serious. I finally left the locker room and went back home, still incapable of understanding what had just happened to me.

Later that day, Bob Gainey held a press conference to announce the team had released me. He said the team would be better without me. That was exactly the same reason he invoked when explaining his decision to the players. I thought this explanation was pure nonsense, since I was barely playing anymore anyway.

He went on to say that I had too many distractions outside the ice, that I was a nuisance to the team, that I wasn't doing the job I'd been hired for, that I wasn't willing to comply with the team's ethics.

I stayed there in front of my television set, mouth open, staring for I don't know how long.

•

At the beginning of the season, I had told the media I wouldn't do any interviews anymore simply because I wanted to concentrate on hockey and nothing else.

I had been injured, that's for sure, and yet I had remained a hard-working player.

I was popular in the locker room, joyful and funny; plus, I was the NHLPA team rep. I couldn't see how that would be a nuisance to the team.

As far as my performances on the ice were concerned, how could Gainey even evaluate them? I was hardly playing anymore, and when I was, Martin was putting me on the ice three or four times a game. You absolutely can't evaluate a player with that kind of ice time.

Ethics? I was ready to sacrifice myself to protect my teammates, even though I was suffering agony most of the time. If Jacques Martin didn't want me to do my job, how could Gainey blame me for that? I truly *wasn't* doing my job, I couldn't deny that, but it had nothing to do with a lack of ethics—I'd been begging to be allowed to do my job. Maybe Gainey didn't know about that, but he could have asked Kirk Muller or even some of my own teammates, and he would have known how much I wanted to play my role.

If Gainey thought there had been some kind of ethical failure, all he had to do was talk to his coach.

•

When the press conference ended, I felt as if someone had hit me three or four times in the face with a shovel.

When I finally came back to my senses, I immediately decided I was going to organize my very own press conference in which I would explain my side of the story. I didn't want my reputation to be tarnished like that without responding. What Bob Gainey had just said was enough to discourage any other team to hire me.

The day after, just a few hours before I would take the microphone in front of the press, a TSN journalist called to ask if he could get a few advance comments from me so that he could insert them on air as soon as the press conference was over.

I told him that if he wanted to know what really happened, he just had to show up at 4 P.M. at the Canadiens' training centre in Brossard. I couldn't help adding, though, that what the team had done was totally lacking in class.

Some team official probably heard or read that quote of mine on TSN, because fifteen minutes before opening the press conference, my agent called me. He told me that someone from the Montreal Canadiens had told him that if I were to attack the team or any of its members they would stop paying me and start looking for possible legal remedies.

For a minute I didn't want to listen to my agent; I wanted to sweep aside with the back of my hand everything he'd just told me. My pride was hurt, my reputation demolished. But my agent convinced me to follow his advice. For the very first time in my life, I spoke like a politician.

Journalists tried hard to get me going, and they all knew by then how to do it. But I remained calm. I told them that I would now go to Haiti and get involved in the reconstruction of the country. As for my career, I promised them that I was going to bounce back somewhere else.

But I was never to bounce back. My career was over. I just didn't know it yet.

Altogether, I had played 695 games in the NHL, scoring 53 goals for a total of 153 points and accumulating 1126 penalty minutes. During that thirteen-year career, I was involved in about 130 fights, losing only five or six times by decision, never by KO.

My last fight was on December 12, 2009, against Eric Boulton of the Atlanta Thrashers.

Maybe it's strange to say, but I really liked Boulton. He was as tough as they come but also a decent guy. I remember the first time I fought him, when he first came into the league. He wanted a shot at me to make a name for himself, and he asked me to dance. When I accepted his invitation, he smiled and asked me not to beat him up too badly. That's composure.

Anyway, that night, years later, Boulton came at me with a hard, wild swing, but I was ready to counter. Things went well for me. The last time I dropped my gloves in an NHL rink, I was on top of my opponent when the linesmen stepped in.

And that was it.

To conclude this chapter, I just want to say that I really do hope the Canadiens win the Stanley Cup someday, for the players, the organization, and for the fans. The city is electrifying when its team wins. The fans are so devoted, they deserve the ultimate prize, the Holy Grail ...

HAITI, *MON AMOUR* 14

I guess coming back to your hometown after making your name somewhere else isn't easy. But it wasn't as though I didn't have all kinds of Montrealers and Habs fans on my side.

I once again received hundreds of emails supporting me. People were sad that the Montreal Canadiens had done what they'd done. Others were really angry at the team, accusing Gainey, Martin, and the whole organization of having manipulated me only to finally take me out to the curb like a bag of trash. But everyone assumed I'd end up playing for another team, and wished me luck.

Members of my family and close friends called me. Some were sad, others were mad, most of them were both. None of them could believe what had just happened.

On a professional level, try to guess where the first phone call came from. That's right—from Sweden. Now that the Montreal Canadiens had released me, the general manager of the AIK couldn't see any reason why I shouldn't put the black and gold sweater of my favourite European team back on. The Black Army wrote emails to me saying quite the same thing.

That offer really tempted me a lot. To escape from Montreal for a few weeks to go to Sweden sounded like the best thing I could do. Far away from North America, it would be easier for me to heal my mental and physical wounds. And I could still play hockey at a competitive level, since the AIK had rejoined the Eliteserien the year before. Moreover, because of the no-movement clause in my contract, the Canadiens were unable to send me anywhere else in the NHL.

So I was all set and ready to pack my suitcase when my agent called, letting me know I couldn't do it. I was still on the Montreal Canadiens' payroll; I was to get the playoff bonuses. In short, he told me that I'd be in breach of contract if I were to accept the AIK offer. Deeply disappointed, I had to decline.

Although the Canadiens had released me, I wouldn't officially become a free agent until July 1, 2010. Until then, it was the team's prerogative to call me back whenever they wanted to. And so when Gainey decided to resign on February 8, only a few days after releasing me, the rumours started that I would soon be back with the team.

I didn't believe them for one second, for the good reason that I didn't think Gainey was the one who wanted me off the team. The guy who was responsible for what happened to me was still standing behind the Canadiens' bench. And I knew for sure he'd do anything to keep me as far from him as he could.

Journalists were calling me, wanting to know my plans for the future. I was still answering that I'd be back, that I would consider any offers I'd get as soon as I could start negotiating, which meant after June 30, when I'd just be one more free agent on the market.

I was still training and working out intensively. That's what hockey players do, and I was a hockey player.

That was when I injured myself again. My herniated discs had gone to sleep when the Habs released me and I wasn't skating anymore. But when I got back to the gym, they woke up in a bad mood. I knew right away that it was now too late.

My comeback with another team, which I had assumed was inevitable, was obviously impossible, even in Sweden.

I couldn't play hockey anymore. So I decided to make it official. At age thirty-three, it was time to retire.

•

Was I melancholy? Did I agonize over the decision? Did I toss and turn at night?

The answer is a quick no.

Don't get me wrong. I love the game. I'm honoured to have played it as long as I did, and at the level I did. I'm proud of what I accomplished, and proud that I never took the easy way out. I got to experience things I'd only dreamed of.

But I was at the end, and I understood that. Thirteen years of fighting the strongest, toughest hockey players in the world is a long grind. As the condition of my back made pretty clear, there's a lot of wear and tear even when you win.

It was more than that, though. Fighting got harder when I had kids. It was tough being away from them. And it was tough doing something for a living I didn't want my kids to see. I'm not saying I had a problem with fighting in the game. But I didn't get into the game dreaming of being a fighter, and that is a complicated thing to explain to a kid.

So I was ready to stop doing it.

Still, I did not like being railroaded out of a game I loved, when I was still among the toughest in the league, by a coach I thought didn't understand the game.

But I didn't have to make excuses. The TSN website posted some of Jacques Martin's thoughts on the game and he exhaustively explained why he didn't believe in the presence of tough guys in the NHL. Without him even realizing it, he'd just told the Quebec hockey world that he was the one who'd gotten rid of me. Thanks for the favour, Jacques.

And when the playoffs began, it became clear to every serious analyst that the Canadiens needed a tough guy among its troops. The press openly asked the question: "Why is Georges Laraque sitting at home with his full paycheque while the team is being pushed around again by the Flyers?" Jacques Martin turned a deaf ear to all those complaints.

Tough guys are a necessity in the NHL, and he was the only one not acknowledging that reality—which is normal, in a certain sense, since he wasn't the one getting punched in the face night after night. But to be respected by his players, a coach has to feel deep inside of him every bit of pain his players are experiencing. Bob Hartley and Michel Therrien were good examples of that.

On January 28, 2010, one week after being released, I was invited on to a popular talk show in Quebec called *Tout le monde en parle*. Aired three days later, on January 31, the show allowed me to set a few things straight. Although I didn't go as far as I do in this book, I was able to give some facts about my side of the story.

After the broadcast I received another round of emails. When people found out how serious my injuries had been, and that I could have chosen to undergo surgery and sit at home collecting my salary, they saw me in a whole new light.

The interview also allowed me to talk about everything that mattered and still matters to me outside the hockey world. The audience discovered then who I really was. I wasn't simply a *goon* who made a living punching people in the face because he loved it.

•

But moving away from hockey didn't mean that my life was going to change totally. Since the beginning of my career, my days had been filled with a lot more than practices and games and team flights. I'd always worked closely with the communities I lived in, helping charities and visiting schools and children's hospitals. I was now going to devote myself to the things that had always really mattered to me.

Now was the time to give back to the world, as I had promised God when I was a young kid, every minute of the dream He had offered me. After having received a lot, I was now going to give.

In the days following my retirement, since I couldn't make the move to Sweden, I started planning to go to Haiti. I knew I could be more useful there than on my couch at home.

Of course, I had dedicated a goal to the Haitian people, but that only told the world that doing something about the tragedy was important to me. Now that I had my chance, I had to follow up and actually do something. The images coming from the island were breaking my heart. They also, at times, made me angry. Watching guys in helicopters throwing bags of food into a starving crowd seemed to demean the Haitians just when they needed respect. No one wants to be fed like a dangerous animal.

On the ground, men, women, and kids were fighting to get their share of that "humanitarian" help. I didn't find it hard to understand them. Anyone who hasn't eaten and drunk for three days would fight for food and water. But sensational news bulletins would show those scenes and suggest that chaos was everywhere in Haiti.

Humanity is capable of accomplishing great things, but for some reason the richest countries in the world couldn't manage to distribute food and water to the Haitian people with dignity. I was outraged.

Then I remembered what happened during the New Orleans flooding tragedy. More than $900 million had been raised around the world to help the disaster victims. Only a third of that money ever made it to the scene of the catastrophe. Much of the other two-thirds ended up paying the generous salaries of career humanitarians who drove around in air-conditioned Land Cruisers and lived in relative luxury. I had the feeling the proportion would be even worse in Haiti.

Thinking I was doing the right thing, I participated in fund-raising events for Haiti, only to find out later that the organizers had kept most of the money to cover their "administration costs." Since collecting funds for Haiti had become a full-time activity for me, I unfortunately couldn't verify everything. For some people, even a humanitarian crisis is an opportunity to make a few bucks.

I was ready to give my own money, a lot of it, but I had to be sure the funds would go straight to the people who needed it. I talked about that to the NHLPA and they immediately agreed to help me find a project and some financing. At first, we thought about reconstructing a devastated school. A worthy project, but not ambitious enough. We had to think again.

I then told myself that, in days of tragedy, the biggest problems the disaster victims have to face, after food and water, are related to health care. I also remembered some images I saw on television in which men, women, and children were medically treated in makeshift shelters where hygiene is something people can only dream of.

In the next meeting we had at the NHLPA, I said that we should be involving ourselves in the reconstruction of a damaged hospital. Everyone around the table thought the project was too much. I promised I would invest myself 100 percent in that goal and not stop until it was a reality on the ground. The charity Hockey for Haiti was born.

And to make it a reality, we had to link ourselves to a recognized non-governmental organization (NGO). I went around to every existing NGO that was likely to help us with the project, analyzing the way it operates and examining its financial statements when available. As I had feared, some would spend 50 percent of the money they collected for their administration fees; others were paying their administrators astronomical wages. I also wanted to see how they functioned when on the ground of a tragedy.

Since the earthquake happened, a lot of observers have criticized the Haitian government for its mismanagement of international help. And it's true—the government's response was far from perfect. Few people, on the other hand, have asked themselves whether the money that was pledged on one side of the world ever showed up in Haiti. That is, you can't criticize the government for mismanaging money it never had the opportunity to spend. By July 2010, only 2 percent of the billions of dollars pledged by countries around the world had actually shown up on the ledgers of the Haitian government. Some still hasn't shown up.

Some NGOs collect funds and then go to Haiti. When on the ground, they hire Westerners to work on their projects. If a construction worker makes around $40 an hour in Canada, how much do you think he'll command to go and work in Haiti? To his salary, you then have to add the money needed for his food and housing, for the insurance he has to get, and for lots of other expenses. That's all money the Haitian people will never see.

Rather than hiring Westerners, if the NGOs hire qualified Haitian workers, it would really help the local economy, and also drastically lower the labour cost of every single project. And the less each project costs, the more projects there will be. A dollar goes a lot further when an NGO spends it locally.

So in our minds it was out of the question not to hire Haitian workers for Hockey for Haiti. The hospital was going to be built by Haitians, for Haitians. Plus, the NGO we were to choose would have to have the lowest administration fees possible. And among all the ones we met, World Vision was clearly on top.

For only 10 percent of the whole budget, World Vision would take care of everything. They've been in Haiti for the past thirty years and will stay there as long as they're needed. And their policy is very clear: they hire Haitian workers whenever it's possible. Last but not least, World Vision is a Christian organization, which is very important in my eyes.

•

A small, religiously tinted parenthesis here. I was born a Catholic. I was baptized and made my first communion. While growing up, I started studying a bit more what that religion was really about. What I discovered by doing so left me both sad and nauseated. Of all the religions in this world, I realized that it was one of the worst—that it had caused countless numbers of wars and crimes, that on numerous occasions it had brought pain and suffering.

In addition, Vatican City, the richest state in the world, owes its present status to one of the fathers of fascism, Benito Mussolini. Did Jesus live in opulence, gilt, and splendour? Vatican City sits on an investment portfolio of uncountable riches, while two billion people in the world can't find enough food to eat each day. Catholics are supposed to venerate the pope when it is said in the Bible that one must kneel only in front of God.

Same thing with priest celibacy, a fundamental absurdity that the Bible doesn't preach at all. On the contrary, the Book says priests should get married in order to be able to counsel married men. These are only a few of the contradictions between Catholicism and the Bible that made me move away from that religion.

Yet, spirituality has always taken a large place in my life. I studied several of the most important religions and philosophies of the world. I even went further than reading books, I actively practised some of them so that I could understand them from within and choose the one that was to suit me best.

After having seen the Spike Lee movie *Malcom X*, I started studying and practising Islam. Over a little more than a month, I prayed five times a day, went to the mosque, and talked with Muslims, including a few imams. My fervour didn't last, though.

In short, I've tried almost all major religions, including Jehovah Witnesses, Buddhism, and Judaism. I almost converted to the latter. I simply love the message carried by the Old Testament and I find a profound beauty in Judaism. I then discovered the thought of Luther, one of the founders of Protestantism.

And as a Catholic whose religious thought began with a criticism of the tradition I was raised in, I suppose I was following in Luther's footsteps.

Today, if I have to define myself religiously, I would say I'm half Jewish, half Christian. Both messages fascinate me in the way they teach us to always put ourselves in the shoes of the other before judging his or her actions in any way.

End of parenthesis.

•

Hockey for Haiti decided to link up with World Vision, but also to the group International Child Care. The institution we decided we would be reconstructing was the Grace Children's Hospital, located in Port-au-Prince, which was almost totally devastated by the earthquake. We contacted Dr. John Yates, who was and still is in charge of it.

After talking to him about the real needs of the Haitian people, we decided we would build a larger hospital than the one we were replacing. The Grace was mostly treating children suffering from tuberculosis and respiratory diseases. Since the needs are huge, the new Grace hospital will treat adults as well as children, and will cover a wider range of specialized medical fields.

When all of this was decided, I started organizing dozens of events in order to collect funds for the project. The NHLPA and the NHL immediately agreed to give $100,000 each. Some players also contributed on a personal basis.

I contacted lots of different institutions, from schools to restaurants, asking them if they were ready to help us raise funds for the project. When I got a yes, I'd help them organize their own campaign. I went to radio stations so that they would organize activities and contests to encourage their listeners to generously give to Hockey for Haiti. I also organized numerous fundraising dinners. The campaign was doing so well that before my first trip to Haiti, a few weeks after the project was launched, we'd already collected half a million dollars.

We left Montreal for Port-au-Prince in the middle of May. Taking part in the trip were people from World Vision and Dan Hamhuis, who was then playing for the Predators but is now with the Canucks. The NHLPA had put out the word to its members that they needed someone to pick up some responsibility for the Hockey for Haiti program, and Hamhuis generously offered his time and support. I really respect him for that. Imagine putting up your hand when someone asks a large group for a volunteer to travel thousands of kilometres to a country in chaos to help out just because it's the right thing to do. It would have been easy for Dan to have done nothing, but he went out of his way to help.

On the plane, the person in charge of World Vision's small delegations told us about the way we should behave once we arrived in Haiti. We had to wear long trousers at all times, for instance, because of all the bugs. It was also totally forbidden to give money to the people who would inevitably beg from us. Finally, we would have to always keep together and stay on our guard.

•

This trip to Haiti wasn't my first. I'd been to the island twice during my youth, but the memories from those family trips basically consisted of a few images of the beach, drinking coconut milk right from the fruit, and eating mangos right after picking them from the tree. I remembered a Haiti that would take a lot of work to bring back.

I also remembered the beggars who would walk naked on the streets. That extreme poverty had shaken me deeply as a kid. And the kids with huge bellies confused me. My parents had told me that few Haitians had enough to eat to properly feed their families. And yet, those children looked overfed. It was only later that I learned that those malformations were due to a disease coming from malnutrition.

Another one of the memories I had from my first two trips to Haiti was linked to an episode I witnessed between my grandmother's maid and a turkey. The turkey lived in the backyard of my grandmother's house, where it could run around freely. I could watch it for hours. It would eat everything it found on its path, even pebbles.

One morning, as I was watching it, the maid came and took it by the neck. In front of my eyes, she then simply cut off its head. And even though it had been beheaded, the animal still took a few steps before falling on its side. I was shocked. How could that beheaded animal still walk? I had nightmares about it for days.

There's a saying that travels broaden the mind. Well, those two trips to Haiti sure had that effect on me, as I never saw my life the same way afterwards. They made me understand how lucky I was to live in a nice house in a rich country. I also promised myself I would never complain about trifles anymore. Haitians were poor and hungry and would still find the strength to smile and sing.

•

In May 2010, I was making my first trip as an adult to my ancestors' soil. The moist heat wrapped itself around us as soon as we arrived.

I made my first mistake as soon as we got out of the airport. I pulled a wad of one-dollar bills out of my pocket and gave one to a very young kid who was asking me for money. With that one move, I instantaneously created a commotion.

From everywhere, people started gathering around me. I really felt the danger and the threats. I gave all I had and looked at that young boy I'd given my first dollar to. He was running away as fast as he could while other kids were trying to catch him and steal that dollar from him. The person from World Vision severely reprimanded me, and she was so right to do so.

Our first destination was the Grace Hospital site. When we arrived there we saw dozens of tents installed to give front-line aid to hundreds of people. The young patients at the hospital welcomed us with beautiful songs I will never ever forget.

The engineer in charge of the reconstruction then explained to us that the vast majority of the small buildings had collapsed because they'd been built with poor-quality cement. I promised him that the new hospital would be built using only best-quality materials.

During the following days, we visited some of the different projects World Vision was conducting in Haiti. We saw lots of farms producing fruits and vegetables and some animal farms, too; we even went to visit a slaughterhouse. World Vision contributions helped create those small businesses, which were now entirely managed by Haitians.

Not only were those visits very fulfilling on a personal level, they also convinced me even more that we'd made the right choice in deciding on World Vision as a partner for the Hockey for Haiti project.

Whenever we were driving along the streets of Port-au-Prince or its surroundings, I couldn't help asking that we stop every now and then. People were cooking food on the streets and I wanted to taste it, talk with them, and try to learn more about their lives. Once again though, people from World Vision would reprimand me.

Even during those five days, seemingly so far from the life I'd left behind, I could not escape hockey or the drama of the Montreal Canadiens. Even in Haiti, I saw the Habs being manhandled by the Flyers. Our trip had had a lot of press coverage and the NHL helped us a lot in publicizing our project. Between periods, fans could see reports about what we were doing to help the Haitian people find their way back to a normal life. Some of them would then ask why I wasn't on the ice protecting the players.

•

When I came back to Montreal, I had only one goal in mind: to continue my fundraising activities. That was when I received a phone call from a guy who is now my friend and partner in business, Nick Brusatore. A few years earlier he'd created a company specializing in what's called vertical farming.

Nick told me that he'd followed my trip to Haiti from his home in British Columbia. He was deeply moved by the situation and wanted to do something to help. He asked me if I had any ideas about how he could contribute to the reconstruction of the country and the healing of the people's wounds. Since his company was producing fruits and vegetables in such large quantities, I told him we could maybe go to Haiti and distribute some of his produce to the neediest people there.

Workers at his company were getting ready to prepare thousands of crates full of fruits and vegetables. In the meantime, we contacted the customs services to find out exactly how to proceed in order to import all that food. But the bureaucratic maze that faced us was so complex to satisfy that, sadly, we had to abandon the whole thing.

Nick didn't want to give up, though, and we soon had a new idea, even better than the first one. We would go in Haiti, buy some food from Haitian farmers, and distribute it to the needy people.

I contacted my friend Pamela Anderson, with whom I had worked in the past for the organization People for the Ethical Treatment of Animal (PETA). She had once told me that she admired what Sean Penn had done for Haiti and felt that she too should do something to contribute.

I told her about the project Nick and I were working on and asked her if she wanted to come with us. She accepted immediately. We did all the paperwork, got our vaccines, and in no time we were ready to go.

Nick paid for everything: airplane tickets, hotel rooms, food, and even the nine bodyguards we had to hire in order to protect Pamela. Even better, he bought the harvests of a whole agricultural field where carrots, potatoes, sweet potatoes, plantains, and onions were growing. We prepared five hundred bags, each one containing twenty-five pounds of vegetables.

Then we went to two camps located near deeply devastated villages in the suburbs of Port-au-Prince and distributed the bags. I was really proud of that because not only did we help people in need but we also contributed to the local economy by buying all the produce in Haiti.

Moreover, if there are still people on this earth who see Pamela Anderson as a brainless bimbo who's afraid of ruining her manicure, well they should have seen her sweat carrying those heavy bags on her back. Respect Pamela! Respect Nick! What they accomplished during this trip was pure altruism, something we don't often find anymore on this planet.

We still had forty-eight hours to spend in Haiti, so Pamela decided to take us to the site of the temporary village Sean Penn had built with the Haitian people. When I arrived there, tears started running from my eyes. It was incredible what the American star had done here. He could have stayed in the comfort of his mansion when the earthquake occurred, but instead he chose to pack a few personal things and go straight to Haiti, not only to finance the establishment of a makeshift city but to build it with his own hands. For months he worked like crazy to make it real. When we visited, more than 60,000 people were living there with enough food and drinking water for everyone.

The next day, after Pamela had left for Russia, Nick and I went to the Grace Hospital construction site. Under a killing sun, some workers were still clearing the place away while others had already started laying the foundations of what would become the future hospital. To show our appreciation, we gave them the bags we had left from the distribution.

On the last day of our trip we decided to take some rest and went to the site of Haiti's Club Méditerranée, which closed its doors in 2000. The sea was beautiful, the sand gorgeous, and we manged to lazily enjoy some of Haiti's natural beauty for a day.

•

That last trip, like the previous one, had boosted my energy and so it was with renewed vigour that I started my fundraising activities again. I wanted to go back to Haiti as soon as possible simply to keep the tragedy in the news. People have the tendency to be moved by something and to forget about it the day after.

I had to wait for favourable circumstances before making my third trip to Haiti, though. I left on July 4, 2011. This time I was joined by Montreal Canadiens star P.K. Subban. Even though he's of Jamaican descent, it was his very first trip to a Caribbean island.

As soon as we arrived, I brought P.K. to the site of the Grace Hospital. I was really impressed by the progress made in the reconstruction, and so was the World Vision president, Dave Toycen, who was with us for the occasion. Moreover, Dr. Yates and his staff were already able to treat more than five hundred patients a day.

It was funny to see how many people recognized P.K. during our trip. It was pretty understandable, though, since some of the 100,000 Quebecers of Haitian origin go back to Haiti in the winter and keep on following the hockey season from there.

The Montreal Canadiens had been very generous with us for this particular trip. They had given us loads of caps, shirts, and various accessories to distribute among the population while we were there. So don't be surprised in the future if you ever see a kid walking down the streets of Port-au-Prince wearing a Montreal Canadiens shirt with the name P.K. Subban on it ...

I was very impressed by the level of empathy and the exceptional maturity this twenty-two-year-old athlete showed while we were in Haiti. At the end of our trip he said to me, "I want to share everything I've seen here with my family and friends. This experience has changed my life for good and for the better. I want it to change the lives of my nearest and dearest."

Before closing this chapter on Haiti, a chapter that will never be closed in my heart, I want to relate one of the most touching experiences I had during that last trip. Two parents came up to me while I was visiting the Grace Hospital site. They told me their children had been saved thanks to the medical care they received from the hospital doctors. When I asked them what their dreams were for their children now, they didn't tell me they wanted them to become lawyers or doctors. They had this simple but touching thing to say: "We want to them to live as long as possible." To hear parents dreaming of something as basic as their kids' health was powerfully affecting for us.

Today, we have exceeded the 1.5-million-dollar mark ...

IN OTHER PEOPLE'S SHOES

15

Those multiple trips to Haiti surprised a lot of people. Some thought I was trying to find myself a new career in humanitarianism; others thought I was doing it mainly because of my Haitian origins.

For those who knew me well, though, those trips were simply following on what had been my life outside hockey for more than a decade or so. I hadn't invented myself an empathetic persona; I'd just started doing full-time what I'd been doing away from the ice for years.

I remember the first visits I paid to hospitals in Edmonton at the beginning of my career. I couldn't help noticing those players who were desperate to leave as soon as possible. They were sighing, looking at their watch ...

That's why I've always been against making those kinds of activities mandatory for the players. I'm convinced that there's nothing worse for a sick child than to feel that his favourite player is bored with him. Far be it from me to blame those players here, though. It's not always easy to go into a hospital crowded with sick children and remain joyful and all smiles. Those kids are often severely ill and they need to think about something else for a while. Not everyone is capable of doing it.

The very first time I visited them, I entered a room where a young boy lay who had just a few days left to live. His dream before dying was to meet Doug Weight.

I stayed in one corner of the room without saying a word. I simply observed and listened. Doug was talking to him in a gentle voice, making jokes. The boy was all excited to have his idol sitting on his bed, so close to him. I immediately saw what kind of impact an athlete can have on the mind and soul of a sick child. I couldn't believe my eyes. Not a single existing medicine could have produced half the positive effect Doug had on this kid. Right there, in that room, I knew I was going to devote myself to them.

That said, I wasn't yet renowned enough to have that same impact. For a visit to really have an impact, you have to be the very one player the kid dreams of seeing entering his room. Yet it didn't take me that long to be appreciated by the kids. I was black, I was a tough guy, but when they saw me, I was always laughing and looked as cuddly as a huge teddy bear in their eyes.

At the end of my first complete season with the Oilers, I was voted the most popular player on the team. That was when I really started to get involved in all sorts of charities and community action. I went to the Oilers' public relations department and told them that I wanted to be part of every single activity being planned. It didn't take long before I was busy practically every single day, visiting hospitals, schools, and day camps … I went to hundreds and hundreds of them while in Edmonton.

Among all the different institutions I was involved with, my favourite was definitely the Stollery Children's Hospital. I would go there as soon as I had some free time and I was part of every single fundraising campaign or event they would organize. My involvement was so intense that the hospital board even put a mention with my name on it on their benefactors' wall.

I also got involved in a campaign the Alberta government started in order to increase public awareness of shaken baby syndrome. I really liked the poster they made for the campaign and the slogan that went with it. Under a photo of me with a baby in my arms was the sentence "Are you tough enough to be gentle?"

I also got involved as a spokesman with the Drug Abuse Resistance Education (DARE) program, which is taught all over North America. I went to several schools in the greater Edmonton region where I was joined by police officers, and together we would try to make the kids understand how dangerous drug abuse could be for their health as well as for their future.

Even though the activities the Oilers were assigning me would have been more than enough for most people, I simply couldn't limit myself to them. Through my website, which I'd launched after my second complete year with the Oilers (www.georgeslaraque.com), I would accept invitations to all sorts of activities.

My favourite one was when fans would invite me to dinner at their homes. Most of those fans didn't have enough money to come see the Oilers live; others could afford it only once or twice a year. I knew they were working hard to manage to feed their families and pay the rent. They were huge fans of the Oilers but could never see their favourite players from up close, much less talk to them. I was pleased by their invitations and would accept them all the time.

At that time I was often asking myself what we, the hockey millionaires, were doing for those hard-working people who were often paying our salaries by the sweat of their brow. We loved to see the stands filled night after night. In that sense, it felt natural for me to involve myself in the community as deeply as I could, to visit those people without whom we would be nothing. It was my way of showing them my appreciation.

When visiting them, I wasn't only there to have dinner. I'd bring loads of Oilers promotional stuff, and would go around the neighbourhood to speak to people. During the off-season I would do that three to four times a week.

When they learned I was visiting fans at home, people in the Oilers' public relations department weren't happy at all. They tried to dissuade me, not only for my own personal security, but also because they were afraid some ill-intentioned person would cook up some allegation and sue me.

We found a compromise. I would keep on visiting fans at their homes, but I'd always bring a friend with me who could act as a witness if something were to go wrong. I had, of course, made a lot of friends among Oilers fans with those visits.

After my fourth year with the team, I had to slow down and then completely cease those visits. Not that I didn't like to do them anymore, but I was so involved in so many activities that I no longer had the time.

I would never say no to charities' invitations, whether it was for a simple event or for a fundraising campaign. Between 2002 and 2006, I received the Community Service Award four times in a row. That award was given to the player who'd been the most involved in charities and various social activities.

Another one of my favourite events of the year in Edmonton was part of the annual funfair called Corn Maze. The organizers had decided that one Monday would be reserved for handicapped persons only. I had so much fun those days. I would go on dozens of rides in various merry-go-rounds with them, hand out candy, and just hang out. I went eight years in a row to this event, called Monday Morning Magic, and magic it sure was.

In all these different activities, what was extraordinary and would make me laugh a lot every time was people's reactions when they met me for the first time. They couldn't believe that the fighter I was, the *goon*, could actually be such a soft, nice person. They would realize that what I did on the ice was a job, and that now they were facing the real me.

If I became so popular in the city of Edmonton, it certainly wasn't only for what I was accomplishing on the ice, but also—and some would say mostly—for what I was doing off the ice. I was involving myself in all sorts of activities, and was generous with my time and money. Most of all, I wasn't being fake in doing it. I loved it and it showed.

I certainly can't relate here all the activities I took part or got involved in. There were so many that even a simple list of them would easily go on for pages. I met so many children struggling with cancer and other severe or fatal chronic diseases that I always wear two yellow bracelets on my wrists in a sign of solidarity with them. These bracelets come from the LiveStrong Foundation created by Lance Armstrong. The champion cyclist had thirty million of those made. He sold every one of them for one dollar apiece, and all the money went to organizations looking for a cure for different types of cancer.

I do remember one time, though, when I was on vacation. I had just checked in at the hotel in Calgary when I received a call from the Stollery Hospital. There was a patient, a young boy named Jordan, who was suffering from muscular dystrophy. He had only a couple of hours, if not minutes, to live. People from the hospital had asked him what was his last dream, and in his little voice he had whispered my name. I bolted out of the hotel, jumped into my car, and drove as fast as I could back to Edmonton. I so wanted to be there before he died that at times I drove on the side of the highway to pass other cars. It took me an hour and a half to make it to Edmonton when it's usually more than a two-hour drive.

When I entered Jordan's room, his family was surrounding his bed. Most of the people were crying and Jordan was very weak. In moments like that, I would always try to instill a positive energy in spite of the dramatic circumstances. I wanted the people in the room to remember their child's last moments as ones of joy. I know that may sound awkward.

People started smiling, and even Jordan was laughing. The electrocardiogram showed that his pulse rate was rising. He was visibly happy and excited to see me. I stayed one hour in the room, and talked to everyone. The boy's parents took me in their arms to thank me.

A week later, Jordan's grandmother had a letter published in an Edmonton newspaper in which she thanked me for my visit. Jordan didn't pass away on the day I came. He stayed alive for a week. According to his grandmother, there was no doubt that my visit had given him the strength to go on. For her, I had allowed the whole family to enjoy Jordan's presence a week more. When I read this, I had tears in my eyes.

In the following years I would often use that example when talking to the other players about the importance of involving themselves in their community.

Nowadays, when I walk in the streets of Edmonton and meet people, they often talk to me about those years. What I love above all is when I meet, often by chance, kids I'd visited years ago in their hospital room. They're adults now, and all of them remember that moment as if it happened yesterday.

Others still send me emails with photos attached, photos of when I visited them. They still thank me for those moments. I was and still am deeply rooted to the Edmonton community. Although it's now impossible for me to involve myself as much and in the same way as I used to, when in Alberta, I never say no to a charity that needs me. And I'm not hard to reach. In Edmonton, everybody has my phone number.

•

When I arrived in Phoenix, one of the first things I did was to meet up with the Coyotes' public relations department. I repeated to them the same words I'd said to the Oilers' PR people. I wanted to be part of all their charities and social activities.

They were quite amazed, since they were used to dealing with players who would hide under the table as soon as the word "charities" was pronounced. And now they were encountering a player who not only wanted to do some, but all of the community activities the Coyotes were involved in.

The same scenario unfolded with the Penguins, but in a different way. Unlike my two previous cities, Pittsburgh contains numerous underprivileged districts. I visited more than once every single YMCA you could find in the greater Pittsburgh region to talk to young kids whose families were grappling with sometimes severe monetary difficulties.

After each practice, someone from public relations would come to the locker room to give me my program of the day. I would talk with the kids, but also play hockey, hide-and-seek, or tag with them. I had as much fun as they did. I've always considered myself a kid imprisoned in an adult body anyway. And when you have fun with kids, they can feel it and they like it.

Even in Pittsburgh I'd receive hundreds of emails a day from fans, old and young, and I considered it my duty to answer every one of them as far as possible. Lots of those emails asked for autographed photos of me. During my second year in Pittsburgh I must have sent at least a thousand of those, paying for the envelopes and stamps myself. Once again I received the Community Service Award.

As you may have noticed by now, I just loved to involve myself in the community. And I must admit that it also helped me break that tough-guy image I had as I toured from one ice rink to another across the NHL. I found it important to show my real self to the most people possible.

My coaches would often suggest that I slow down a bit, take some time to rest. What they didn't understand, until I would explain it to them, was that it was my personal way of recharging my batteries. When I'd give energy to kids, they'd give it back to me a hundred times over.

Arriving in Montreal, I wasn't going to change my ways a bit. My reputation had preceded me anyway. Seeing me entering their offices, the people in the public relations department told me they'd been waiting for me and that they would assign me so many different activities I wouldn't be able to keep up the pace. They had already gone ahead and put me in charge of the Montreal Canadiens fan club. They even gave me an assistant, Geneviève, who was going to be in charge of my agenda.

The Canadiens are definitely one of the NHL teams that gets the most requests as far as community services are concerned. So it was no surprise to me that I was more in demand in Montreal than ever before. I would answer all those requests as far as it was possible. I visited the Ste. Justine Hospital, the Montreal Children's Hospital, and the Jewish Hospital several times. I also visited the young kids of Montreal Nord and Parc Extension, two of the most underprivileged districts in Montreal, where the Haitian communities are significant.

After Montreal released me, I was still answering lots of demands the team was receiving. I believed and I still believe that I had been a great ambassador for the Canadiens.

●

All throughout my NHL years, I always tried to push my teammates to do more for the community. Professional athletes are not above the masses, for the simple fact is that they owe to the masses the paycheque they get every two weeks. And they should always remember that, after all, they only put on a show, nothing more.

When I'd walk down the streets of Edmonton, Phoenix, Pittsburgh, or Montreal, people would often stop me and ask for autographs or to have a picture taken with me. I've almost always taken the time to answer their requests. I believe it's very important for every player in the NHL to convey a good image of themselves to the fans. For a lot of people, we, professional athletes, are models, and we should always be equal to that image we project.

Too many times have I witnessed professional athletes acting like morons with fans. These are usually the ones driving around in their $100,000 convertible sports cars wanting to be seen. They love their popularity for all the privileges it brings them, like entering a trendy nightclub without having to wait in line. But they won't hesitate a minute to brush off a fan who only wants an autograph. They want to be seen but not approached.

Way too many celebrities act like that. I've always thought that if they don't like people, why don't they stay in their homes? To be a popular figure has a lot of advantages, but it also has its downsides. You have to accept both to be a well-balanced human being.

•

As I've said before, I have always been a man who wants to meet other people, especially if they don't have the same kind of standard of living as I do.

During the spring of 2011, university students invited me to spend twenty-four hours in the shoes of a homeless person. They wanted to collect funds for shelters and to increase people's awareness of the life conditions of those they see every day without mixing with them.

I talked with a lot of homeless people during that time. One man in particular, named Jean, was definitely one of the most intelligent people I've ever met in my life.

Jean was living in the streets because he chose it. He has a cellphone and he takes it as his duty to bring clean needles every day to other homeless people who inject themselves with drugs. He told me that some homeless people are a lot richer than a lot of hard-working people who struggle to make ends meet. He told me we were robots, always forced to do things, always watched over, when he felt free. We rode our bikes around the city. I couldn't believe the shape he was in; I had trouble following him. And he was smoking …

That was an extremely rich experience. And it was so because I allowed myself to open my heart to another. To be able to put oneself in other people's shoes is my philosophy. Too many people on this earth denigrate difference instead of trying to understand it.

Sometimes I joke that I'm so busy now that I wish I could go back to playing professional hockey just to take a break for a while. Close friends and relatives often tell me that I'm doing too much, that I should relax a bit. I have only one answer to that: if everybody was doing a bit more, maybe then we could do less.

OF MONEY AND BUSINESSES

16

I have to admit right from the start of this chapter that I've been blessed enough never to have experienced a lack of money. I just hope that knowing how lucky I've been will help ensure that I never do find out what it's like not to have enough to go around. In my experience, it's when you think money comes easily that it seems to lose its value. And that's when it slips through your fingers. I've had enough money vanish over the years that I hope I've finally figured out how to hold on to it.

Despite the regular encounters with my father's belt, it wasn't as though I grew up deprived. My siblings and I didn't miss out on anything at a material level when I was young. We weren't spoiled, that's for sure, but we could always count on the essentials, and even quite a bit more.

During my teenage years, I had a few minor jobs. Like a lot of North American kids, I started my "career" flipping burgers in a fast-food restaurant. The pay was pathetic, but I sure never worked that hard in all my life. I couldn't believe the number of tasks I could be asked to do in just one minute.

When I'd finish my shift, I was so beat I would fall asleep right away. After two months of that inhumane treatment, I simply quit and started advising my friends against making the same mistake I had.

As an adult now, I always tell my business partners that when they want to hire someone, never turn their noses up at a candidate who once worked more than a few months in the kitchen of such a restaurant. If you're looking for a hard worker, that candidate sure is one. (Interestingly, McDonald's in the United States accepts exactly the same percentage of applicants as Harvard does. So it turns out that I've been right all along—working in a fast-food restaurant really is an elite preparation for a career.)

After that I worked in a convenience store. Compared to my previous job, it was sheer luxury. In fact, the only problem with that line of work was that there was so little to do that I would literally eat my paycheque. I'd just sit there behind the counter, gobbling down chips and chocolate bars, waiting for someone to come in.

I stayed there a few months until I found a better work as a technical assistant for Canadian National. That was my last job before signing my contract with the Edmonton Oilers, which would change my life for good.

As I said earlier, that contract came with a signing bonus of $275,000. What does a kid who's worked in a corner store do with more than a quarter of a million dollars? All kinds of things. Some of them ridiculous (like buying a colossal sound system for an SUV), and some of them a bit more generous. I immediately shared my good fortune with my close relatives—and people I hadn't heard from in years would suddenly reappear.

Total strangers and distant relatives shamelessly asked me to lend or even give them money. Some wanted me to endorse loans for a car or a house, others wanted me to invest in their business. It was frankly an unbearable period to experience on an interpersonal level.

After my father left Quebec for Florida and I was living at my mother's, I decided to involve myself in my young brother's education. Jules had been living with my mother for a few months by then, and things weren't going so well for him. He had a rebellious side that the sweetness of my mom couldn't control. Worse, he was becoming less and less interested in his studies. So I made him a deal. If he finished high school, I would buy him a brand new car. He kept his promise and so did I.

At the beginning of my career, I would spoil my brother so much that one of my training partners, Stéphane Dubé, who would later work a bit with the Montreal Canadiens, would joke about it. He once said that Jules had the lifestyle of an NHL player without having to play in the league. I still tease my brother with that from time to time.

I've got to say, though, that Jules has turned out to be a great guy—and I can't take credit for that. But if some of the money that came my way helped out at all, that's a pretty good argument against the idea that money can't buy happiness. Because helping out makes me very happy indeed.

●

Young people can do some pretty foolish things. And young people with a lot of money are a lot more foolish than most. I was no better myself. After getting rid of my Jimmy, I fell into a strange madness. I became addicted to luxury sports cars. My garage featured a variation of the typical young guy's dream: a Dodge Viper, a Carrera Porsche, a BMW Z8, an M5 …

Buying those cars was foolish, of course. And the way I drove them was even worse. I remember times when I'd push the speed up to three hundred kilometres an hour while talking on the phone with my brother and steering with my knees. At that kind of speed, cars in front of me would swerve to the side to let me pass. If I could grab that younger me by the scruff of his neck, I would teach him a lesson.

I also bought myself a motorbike—a Suzuki Hayabusa, in fact, the fastest production bike ever made. I crashed it the very first day I had it. I was lucky to escape without serious injury, and figured I shouldn't push my luck. I took the bike straight back to the dealer, knowing I was going to kill myself if I kept it even one more day.

Even my teammates knew I was headed for trouble. Dennis Bonvie staged an elaborate public intervention. He convinced a police officer to come into the dressing room and pretend to arrest me for dangerous driving. I was terrified when I thought I'd finally been caught. But do you think I learned my lesson? As soon as I figured out it had all been a hoax, I was right back behind the wheel, driving like a jackass.

I remember exactly when that craze for fast cars stopped. It was on September 29, 2003; I was twenty-six at the time. The night before, Atlanta Thrashers player Dany Heatley had been involved in a serious car accident as he was driving his Ferrari 360 Modena at high speed. He lost control of the vehicle and smashed it into a pillar, splitting it in two. Heatley and his passenger, teammate Dan Snyder, were ejected from the car.

Heatley got out of it with a broken jaw, a severe concussion, and some minor injuries. Snyder wasn't as lucky. He suffered a skull fracture, and would die from his wounds six days later, on October 5.

From that day, I started selling back all my sports cars, convinced that if I kept them I'd be the next one on the list. Moreover, I was already quite involved in the Edmonton community. I didn't want to see my face on the front page of a newspaper because I'd been arrested doing three hundred kilometres an hour on the highway. I would have lost all credibility.

•

A professional hockey player can make a lot of money during his career, it's true. But that's not the case for the majority of them. Plus, you have no clue as to when your career will end. Not a lot of people know that an NHL career lasts an average of five years. I was lucky—mine lasted almost thirteen. But going in, there was no way of knowing that. It could have ended at any time. I could have been injured much earlier in my career, or my back could have held out and I could have played a few more years. (Perhaps as my fighting skills diminished, I would have reinvented myself as a goal-scorer.)

People from outside the game often see only the glamour of a hockey player's life. I won't deny that it does exist—an NHL player lives a pretty good life. But the perks hide a lot of things. Let's take the example of a player earning a million dollars gross a year. You take off from that amount the taxes he has to pay and you're down to $500,000. He has then to pay the NHL escrow, which is about 10 percent of his gross revenue. Now he has $400,000 in his pocket. Not bad, of course, but that's not all.

When he's on the road, the team books the hotels. He gets an average of $80 a day to cover his meal and hotel expenses. Needless to say, it's not enough to cover everything. Most players will spend another $30,000 on the out-of-pocket expenses of constantly travelling and being in strange cities.

When you add to this the season tickets he buys for family members, his mortgage and car loans, and his professional insurance fees, the millionaire we started with might, maybe, save $100,000 a year. And that's if he's cautious with the way he spends his money and lives in a city where the cost of living is reasonable.

I know players who earn $600,000 to $700,000 a year in Los Angeles or New York. Some have to live with roommates to be able to save a bit of money for their post-career life. And as I said earlier, you never know when that post-career will start.

I'm not trying to make anyone cry here. NHL players aren't pitiful, I sure agree about that. And yet most of them are a lot less rich than what people seem to think.

•

Having money when you're too young can also bring its own load of problems; and I'm not talking here about people trying to swindle you. That will come later.

When I said at the beginning of this chapter that I'd never known what it was like to be out of money, I omitted one episode of my life that occurred during my first complete season with the Oilers, in 1999–2000. At that time, I used to watch a television channel that broadcast, among other things, roulette championships.

I got totally addicted to those shows, and would try to analyze the game to see whether there was some foolproof recipe for winning. One night, I had some kind of insight and was absolutely convinced that I'd found the perfect system to get rich playing roulette.

My system consisted of simply doubling my bet every time I lost. I would only bet on the colours, blacks or reds. For instance, I'd bet $10 on the reds. If the blacks came out, I would then bet $20, always on the reds, then $40, $80, $160, and so on. When I'd win, I'd start again with a $10 bet.

The night I found that system, I figured I was a genius, nothing less, and decided I would go straight to the casino to become a millionaire.

The only problem I hadn't thought of, and not the least, was that the reds or the blacks could come out ten or fifteen times in a row. If I'd bet on the colour not coming out, the stress would build up more and more. Then I would finally win, but all I'd be getting back was my initial $10.

Moreover, there were times when I'd hesitate. When the bets were up to $1280 or $2560, I would sometimes skip a turn. Of course, that was usually the time my colour would choose to come out, making me lose all the previous bets. I'd be furious for a second, swearing I'd never gamble again. And a moment later, there I was trying my luck once more.

In only a few months I'd lost over $100,000 with my brainwave. I decided to stop, not because I didn't believe in the system anymore, but because my bank account was empty. I started loading my credit cards as well as my line of credit. The only thing I could do was watch the interest fly sky high and wait for my second season to begin so that I could settle my debts.

Nowadays, when I enter a casino, I don't feel any kind of pressure to rush to the roulette table. I've learned my lesson.

•

Let's talk about fraud now. I can't count the number of times somebody has tried to swindle me. There are far too many examples to even bother keeping track. Some people are capable of real genius when it comes to prying money out of others. I learned that at my expense quite a number of times.

If I managed to foil 99 percent of the plans made behind my back, some people were able to outsmart me a couple of times. There are two main reasons why they succeeded: first, I totally admit it today, the artlessness of my young twenties; and second, the fact that the people who managed to get their hands into my pockets were above all suspicion. At least, that's what I thought.

It sometimes gets me really angry to think about the amount of money that was stolen from me right in front of my eyes. Furious at those crooks who abused me, of course, but mostly just furious. I can easily say today that I was robbed for around $500,000 over the years, and maybe—probably!—even more.

One example among many others. There was a man I'd known for a couple of years. I was getting along really fine not only with him but also with his whole family. I'd spend great quality time with them. One morning he called me with a sob in his voice. He was waiting for some of his clients to pay him. They owed him quite a lot, but they were creditworthy and it was only a matter of time, maybe a few weeks, before they could pay him.

The problem was, his own creditors wouldn't wait any longer and were just about to seize his house. He begged me to help him out, to lend him the money he needed to save his home. He also made me promise that I wouldn't talk about it to his wife, since she was emotionally very fragile at the time.

Gradually and over only a few weeks, I lent him about $150,000. He was the owner of a small rug and carpet company. Since I'd known him, he had always been a very stable man, very serious in his business and in every aspect of his life. In short, I wasn't worried at all and had full confidence in him. A few months later, the cat finally got out of the bag.

We discovered that for the past two years the man had been a drug addict and had gone so much into debt that prison was now awaiting him. Of course, I would never see the colour of my money again.

I had lots of other smaller unfortunate experiences in the same vein, but I managed to get out of them before it was too late. Some people, for instance, asked me to lend them money for a week or so, the time it would take for their bank to accept a second mortgage. I'd learn later that the bank was in fact ready to seize the house.

When I think about all those things today, I guess I was lucky in spite of all my mistakes. During my years in the NHL I've earned about $7 million gross. I know this is a lot of money, but when I think about how generous I've been with friends and family, with all that I've wasted on sports cars and the rest, and with all the money that was stolen from me, I can't believe I'm not living on the streets today.

•

If I'm not totally in debt today, in my mid-thirties, it's also because I met people, men and women, who had solid projects I linked myself to.

The very first business in which I invested without losing any money was a fitness centre called Body By Benett in Edmonton.

Gradually, I invested $150,000 in the company. With this money, my other partners opened a second centre in Edmonton.

But because of our high level of debt, it would have taken too long to begin to see a return on my investment, so I decided to buy back my share of the company. I got exactly the same amount back that I'd originally put in. I had finally made an interest-free loan. Well, I'd tell myself philosophically, at least I had the opportunity to work out for free for three years.

In 2009 I finally decided to invest in the one thing I was an expert in: hockey. A Montreal company named WeTeam Ice was specializing in the installation of synthetic ice. Their supplier was the Florida-based company Super-Glide, whose product is still head and shoulders above anything else in the world today.

But history repeated itself. WeTeam Ice was managed in a cavalier way by its president. I had already invested $200,000 in the business and the product was absolutely excellent. Even today, I skate on this synthetic ice, and I love it. After skating on it for a while, you can barely tell the difference. The only problem was the administration.

Soon the company was deep in debt. This time, though, I decided not to let the project miserably collapse. The only thing that had to be done was to modify the managing methods a bit and the business could work perfectly fine and become very lucrative.

One of my partners in the WeTeam Ice venture, David Ettedgui, had really helped me out when I moved to Brossard after being hired by the Canadiens. Not only was he a big investor in the company, but he was also the manager of a huge furniture store. We would talk a lot on the phone, at first about the new furniture I needed for my new home, but later about the future of synthetic ice. We both decided to leave the sinking ship called WeTeam Ice and try to market the same product under a different name. Then we met the president of Super-Glide and managed to convince him we were the right people to make it work in Canada.

At the same time I met a man named Marc Fillion, who was installing the domotic system in my new house. I immediately noticed that he had a very structured mind and an exceptional methodology in his work. I talked to him about the new synthetic-ice project, and he helped us a lot, David and I, in starting the new business.

Only a few months after we started, the debts disappeared. Today our sales are exceptional and still progressing. We're now installing synthetic-ice rinks in a few countries outside Canada, even in tropical countries.

I went on to become a partner in other businesses, but on a smaller scale, mainly as a spokesman. These include companies like Octane and TekSavvy. TekSavvy is a small company taking on bigger competitors—something that was bound to appeal to me. TekSavvy fights so that Canadians can have options; that is, they're fighting to break the national duopoly that still exists today between telephone and cable companies.

When TekSavvy approached me, I was excited about joining a small company and helping them expand. At the same time, I was happy to get involved in the many charities the company supports, including the YMCA, the Rotary Club, United Way, Chatham Minor Hockey Association, and Exceptional Riders. To my great surprise, TekSavvy has stepped up big time with financial support to join me in my reconstruction of Grace Children's Hospital in Haiti. We've also worked together on TV ads that reflect my personality in order to get our name known across Canada as the number of subscribers grows every day. The company is also very environmentally conscious.

●

And that brings me to the subject of the next chapter: ecology. A passion, a conviction, a way of life ...

THE GREEN GIANT 17

For as long as I can remember, I've been very careful about what I eat. In a certain sense, I've never really had a choice, since I'm genetically predisposed to gain weight at a very fast pace. If I stop training and start eating everything I want, I can gain forty to fifty pounds in no time.

Moreover, ever since the experience I had working in a fast-food restaurant, I've always avoided the food—less because the restaurant exploited me for two months than because I'd seen with my own eyes what was in the food and the way it was prepared. Anyone who's worked in the kitchens of these types of restaurants and still eats what they serve can clearly be considered a masochist.

On the other hand, I was eating meat almost every day. To me, nothing was more natural. Believe it or not, and call me naive if you feel like it, but for a long time I assumed the meat we eat came from animals that died of natural causes. As a matter of fact, I'd never much thought where meat was coming from at all. But things have changed a lot for me ...

I became a vegan overnight. It was around the end of April 2009 in Boston, when the Montreal Canadiens were to play the first game of the playoffs against the Bruins. To be a vegan, for those who don't know what it means, consists of not eating meat, just like a vegetarian, but it goes a bit further. A vegan won't eat anything that contains any animal protein in it: no eggs, no dairy products, no commercial bread that has milk in it.

But to fully understand what happened to me and made me dramatically change the way I was eating, one has to go back a few months before that pre-game in Boston. I was visiting a friend of mine, Sandrine Balthazard, who had been a vegetarian for a couple of years already, and during our conversation I told her about a movie that had forever changed my life and the way I perceived it. It was called *Pay It Forward*, directed by Mimi Leder.

At one point I asked Sandrine a trivial question that would later prove to be not that trivial at all. I wondered why all the couches and armchairs she had in her house were made out of cotton and not leather. After all, nothing is less practical than cotton when it comes to cleaning it. A simple spilled glass of juice on a couch can make a mess almost impossible to clean, whereas with leather, just a little sweep with a cloth and the job is done.

Sandrine started talking about animal rights, and about the way animals are badly treated around the world solely for human use. I was listening, but everything she was saying was so new to me that I remained skeptical. That's when she said, "Georges, you told me that a movie changed your perception of life. Well, a movie changed mine, too." Saying that, she put a DVD in my hand. I looked at it. The title was *Earthlings* and it had been made by Shaun Monson. Sandrine said, "Watch that movie and we'll talk about it afterwards."

That DVD remained on my shelf for weeks. Whenever I'd talk to Sandrine or meet her somewhere, she would always ask me if I'd watched it yet. Each time I would tell her I hadn't, saying I hadn't had the time, or any other excuse to get me out of it. To tell the truth, I wasn't planning to watch it at all. An animal documentary? Frankly, I couldn't care less …

Back to Boston now. Since Sandrine had insisted so much, I'd taken the DVD with me, more as a reflex than anything else. I looked at the time on the alarm clock in my hotel room and realized I had an hour and a half to kill. I thought to myself, "Okay, I'll watch it, then she'll stop harassing me."

I put the DVD in the player, pressed Play, and got ready to be bored or fall asleep. Instead, I went from one trauma to another for the next ninety minutes. That movie—often filmed amateurishly because some scenes were captured with hidden cameras, sometimes at the risk of the camera operator's life—is a powerful summary of all the cruelty that humankind is capable of committing against animals.

Breathtaking and blood-curdling images were jumping out at me. I went from a slaughterhouse to a scientific laboratory, from an illegal farm to a zoo, from illegal hunting in Africa to seals on an ice floe. I started crying like a baby, my limbs shaking like a dead leaf.

As soon as the film ended, I called Sandrine. I thanked her from the bottom of my heart for having made me discover this precious documentary that had opened my eyes to so many cruel realities I'd never suspected existed. And with that tendency of mine to always go to extremes, I decided right away to become a vegan.

I also promised myself I would go even further. In some way, I wanted to make up for lost time. I was going to stand up for animal rights. I would show that movie to as many people as I could. The public had to know.

← At the Bell Centre, another tough game against the Boston Bruins (Andre Ringuette/ National Hockey League via Getty Images)

...ause of
...alary, I
...d not be
...ised to
...aded."
...orges
...que,
...ppointed
...his ice time
... arriving with the Canadiens

CONGÉDIÉ
PAGES 108 À 111

Une AUTRE ÉPREUVE pour Laraque

Another test for Laraque
(Journal de Montréal)

↑ Training with the famous Jeff Buttle and David Pelletier, and of course, the superb and supremely courageous Anabelle Langlois (Perry Mah)

← Getting out of the hospital for the third time during *Battle of the Blades*

Our first performance
on *Battle of the Blades*
(CBC)

Safari at the Ngorongoro, in Tanzania—a dangerous encounter with an elephant

← Dancing with the Maasai tribe

→ The group for the Lani Foundation expedition

Laraque prie pour Haïti

Laraque prays for Haiti

←↑ A visit to Haiti with P.K. Subban, July 2011

↓ Another visit to Haiti with Dan Hamhuis, May 2010

21

↓ With PETA's CEO,
Ingrid Newkirk

↓ With *Earthlings'* director
and producer, Shaun Monson

↓ My very first protest, against
the fur industry, in May 2009

← The shaken baby syndrome campaign in Alberta (Used with permission)

↑ My friend and business partner in vertical farming, Nick Brusatore

→ Our team for the Montreal–New York relay run for the Esprit de Corps foundation

Are you tough enough to be gentle? It only takes a **MOMENT** Shaken Baby Syndrome Take a Break - Don't Shake

The Gay Pride March in Montreal, July 2010—I was there as deputy leader of the Green Party

A really moving moment—meeting the Dalai Lama on September 7, 2011 (© FlashQuebec Inc.—Kurt Jawinski)

When I got back to Montreal, I almost immediately called Anne-Marie Roy, a nutritionist renowned for being a vegetarian. I told her that I'd become a vegan and that I needed some help to build myself some menus, since I didn't know anything about it.

We went together to a big natural and organic foods store. There, she spent about four hours explaining to me what foods I should choose to replace what I used to eat. I was discovering foods that I didn't even know existed. And what stunned me the most was that they were a lot more nutritious than the ones I'd been eating until that night in Boston.

The first menus I made for myself were pretty simple, since I had to get used to all those new tastes. It wasn't that obvious in the beginning to replace, for instance, the cow's milk in my cereal with almond or soy milk.

•

The first thing I did in practical terms in support of animal rights was to join a demonstration against the wearing of fur. It was the first demonstration I've ever been at in my life. A big fur traders' convention was being held at the Palais des Congrès in Montreal, and the demonstrators were massed right across the street.

I went there with my cousin Thierry. When we arrived, I saw dozens of people, some with multicoloured hair, others dressed like hippies. In short, a colourful crowd, and a hundred miles away from the people I was used to hanging out with. It felt good. And there I learned that it took at least fifty animals to make just one coat.

The press, but also the police, arrived. I was so happy to see that kind of mobilization. Some people from the convention, who had come out to smoke, would insult us. Cars passing by were doing the same; others were honking their support.

While there I met Sameer Muldeen, who was head of a vegetarian association and whom I had spoken with on the phone a few times before. He offered to teach me even more about animal rights and foods that don't contain any animal products. In the days to follow, he taught me a lot of things on different subjects. He also gave me practical information, things as simple as the restaurants I could now go to. I sure wasn't going to be seen in a steak house anymore.

Sameer wasn't the only one who helped me in my new life. Quite a few people were generous with their time and gave me lots of advice and information of all kinds to help me make the transition in the softest way possible. Of course, I was also doing lots of research on my own on the internet.

A few days after the demonstration, I went to a vegan event. There I met a man who suggested something quite strange. He told me that, since I had just begun being a vegan, I should go to the Heart Institute and take some tests, which would give me a global portrait of my physical condition. "Then," he said, "you go back again later, take the same tests, and see for yourself the difference that becoming a vegan has made for your health." That sounded like a challenge, and I like challenges.

I followed his advice. The before-and-after difference was spectacular. Even though I was a high-level athlete, my physical condition had gotten a huge boost from changing nothing in my routine except the way I was eating. My blood pressure, a little high before, to the point that I had to take a light medication, had stabilized itself naturally. My asthma had almost completely disappeared.

Another difference I felt almost instantly was the way I would feel after dinner. Before, when I was still eating meat, I'd leave the table feeling a little weariness, even some fatigue when the meal had been very rich in meat. Since I'd become vegan, it was the absolute opposite. I was full of energy, ready to run a marathon.

During the summer, as I commuted between Montreal and Edmonton, I started to tell friends, family members, and even people in the streets and the press about my new vegan status. Some kindly laughed at me, saying that a big guy like me couldn't survive without eating meat; that next season I was going to be weak and every tough guy around the league would easily beat me.

In Alberta I was of course spending a lot of time with my children. Their mother became largely vegetarian and started eating only organic food. The kids became partially vegetarian, their mother giving them some chicken and some fish occasionally. When they were with me, though, they were a hundred percent vegan.

Every time I was back in Montreal, I would organize showings of the movie *Earthlings*. For the premiere, I rented one of the theatres in the Guzzo complex in downtown Montreal and invited the producer to join us. All in all, I organized about thirty-five showings. Each time it cost me between five and ten thousand dollars, but the money was nothing; I wanted people to see the movie. And those showings weren't only about the movie. I would have a sample of vegan items prepared with a wide selection of different foods so that people could actually taste all sorts of things.

The public attending the showings were deeply moved. Some would cry, others were shocked, outraged. Many of them told me afterwards that they were going to change their habits from then on; others reacted exactly as I had and decided to go vegan right away; some even wanted to get involved in the animal-rights movement. Only one scene in the movie made the crowd exultant with joy. It was when an elephant revolted against its torturers and kicked them with his legs and trunk.

A few of my teammates from the Canadiens came to some showings; among them were Scott Gomez, Mike Cammalleri, Benoît Pouliot, and Maxim Lapierre. Some members of my family also came. My sister became a vegan after having seen the movie and listened to the conference I gave after the showing. My mother came to one of the showings too, but for a different reason: she wanted to make sure her son hadn't been recruited by some kind of sect. She couldn't conceive that a Haitian, especially one of my size, could live without eating meat. After the movie, though, she told me she understood my reasoning.

Some, including members of the press, accused me of falling into sensationalism. That assertion would inevitably make me laugh. *Earthlings* wasn't any more sensationalistic than a news bulletin. Others told me the movie was propaganda and that I was part of it. But if informing the public about the bad treatment animals have to endure to end up on our plates is considered propaganda, then that's exactly what I was doing and I was proud of it.

I've always thought that one of the worst enemies of humankind is ignorance. With those screenings, I only wanted the public to know what was happening behind its back. In my eyes, three main things are to be learned from *Earthlings*. First, animals suffer agony to end up on our plate; second, eating meat is a detriment to our health; and third, the meat industry is extremely harmful to the environment.

•

During the same summer, I told the Montreal Canadiens organization that I'd become a vegan and that I wouldn't be able to share the same meals as my teammates. Everybody was, of course, already informed of the news. What helped me a lot was that the GM, Pierre Gauthier, was also a vegan. The organization then agreed to change some of the menus to adapt them to my new reality.

When training camp started in September, the guys couldn't believe their eyes. How did I manage to keep such a muscular mass without eating any meat? Suddenly, some of my teammates started getting interested, if not in veganism, at least in vegetarianism. Many of their spouses had already adopted a no-meat regimen. But what really convinced them of the virtues of that regimen was when they started eating less meat on game days.

A carnivore forces his body to use 80 percent of his energy to assimilate what he's just eaten. Why not keep that energy to play the game?

Some players also stopped drinking shakes made out of cows' milk, which, without their even realizing it, were fattening them. They started drinking beverages made from water, soya milk, or almond milk. And they could feel the immediate difference in their bodies.

I want to be clear here. I have nothing against the milk producers. They do their job. But I do have something against the ones telling us that drinking cow's milk or eating products made from it should be part of a sane diet. The fact that we're the only mammals to drink another mammal's milk should be enough, according to me, to discourage us from drinking it; but to add to this, more and more studies tend to prove that drinking milk is also harmful to our health.

First, milk acidifies our system, forcing it to produce a lot of mucus to absorb and assimilate it. Second, contrary to what people might think, cow's milk decalcifies our bones and contributes to the loss of iron in our blood. If you're looking for iron and calcium, simply eat green vegetables.

I admit it, I became pretty extreme in my position against the milk and the meat industries. During the conferences I gave right after the *Earthlings* screenings, I used strong images to dissuade people from eating meat. For instance, if I took a glass, cut it into my arm, and let the blood pour into the glass, would you drink what's in the glass? Of course not. If I did the same with a cow, would you drink what's inside the glass? Of course not, again. And if I were to wring your steak over the same glass, would you drink it? Again, no. I would then tell the audience that that's exactly what they were doing when eating meat.

I would also talk a lot about slaughterhouses, saying that I was convinced that if people saw the way the pigs' throats are cut, and knew that most pigs are still alive when the slaughterhouse workers start tearing them apart, they wouldn't eat any pork or bacon anymore.

Moreover, a vegan regimen transforms the body into an alkaline environment. Scientists know of hundreds of diseases that can't develop in such an environment. Meat and products made from animal proteins will acidify an organism, making it vulnerable to those same hundreds of diseases.

On the environmental side, I would inform audiences of the fact that the meat industry is responsible for 20 percent of the greenhouse gas emissions on the planet, and that eight kilograms of grain are needed to produce only one kilogram of meat. We cut down thousands of hectares of wild forests to plant the grain that will feed the animals.

Everybody knows nowadays that we'll soon suffer from a lack of water on this earth. Still, we go on wasting billions of gallons of water simply to make the animals grow. And I'm not even talking here about the pollution created by the transportation of meat from the place the animal is killed to where its meat will be sold. If, fifty years ago, eating meat could be considered a necessary evil, it's definitely not the case anymore. And over those same fifty years the animal production system has changed quite a lot. The widespread use of antibiotics and other strange products is literally poisoning the meat people now eat. Some scientists see a correlation between the use of antibiotics and the fact that today teenage girls reach puberty at a younger age than even a few decades ago.

But numerous people would tell me that *Earthlings* was showing a reality that had nothing to do with what's happening in Quebec and in Canada. In that sense, journalist Yvan Martineau from the CBC did me a great favour.

The show *La semaine verte*, for which he worked, had shown some excerpts from the movie. Martineau then went to visit some farms in Quebec and elsewhere in Canada to see if what *Earthlings* was depicting was also happening here. And in his report he showed how Canadian farmers castrate the pigs, cut their ears, and pull out their teeth—all without anaesthetic.

Martineau was clearly proving with his report that industrial farmers are no better in Canada than they are in any other country. I'm not denying the fact that certain exceptions exist in smaller, local organic farms. But they're far from being the majority, and the animals still suffer in the end.

To extend my involvement in the vegan movement a little further, I became a partner in the restaurant Crudessence. It all started when I first met the restaurant's owners, David Côté, Julian Giacomelli, and Mathieu Gallant. While talking with each other, we quickly realized that we had the same ideals and the same philosophy. They also had a knowledge I hadn't, a culinary one. I tasted their hamburgers, their lasagne, and their cheesecake. Every single dish was awesome, so flavourful, and had been prepared using only raw organic products.

Eating raw food isn't a new concept, but it was very unusual in Quebec at the time. When eating raw food, our body absorbs more minerals and vitamins while needing a lot less energy to digest it. I started eating raw food all the time and soon realized that I was a lot more energetic, had a greater ability to concentrate, and needed less sleep.

When I became a partner in Crudessence, we opened a second restaurant, still in Montreal, and a cooking academy. Since the four of us are really ecologically conscious, we started greening some roofs in Montreal and giving workshops at corporations and schools. Our message is simple: eating well means taking care of yourself, and taking care of yourself means taking care of the environment.

I also became a spokesman for the VEGA company, founded by triathlete Brendan Brazier, himself a vegan. Brazier and his associates produce a wide variety of vegan products that are not only excellent for your health but also very popular among hundreds of high-level athletes.

I began touring schools, universities, and hospitals to promote the vegan regimen. I chose these locations because I really feel they should be the first ones to give the example. I've always asked myself why, after open-heart surgery, patients are served ham and Jell-O ...

•

One morning, towards the end of summer 2010, I was leaving a yoga session when a man and his daughter came up to me. He told me his name was Howard and that he really appreciated my involvement in animal rights. He also told me he had a recording studio and that if ever he could be of any help, I should call him with no hesitation. I took his card politely, telling myself that I really couldn't see when I'd ever need a recording studio.

Knowing all the visibility I was giving his movie *Earthlings,* the producer called me two days later and asked if I'd be interested in recording the French version of the movie. The English version had been done by actor Joaquin Phoenix, a well-known vegan. Given the importance of language here in Quebec, I thought the idea was excellent, so I decided to accept.

That was when that impromptu meeting with Howard popped into my head; what an incredible coincidence that had been. So I called and asked him if his offer was still on. He agreed to do the whole recording at no charge. He sure didn't know what he'd just gotten into, and neither did I.

I'm no actor, and playing in a few movies sure didn't make me one. I had never practised my voice, and wasn't used to putting different intonations in it on command. We decided we would hire a French voice coach who would stand beside me for the whole recording session.

I thought I would wrap it up in about two hours. It took me fifty! When it was done, we decided to release it on DVD. The movie had a new title in French, *Terriens,* and I started showing it in regions outside Montreal. To this day we've sold over 10,000 copies of it.

•

Following a demonstration against the hunting of baby seals, officials from the PETA organization contacted me to ask if I would act as a spokesman. I knew that PETA was often criticized for its radical ideas and its somewhat controversial actions. Yet I was absolutely sure, and still am, that without them, animal rights would be a thing of the past. Humans kill 53 billion animals every year, 100,000 a minute. For medical research alone, 19,000 a minute are killed. And I must say I'm pretty skeptical when it comes to the usefulness of that research.

I also campaign against zoos. In mid-December 2010, I sent a letter to the mayor of Edmonton in which I offered him $100,000 so that one of the city zoo elephants could be moved to a sanctuary in the United States where it could end its days in peace, quiet, and relative freedom. Lucy, that's the name of the elephant, was thirty-five years old and was wasting away a bit more every day. Bad treatment had pushed her towards depression.

The letter was published in Edmonton newspapers and made some noise. PETA had been trying for a while to put pressure on the zoo so that Lucy could be moved somewhere else, in vain. Veterinarians from the zoo were denying everything PETA and I were saying. But independent vets who had access to the animals were clear about the bad condition Lucy was in.

The nephew of the woman who had brought the elephant from Asia wrote to me to give me his support. In his letter he even said that his aunt, just before dying, had said that the animal would be better off out of that zoo. The affair isn't over yet, and the pressure keeps mounting on both the institution and the mayor.

Since we're talking about elephants here, I have a small anecdote about what happened to me while I was in Africa in July 2011 for the Lani Foundation, whose goal is to try to prevent suicide among young boys and girls.

We were visiting the wonderful conservation area of Ngorongoro in Tanzania, definitely one of the most beautiful places I've ever seen. At lunch, our group, along with some tourists, was sitting in an area specially reserved for eating. While we were having lunch a huge elephant decided he would pay us a small visit. Everybody slowly stood up and started moving in the opposite direction from where the elephant was coming. I did the contrary.

I walked towards the animal, making long strides with my camera in hand. I was about five metres from it, fascinated, taking pictures. The rangers had been yelling at me to get away from there for about five minutes. I couldn't hear them because of the strong wind and my excitement. Now it was too late anyway ...

The elephant had decided to slowly start walking towards me. Its ears were moving up, which I knew wasn't a good sign. I suddenly realized how stupid I'd been to get so close to it. I was really panicking now.

I started slowly walking backwards, zigzagging. The elephant began zigzagging to the same rhythm, following every change of direction I made, staring me in the eye. Although I'd had no experience with elephants, I immediately understood that if I were to start running it would charge me.

I was about to close my eyes and get ready to be pulverized by a six-ton monster when the rangers' Jeep arrived. The ranger slammed on the brakes and stopped the vehicle right between the animal and me, which made it pause long enough for me to jump in the truck and get away. I don't think I have to tell you how upset the rangers were with me—and for good reason, since an elephant could flip over that Jeep without a second thought. That ranger had taken a real risk to save me.

I'm also very critical of circuses that use animals to do tricks. The spectators may like what they see, but I'm not sure they would appreciate it as much as they do if they knew what goes on behind the scenes.

Do they really think you can convince an elephant to sit on a chair simply by feeding it some hay? Of course not; the tamer has to hit it violently and repeatedly. He has to terrorize the animal, make him starve for days until the elephant finally knows who's the boss. Moreover, circus animals spend 95 percent of their lives chained to a stick.

In short, and I guess you've understood it by now, I'm against all abusive uses humans make of animals. And that includes the famous Old Montreal calèches.

I'm truly convinced that as long as humans don't respect animals as the living beings they are, with rights of their own, they won't be able to respect each other either. This might have nothing to do with it, but in a recent study I've read, it appears that the vast majority of serial killers grew up being abusive to animals …

•

When I was interviewed on the *Tout le monde en parle* talk show, I had of course to answer a series of questions. One of them was pretty simple: Was I more Liberal Party or Green Party? I answered Green Party, of course. The morning after the show aired, Sameer Muldeen called me. He said that he was a member of the Green Party of Canada, and that the deputy leader of the party, Jacques Rivard, wanted to know if I'd be interested in joining. I accepted, since to my mind, environment and health go hand in hand. A cleaner environment means better health for every one of us.

A few months later, Rivard quit the Green Party to join the ranks of the Bloc Québécois. Our president, Elizabeth May, came to see me. She offered me Rivard's seat.

I told her I was honoured by her proposition, but that I couldn't possibly accept, especially given the huge amount of time I needed to put into my involvement for Haiti. She sure knew how to be persuasive, though. She told me that there were 308 electoral districts in Canada and that my presence alone would help every one of our candidates in every district.

She added that, in election after election, an average 40 percent of Canadians weren't using their right to vote. Among those people were a majority of young adults, most of whom were cynical about traditional politicians. She thought that a guy like me would stand out in sharp contrast to what voters were used to. My presence, she said, could maybe push some of those non-voters to join the Green Party, or at least to go out and vote on election day.

I did accept her offer. I thought it would give me a new and higher platform from which to speak about animal rights and veganism. I might also help convince some people about the necessity of adopting new ways of seeing life, more in phase with the environment. If, by accepting that role, I could make even one person change his or her mind about the environment, then it would be worth it.

The more I thought about it, the more convinced I was that it was a great idea to have accepted. It would also allow me to speak about gay and lesbian rights, which I'm a strong advocate of; and the same with Aboriginal rights. I find it horrible what, as a collectivity, we are doing to them. And the hypocrisy we showed in the Opening Ceremonies of the 2010 Winter Olympic Games gave me nausea. Canada had decided to honour Aboriginals during that ceremony, when on an everyday basis we treat some of those nations like trash. They are denigrated, insulted, parked in reservations. Some communities don't have electricity in their territory, or even running water. But to the world we were going to show how as a country we respect our First Nations.

My voice in favour of legalizing marijuana could also be heard. I'm convinced that such a measure could help get rid of a certain form of criminality while giving the government a new source of revenue.

I could also start campaigning in support of the legalization and supervision of prostitution. The Dutch situation tends to prove that these measures would greatly reduce the number of abuses prostitutes are victims of; as well, and some may say it's not related, the Netherlands still has one of the lowest rates of rape in the Western world and a much lower crime rate than Canada.

Becoming a member of the Green Party also led me to change another of my habits. Before that, I used to drive a Cadillac Escalade, obviously not a very ecological choice. I decided to sell it and associate myself with Montreal Autoprix, a used car dealer. I now drive used hybrid cars, another great way to recycle.

When I accepted Elizabeth May's offer to become deputy leader of the Green Party, I did it on one condition: I would do the job as a volunteer, since it was out of the question for me to ever try to get elected. But now ...

The last federal election, in May 2011, might have changed my position on that a bit. I simply adored every single minute of that campaign. The meetings with the electors, the way ideas were debated and points of view exchanged, the devotion of every single one of our volunteers and candidates, and the supreme intelligence of our president, Elizabeth May, were all new to me and made me discover one face of politics I didn't know existed.

And when Elizabeth was elected in the Saanich–Gulf Islands district, becoming the first ever Green member of Parliament in all of Canada's history, the moment of magic we all experienced together was purely extraordinary. So, maybe next time ...

•

I was invited to David Suzuki's house to celebrate Earth Hour on March 27, 2010. Earth Hour has been held every last Saturday in March since 2007. It began in Sydney, Australia, when more than two million people and two thousand companies shut down their electrical power for an hour to protest against climate change. At Suzuki's house that day, "green" businesspeople mixed with environmentalists for a fundraising event. Among the former was Nick Brusatore, the same man I talked about in the chapter on Haiti. It would be our first meeting. As a big hockey fan he came up to talk to me, but after a few words about the game he told me he'd read most of what was on my website. He liked the fact that, as something of a celebrity, I was using that status to try to make things change in our world.

We talked for a very long time. Nick had thousands of different projects he was involved in, and to be honest, he was making me dazed talking about them all. At the end of the evening, we exchanged numbers. He told me he really wanted us to see each other again, as he could easily see me playing a role in some of his businesses.

For the next few months he kept trying to reach me either by phone or email. I was ignoring both. He would insist so much that he was exhausting me. I sincerely regret that indifference, since today we are as close as brothers.

He finally managed to reach me one day. He told me he'd watched one of the videos on my website where I talk about all the racism I experienced when I was young. Nick said he felt close to what I was saying because he too had suffered from a lot of discrimination in his young days. At the end of the phone call I invited him to Edmonton for a few days so that we could talk about all those projects he either had in mind or that were already going on.

I went to pick him up at the airport and, soon after he got in my car, I knew we were going to be friends for life. We've been seeing each other a lot since that day, and I now feel that I'm a part of his family.

The main project I'm involved in with Nick is the one I talked about a bit in the chapter on Haiti. A few years ago, Nick co-founded a vertical-farming company named TerraSphere, which he sold a few years later. Thanks to a high-tech process developed by Nick and some of his colleagues, vertical farming is able to produce fruits and vegetables on a large scale using no polluting agents. Light and water are precisely controlled at all times, which allows for optimal growth and productivity while preventing any wasting of water. Plus, because the hydroponic cultures are built in tiers, each square foot of the facilities is used to its fullest potential. Production lasts all year long and can be installed virtually anywhere, even in the desert, since the cultures are located inside giant, ultra-sophisticated warehouses. A supermarket could, for instance, install a vertical farming facility right next to its building, meaning no transportation costs and no pollution.

I agreed to become a partner in his business not only because I love the friendship Nick and I have, although that definitely played a part in my decision, but also because every one of Nick's vertical farming projects answers my environmental, vegan, and humanist beliefs in the best way possible. In spreading that technology throughout the world, lots of malnutrition problems could be solved with a little more goodwill from our politicians.

I strongly believe in a better future for this planet, and I think companies like Nick's are part of that better future.

THE PRESS AND ME

18

Right from the beginning of my career, the press and all the other media have been fascinated by me. During my first years, the approximate way I would speak English didn't make me very attractive to journalists. But rapidly, as I got more and more fluent, I became a favourite of the press.

I didn't have any secret recipe. I was simply saying everything that would come to my mind. And since clichés like "Guys have to give it 110 percent in the third" or "We've got to keep our feet moving and get bodies to the net and the puck is going to start going in for us" never cross my mind, journalists knew they wouldn't get them from me.

When I was happy, people would know it at once. When I was mad, same thing. I wanted only one thing: that the fans paying my salary got the truth, not canned comments prepared by the media relations department. And even if I'd wanted to play the cliché game, I would have made a fool of myself—I'm just not fluent enough in that language to communicate in it.

I was and still am too direct and too frank. It would have been obvious that I was playing a game if I were to say things like "We worked hard in the corners." What a ridiculous expression, by the way. I've spent over thirty years of my life on ice rinks and I'm still trying to find the corners.

As the years passed, I started "playing" with the media and the press. I had realized, of course, that the more exuberant my words were, the more the journalists would come back. That's why, after three or four years in the NHL, I started seeing my relationship with the media as a show. I was waiting for them with a big smile.

Several journalists and some of my teammates started speculating that I would end up in the media after my career. It was thanks to the program director of an Edmonton FM radio, James Stuart, with whom I'd started getting on well, that I made my debut in the entertainment business. Gradually I experienced different things, and began performing little comedy sketches, being a deejay, reading small poems on the air. For several months I even co-animated a show about love and relationships called *Summer Loving*. Thanks to the doors Stuart opened for me, during my years in Edmonton I became very comfortable in front of a microphone. And the more comfortable I got, the more my declarations to the press gained in quality and wit. By the end, I was talking hockey and sports with the notorious analyst and anchorman Bob Stauffer.

Never would I have thought those small first steps would one day lead me to become part of CBC's Canada Reads. On February 2011, five Canadian personalities were chosen to defend a book they thought every Canadian should read. I couldn't believe I was among them. The panel around host Jian Ghomeshi's table included Debbie Travis, defending *The Birth House* by Ami McKay; Ali Velshi, defending *The Best Laid Plans* by Terry Fallis; Lorne Cardinal, defending *Unless* by Carol Shields;

Sara Quin, defending *Essex Country* by Jeff Lemire; and then me, defending *The Bone Cage* by Angie Abdou.

I definitely had a lot of fun arguing and debating in defence of my book. In my mind, Angie's was by far the best one and the most essential book Canadians should read. It tells the story of a male wrestler and a female swimmer on the road to the Olympics, and all the struggles and pain that journey involves. When I read that book, it really resonated with my own experience. In the end, Ali Velshi won with the humorous and political *The Best Laid Plans*. I still can't believe I was part of that panel.

But when I arrived in Phoenix, that was far in the future, and I was a long way from the CBC and Edmonton's non-stop media environment. I missed my relationship with the press. Without going as far as saying I was addicted to it, I really enjoyed playing with journalists. Not only were the stands almost empty when we were playing at home, but journalists were totally absent in the locker room. Lots of my teammates loved that situation, since they saw the press as a nuisance.

But for me it was the contrary. I had the sensation that whatever the team was doing, winning, losing, nobody cared at all. We could win a game 5–0 and we'd get just a brief article at the bottom of a page. As for the electronic media, they simply ignored us. We could have played in clown uniforms and I don't think the local press would have noticed.

Once I was in Pittsburgh I started to breathe again in every respect, including in terms of my relationship with the press. After my time in Phoenix, I had the feeling once again that hockey was of interest to journalists. Not only would I be giving interviews all the time, but I was also asked by a few local radio stations to deliver some mini-reports on various subjects. I would record little promotions for the team as well. So I was all ready for the Montreal media pressure.

●

As soon as I got to Montreal, after the foretaste I had with Jean-Charles Lajoie two weeks or so before my arrival, I realized pretty quickly that two things were making the press different there from anywhere else in the NHL. First, they loved to make much ado about nothing; second, they enjoyed complaining so much that it sounded pathological to anyone coming from outside.

As I said before, I had decided I wouldn't change a bit just because I was in Montreal: Georges Laraque is Georges Laraque wherever he is. I'm always the same person. Of course, I became one of the favourites for the gossipmongers.

Most of the players in Montreal complied by the rules the Canadiens had set. Not a single one of them would have told the press, like I did, that they wouldn't have signed in Montreal if they had known they wouldn't be playing more. They probably would have said the following: "I understand the coach. I've got to work harder to get back into the lineup and make the most of my opportunities." Sound familiar? If you live in Montreal it sure does.

Another thing that really bugged me in Montreal were the pseudo-analyses some observers would make based on my statements. I was always saying what I wanted to say. But instead of simply quoting me, they would try to read between the lines even though there was absolutely nothing there.

Among the worst poisons in the Montreal sports press was Bertrand Raymond, one of the most inept paper-pushers I've ever seen. The only good thing I can say about him is that thank God he's not writing anywhere anymore. That man, who knows absolutely nothing about hockey, spent the whole year and a half I was with the Canadiens attacking me with lies full of venom.

•

Open-line radio shows have been very popular all across North America for quite a while now, but in Quebec, especially when it comes to discussing hockey on the air, it's almost a religion. The priest/anchorman is there to receive the confessions of the faithfuls/fans. But instead of celebrating in dignity and respect, they prefer to imitate the worst television preachers you can sometimes find on cheap local cable stations in the U.S. Deep South.

On television it's a bit different. The priest adopts a posture of solemn neutrality and then goads his guests into the most outrageous positions he can get them into. The more impetuous the guests are, the happier the grand priest.

It may sound like a caricature, but for somebody coming from outside Quebec, that's how it would look and sound. Sure, the media in Edmonton treats hockey with all the solemnity of religion, and no NHL player could ever doubt that in Toronto the Leafs take on the importance usually reserved for things like foreign policy, unemployment, political scandal, and probably natural disasters. The hockey media in Canada just can't give fans enough. But even compared to the rest of Canada, the Montreal media is intense, and the talk-radio shows are the most intense of all.

I don't mind those shows being on the air. Who am I to say what should or shouldn't be on the air? What I dislike about them, though, is not that they take hockey too seriously—hey, *I* take hockey pretty seriously. What bothers me is the dishonesty. Those shows mislead listeners into thinking everything is improvised, when in fact it's all staged in advance.

Producers look for two major ingredients: first, and most important, bitter criticism; and second, almost as essential as the first, verbal confrontation. And if you want the soufflé to be a perfect success, the Montreal Canadiens must be on a losing streak. The longer the streak, the higher the soufflé will rise. Unfortunately for these misters, they don't have any control over that one. Because if they did ...

It's not hard to find listeners deeply imbued with negativism for the first ingredient, since most fans have been inoculated with that virus from birth. But to make sure the verbal row really takes off, the producers of those shows must do a little bit of staging.

Thus, before the show begins, the producer cherry-picks the callers, who all have to declare before they go on air what they want to talk about. That way, the producer can make sure that a caller who thinks the team's dismal performance can be blamed on this or that player will be confronted by another fan who thinks that player is the heart and soul of the team. It's never by chance that those two guys end up going at it.

In other words, if you can find one person who thinks Player A is a bum, and one person who thinks he's a solid player, then you can manufacture a crisis by putting the two fans on the air and giving the impression that they're talking about what everybody is talking about. The morning after, fans go to work and discuss the show with their colleagues, thinking they've been witness to a genuine argument on the air—that is, thinking the issue that sparked the heated argument they just heard must be nagging the team. They comment on it, argue about it, keep the previous evening's entertainment going.

Except that what fans and their acquaintances are discussing has nothing to do with reality. Most of the time it's pure fiction. I find it pathetic that this kind of nonsense can be passed off as reality. I call that laughing at the fans.

During my first year in Montreal, journalists would often come to see me or call me and ask me to forgive them in advance because of what they were going to say about me on a live show later that night. Some would even ask for my permission. No one needs my permission to tell the truth. And no one should ask anyone's permission to lie.

But sometimes it's more complicated than just telling the difference between lying and telling the truth. Some journalists agreed to "virtual contracts" with the francophone players on the Canadiens. The terms of the contracts are simple. The player will give the journalist privileged information and in exchange the journalist promises he or she will never attack the player in any way.

I could give many examples of this situation but will offer just one. After a tough game that we'd lost because Carey Price had given up a bad goal, Andrei Markov was so mad going back to the locker room that he went a bit berserk and started breaking things.

Not a single player talked about it to anyone. Still, half an hour later, the news was reported during one of those trash TV shows. Only a player in contact with someone on that show could have leaked that news.

We all knew who those players were in the locker room. If you ask me who they were, I won't give you names. But it's pretty easy to know. They're the ones nobody ever criticizes. So I guess you know it wasn't me.

•

Not a lot of players got as much attention from the Montreal press as I did in such a short stay. Journalists and analysts were attacking me all the time. Yet, when I would coldly analyze the situation, I really couldn't understand why.

I wasn't mean to my teammates. I never publicly denigrated my coach, although I wished I had in the end. During the last six weeks before I got released, I wasn't even playing. I was basically spending my time working for charities.

I played only sixty-one games for the Montreal Canadiens, but when I look at the press coverage I got, it seems to me as if I'd stayed ten years with the team. And all that attention, even if it was negative, brought me under the spotlight and gave me opportunities I wouldn't have had without it.

The more I was attacked in the press, the more my email inbox was filled with support messages from fans. So those denigrating journalists did me a favour, even though it wasn't their intention. And if today I'm part of the Quebec mediasphere, participating in the show *Le Match* on TVA Sports, I owe it in part to them. Which proves the publicists are right when they say, "I don't care what they say about you, as long as they say something, and as long as they spell your name right."

I agreed to be a part of *Le Match* solely because the concept was totally different from what could be seen on other television channels. The producer, Éric Lavallée, had promised me that the team of observers we would be forming wouldn't be on air to stab other players in the back. I would never do that. There are about seven hundred players in the NHL. They had to outclass millions of others to get there. Respect!

Another thing I love about our team at *Le Match* is that we're all young analysts who know what we're talking about when we discuss today's hockey. Everyone around the studio was in the NHL a couple of years ago. I have nothing against old people, understand me. I simply don't think that somebody who hasn't played or coached in the NHL for the past ten years can really understand how hockey has evolved recently to become the game it is today.

•

When I look back, I can't think of a single declaration I've made that I regret today, probably because I've always said what I thought. When you don't lie, your heart stays light …

OF SKATING AND OTHER HOBBIES

19

My retirement had barely been confirmed when I received a phone call from Christine Simpson, sister of former NHLer Craig Simpson and director of *Battle of the Blades*. She wanted me on the show, but I saw no reason to accept. The way I saw it, figure skaters were slender, elegant little guys. It's been a long time since anyone has thought of me as slender or little. And there's only one person in the world who thinks of me as an elegant skater. (Thanks, Mom.)

I don't mind laughing at myself and being laughed at, but I had to draw the line somewhere. And there was no way I was going to make an ass of myself on national television. I'd heard stories that Wayne Gretzky didn't like to skate next to Paul Coffey because he knew Coffey was the smoother skater and he hated to look second best. If even the Great One didn't want to look bad beside a guy on his own team, how was I supposed to feel performing beside—and against—some of the best female skaters in the country?

Christine would call me back frequently, though, always trying new ways to convince me to accept. Every time, I would say no. All I had to do was think of myself performing pirouettes as cringing fans and fellow hockey players looked on in horror, and it was easy to say no.

Still, despite everything, she did find a way to make me say yes.

I was really busy at that time working on the Hockey for Haiti project and the reconstruction of Grace Hospital. Haiti had totally vanished from the news, even though help was still desperately needed on the island.

Christine told me that having me on the show could be a good way to bring Haiti back to the headlines. With the show's ratings approaching two million viewers, I convinced myself it was worth a try. If it was for the benefit of Hockey for Haiti, I was ready to make a fool of myself. When I accepted, she promised she would show some images from my first visit to Haiti.

The producers and Christine decided to give me Anabelle Langlois as a skating partner. I really think they paired me with the best simply because I was the worst skater among the former NHL players who were going to be on the show. Anabelle and her partner in life as well as on the ice, Cody Hay, had been the Canadian pair champions in 2007–08 and were just coming back from the Olympics, where they had finished ninth.

I had to get made-to-measure figure skates. My feet were definitely too long and large for the existing ones on the market. There I was at home, looking at those huge blades, thinking I really didn't know what kind of adventure I was throwing myself into. The only thing I was certain of was that I'd have to work hard. Since I knew Jamie Salé and David Pelletier, I had a good idea of how difficult this sport was.

Anabelle and Cody were living in Barrie, Ontario. They accepted my invitation to come live in my house in Brossard so that we could start our training. I also hired Julie Marcotte as a personal coach and choreographer so that I could make faster progress. It was she who first guided me, helping me learn some moves and trying to teach me to skate differently. I was so unstable on the ice when we started that I felt like calling Christine Simpson to tell her I simply couldn't do it. But Julie's brother and Amélie Fortin also helped me a lot in the beginning. And Anabelle, Cody, and I would also go to Edmonton for training sessions with David Pelletier, who was working for the show.

Even though I sometimes felt like calling the whole thing off, I was still Georges Laraque and decided that my only goal was to win *Battle of the Blades*. The producers of the show had organized a poll, and according to the responses, I had no chance whatsoever to finish first in the competition. And I can't say the oddsmakers were crazy. I mean, I was up against a thousand-point scorer in Theo Fleury, a speed merchant in Valeri Bure, an accomplished skill guy in Russ Courtnall, and Patrice Brisebois—a guy who skated as effortlessly as anyone in the NHL. Okay, maybe Kelly Chase, P.J. Stock, and Todd Warriner weren't the most stylish skaters ever to play the game, but I knew they weren't guys who would go down without a fight either.

The odds were against me, and I knew it. And, as usual, that just fuelled my determination.

Anabelle and Cody had the same kind of motivation. We worked very hard so that I could make some quick progress and begin doing some moves as early in the process as possible. Every day, three hours a day, we would skate together, trying to adapt to each other.

I'd spent the last thirty years skating like a hockey player, and now I had to try to change it. I tried and tried, but couldn't seem to find the switch in my mind that would allow me to do so. Anyone who's ever seen figure skating knows the blades have serrated picks at the toe. What might not be as obvious is that the blades are wider, longer, and heavier and have a deeper groove down the centre. They are much, much harder to master than hockey skates, and the boot doesn't give as much support as a modern hockey boot. It was like trying to get around the ice with blades several sizes too big and with my skates untied. It took me a week not to fall down every three steps.

The lifts and carries we were practising had a very high level of danger. But going into it, I had no idea—it was figure skating, right? It might be difficult, but dangerous? For a hockey player?

Anabelle and Cody quickly sorted me out. As I talked to them about their sport, I found out that Anabelle had suffered four severe concussions during her career. Her courage and fearlessness were exceptional. And now she'd placed all her confidence in me. That made one more person I couldn't let down.

Our coaches were pretty amazed by the types of lifts we were able to do, since they were usually reserved for the professionals. The only reason we could quite easily do them, besides Anabelle's courage, was because of our size difference. She's under five feet tall and weighs less than a hundred pounds. And I was around 275. Let's just say that for me to lift her up in the air was no great challenge.

Lifting I could do. I would do the lifting, and she could do the skating. If it had been a lifting competition, I wouldn't have had anything to worry about. One thing was for sure: the less I'd have to skate, the better I would feel.

I remember one day when we wanted to relax a bit and forget about the competition, and so we decided to go and take a salsa class. After all, maybe it would help me move a bit better. My sister gave those kinds of classes at the time. After the class, Daphney told me that I was a desperate case. To be honest, I was as supple as a street light.

After a few weeks of training in Brossard, Anabelle, Cody, Julie Marcotte, and I decided to go to Edmonton to work a bit with David Pelletier. We stayed there for a couple of days and, right before we left, Julie told us she wanted to teach us how to do the chainsaw, one of the most dangerous moves in figure skating.

Invented by Lloyd Eisler and Isabelle Brasseur, that move required Anabelle to hold herself by her arms around my neck while I made her spin around at a crazy speed. Besides Eisler and Brasseur, nobody has ever tried it in a competition. On dry land, we were able to do it without any problem. Then we attempted to do it on the ice and succeeded. All around us people couldn't believe we could actually do it.

We were now at the point of learning our first choreography. Jeffrey Buttle, world champion in 2008, was to design it. Included in that ninety-second sequence was the chainsaw, of course, and a moonwalk session. I was so proud that I could finally do it.

We also had to find a song. For the first choreography of the season, every participating hockey player had to pick music that represented his career. I chose "Eye of the Tiger." Not only for me, but also for Anabelle. She really was a tiger and wasn't scared of anything.

Jeffrey taught me different moves, from the waltz to spirals. We would do a backward spiral that nobody else was going to try, and a double salchow, which only a few pairs would have in their routines. Even though I wasn't a good skater, we knew now that we had a program to stack up against anyone's.

We left Brossard for Toronto, where the competition was to be held, wanting to be on site to round off our preparations. That was when I realized how big *Battle of the Blades* was—a real media craze was surrounding the show, and for once it wasn't only the sports journalists who wanted to talk to me.

The day before the first show, we met the dresser team. We had to decide what we were going to wear for our performance. They suggested I wear a sleeveless T-shirt. We got dressed and went to try our choreography with our costumes on. But by the time we got to the chainsaw, we realized it would be impossible. Anabelle's skin would stick to mine.

The organizers told us I should try to put some oil on my skin so that the friction would disappear. That was a very, very bad idea. Cody oiled my shoulders, and Anabelle and I went back on the ice to try the move again. Right when we started, I could feel that the oiling was a big mistake. Anabelle was turning fast. Too fast to hold on. At the end of the sequence, she lost her grip around my neck.

She was going to fall headfirst onto the ice. In a desperate attempt to prevent that from happening, I tried to grab her legs so that she would fall on them. By doing so, one of her skates hit my face and deeply cut me. The shock was so violent that I fell to the ice and lay there on my back.

I was out cold. People around came to the rescue while I was unconscious, and when I came to, my face was covered in blood. I had probably experienced a small concussion. KO'd in practice in a figure skater's costume. But my first thought wasn't *How on earth did I end up in this situation?* My first thought was *Have I lost an eye?*

On the way to the hospital I was now fully conscious and Anabelle was crying. Without informing us, the producers of the show had already counted us out. Everybody thought it was all over for us. When we got to the hospital, an intern came to see me—and made the mistake of telling me it would be his first time sewing stitches.

From my gurney, I protested. I wanted a confirmed doctor to do those stitches. I might have felt differently about a cut on my arm or something, but no one wants a rookie doctor practising his or her stitching on your face. Fortunately, one of the hospital staff recognized me, and after asking me if I really wanted to be on the show the next day, he did his best and sewed my face up.

When we got out of the hospital, I was still pretty shaky. But I told Anabelle that if we wanted to hold on to our chance to go to the second round, we had to do that move. And I had to try it once again to be confident enough for the show.

She tried to dissuade me from attempting it again, saying that she didn't think we needed it to get to the next round. But I was as stubborn as my father ever was, and I managed to bring her back on the ice so that we could try it once more. There I was, stitched up, bandaged up, and more important, wearing a shirt with sleeves.

And everything went fine.

●

The day of the competition finally arrived. After all the practice, it was go time. Time to see if we could pull it off with millions watching. I arrived in my dressing room pretty early in the morning. My mother and sister had made the trip to Toronto for the occasion, but when my mom came in and saw the stitches, she immediately asked if I was going to try the move again. I said yes. She became really nervous and left the room.

When our hour came, Anabelle and I did our choreography without a single mistake. We were invited to the second round. I know the chainsaw helped get us through, but I think the story of my stitches may have had something to do with it as well.

Still, we got eliminated in the second round. Even before putting one blade on the ice, I already knew it. Nobody behind the scenes was acting the same with me.

After our elimination, the producers told us that one of the eliminated couples would make a surprise return in the middle of the season; even the other couples in the show wouldn't know about it. So we were ready to get back to work and make our second chance pay off. But that turned out to be a very bad idea. Because now it was Anabelle's turn to injure herself for this puppet game.

It was an unfortunate fall while we were training. We never saw it coming. We were practising a triple twist jump that we'd done successfully dozens of times before. As usual, I threw her in the air, but instead of staying there to catch her back, I fell down on the ice. She fell heavily on her knees and started screaming like crazy. I'd never seen anyone suffer like that—I really thought both her kneecaps had exploded.

The ambulance came a few minutes later. On our way to the hospital I was totally devastated. As soon as we arrived, a doctor sewed a few stitches on one of her knees. On my Twitter account I left a note to my followers informing them of the accident and asking them to pray for Anabelle, telling them that our *Battle of the Blades* adventure was over, but that I didn't care—only her health mattered to me.

The doctor finally came to examine her knees. She wasn't hurting at all anymore. She looked straight at me and said simply that everything was perfect, that we could do the show the next day after all. Not only could I not believe my ears that she was feeling all right, but it was out of the question for me to go on after what we'd just lived through. But Anabelle told me it was her choice, not mine. As I carried her on my back to the hotel, I couldn't understand what had just happened. How in the world could she have healed so fast? That seemed like a miracle to me.

We tried the triple twist jump a few more times and nothing bad happened. But then the morning before the show, when we met for breakfast, Anabelle told me that she'd had a nightmare about the accident and didn't want to try the move again. I understood her feelings. We were eliminated for good.

•

Battle of the Blades had been an exceptional experience for me. I had the opportunity to work with the best trainers and the best skaters the world had to offer. That experience also made me realize that figure skating is a sport far more dangerous than hockey, and a lot harder in some respects. Nobody gets out of the experience without getting injured. Every former hockey player involved in the competition that year had learned that too.

Figure skating leaves absolutely no room for mistakes. When you fall, there's no padding to soften the impact of your body hitting the ice. Every time a figure skater falls, he or she can die. It's an extreme sport. Think about it. For thirteen years, the toughest hockey players in the world had thrown everything they had at me. But in the end, it was a woman who stood four foot eleven and weighed ninety-seven pounds who gave me the worst injury of my career.

Yet, I really fell in love with it. To achieve something difficult, to seduce a crowd—those things had filled a void after my retirement from hockey. I can never thank Anabelle and Cody enough for what they allowed me to discover. I was so lucky to meet them and work with them.

After that adventure, I really thought I'd never hear about figure skating again. Boy, was I ever wrong. Some skating clubs began calling me from all around the country, starting with the one in Barrie, Ontario, where Anabelle and Cody were living. In just a few weeks my agenda was filled.

Not only did the clubs invite me to do figure skating exhibitions, they also found me partners, since Anabelle couldn't free herself that much. I started dancing with numerous skaters across the country. I still do, and still will. My weekends were now booked ... for years to come.

•

Besides loving the sport and the fact that it keeps me in the best possible shape, what I really like about doing figure skating exhibitions is that I help to burst a lot of stereotypes. That's the main reason why I agreed and still agree to perform all those shows free—I think the message I'm trying to send has a bigger impact than it would if I were being paid for them. Plus, let's just be honest here, I'm not a good enough figure skater to get paid.

Parents started writing to me, asking me if they should let their son attend figure skating classes. I always answered yes, explaining to what extent that sport is extreme and a lot harder and more demanding than hockey.

Figure skating had brought me to the hospital three times in only a few weeks, something that had never happened to me during all my hockey years. And if ever again someone calls a kid who figure skates a faggot, the tough guy in me might reappear ...

•

Life leaves me some free time now and then. Not much, I admit, but I always try to live it to the fullest. And when those times happen, my favourite activity has to be karaoke. I'm fanatical about it.

I never travel without my microphone or my karaoke sound system and the ten thousand songs it contains. I know hundreds of songs by heart, mostly ones sung by women.

Don't think I'm a good singer, though. I have absolutely no talent at it whatsoever. When I sing, I'm so out of tune it would probably make you want to leave the place. But I don't care, I just love it!

Whenever I can, I organize karaoke parties with friends. There's a place called Pang Pang on McKay Street in downtown Montreal where I often put together karaoke parties. I even sometimes rent the place for myself ...

My passion for karaoke is a direct consequence of the passion for music I've had since I was a kid. But don't ask me what my favourite types of music are: I wouldn't be able to answer you. It would be a lot easier to say the kinds of music I really don't like. There are only two of them.

I'll start with the one I really can't stand: country music. I'm allergic to it. And for someone like me who's lived full-time and now still lives part-time in Alberta, trust me, if I could have gotten used to it, it would have happened by now.

In the Oilers locker room, it would often happen that a player would play a country record. I'd rush to the CD player and simply turn it off—and sometimes I'd even take the CD out and hide it. It happened in Montreal too, since Carey Price is a big country music fan.

The second type of music I don't really like, but that I don't despise as much as country, is rap music. I've always thought, and I know I'm probably wrong, that this style of music is made up of a load of bad words put one after the other until the singer has enough of them to call it a song.

What's strange about the fact that I don't really like rap music is that I've met some of the greatest hip-hop artists around. I met DMX in New York. I also met Snoop Dog in Edmonton. The guy even spent the first half of his show wearing my Oilers shirt. When I went to meet him backstage after the show, I really tried hard to understand what he was saying to me, but I lost half of it because of his accent and the words he used.

I also met 50 Cent, still in Edmonton. He too started his show in the Oilers arena with my shirt on. The only mistake I made the night of his show was to bring my mother with me. I was renting a suite on an annual basis at Rexall Place and would offer it to sick children for every game. When there was a concert in the arena I'd bring some friends there, and that night, my mom too.

Ten minutes after the concert began, my mother started feeling a bit dizzy. She didn't understand what was happening to her, but I knew right away. Hundreds of marijuana joints were being smoked in the stands right below us and the smoke would all end up in the suite. A friend took her home.

Even though I like to attend music concerts, I'm not someone who goes out a lot. I sometimes join friends in a bar, but I almost never drink. I know when reading that last sentence, some of my friends will accuse me of lying impudently. But those very same people will probably fall off their chairs when they read what follows.

I have the reputation of being a man who can hold alcohol like no one else. I can drink dozens of shooters and still walk straight. Am I that resistant?

Every time my friends and I walk into a bar, I go see the bartender right away and order a series of shooters for everyone. Then I tell the waiter that, in the glasses he serves me, I don't want the same thing as the others. If I order tequila, there will be water in my glass. Jägermeister? I'll be served cola. Sour Puss? Give me that cranberry juice, waiter!

To make sure my friends don't suspect anything, I always play the drunk guy. I've become very good at imitating it. After those boozy nights, I sometimes take a cab because I'm not supposed to drive in the state I'm in. With all the alcohol I drank, my friends wouldn't let me take my car anyway. But once in the taxi, I ask the driver to go around the block and let me off at my car. Then I safely drive home …

Sorry guys!

•

As shocking as that may be, I have a still more astonishing confession. Even after a lifetime of playing hockey, I hate beer. Many people may assume that it's impossible for a hockey player to hate beer, but I promise you, it's not. Almost impossible, maybe, but not quite. I can taste the difference between the brands, but for my palate, the variety of flavour goes from strong urine to diluted urine, always with that sharp, acrid taste I hate.

As a matter of fact, I like only one type of alcohol, and it's red wine. Even then I only drink one brand, called Caymus, a great, savoury Californian wine. The first time I had a sip of it I just fell in love with that nectar, and ever since then I've been convinced that it's the best wine in the world. I have about two hundred bottles of it at home.

I know that's no collection, unlike the one owned by the Canadiens' physical trainer, Pierre Gervais. Not only is he a man of heart and class, but he's also a fine oenologist. He must have about twenty thousand bottles in his cellar, and he can recognize almost any kind of wine just by sniffing it.

To his mind, the Caymus is an okay wine, but nothing to be compared to a Petrus or an Yquem. I was so obsessed with the Caymus that Gervais ended up printing a special Montreal Canadiens shirt with the number 00 and the name Caymus on it. I still have it, of course.

The funny thing is that when Mike Cammalleri joined the Canadiens, we got onto the subject of wine. Of course, I started to talk about the Caymus, and Mike said it was his favourite wine too. The whole team yelled in unison, "NO! NOT YOU TOO!" I had just made myself an ally, to the great displeasure of my teammates ...

•

Among the other hobbies I have, I must mention the movies, social networks, and soccer.

I love historical movies. It always takes me four or five days to finish a film, though, since I invariably fall asleep after fifteen minutes only to wake up as the closing credits start.

As for social networks, I simply couldn't live without them. I confess I'm deeply addicted to Facebook and Twitter, and there's not a day, if not an hour, that goes by without me leaving messages on them.

I said this earlier, but I just love soccer, which is definitely my favourite sport among all. Every summer I gather some friends and we play against elite women's teams. Why against women? Simply because if we played against men, it would be far more physical and the risk of injuries would be too great.

The fact that we play against women doesn't make it easier for us, though, and scores like 8–0 against us are not a rare thing.

TO YOU TWO ...   20

I've fought all my life. And I'm not only talking about the fights I had on the ice. My whole existence has been a succession of struggles to win, of challenges to complete, of barriers to smash.

I've always set myself goals that seemed impossible to achieve and have always achieved them. I've always had the craziest dreams; they all became reality. I'm not better than anyone, far from it. Anybody who's ever heard me sing will agree. But I always wanted to be free.

Everybody has a different definition of what the word *freedom* means. In my eyes, being free means a lot more than doing whatever I want, whenever I feel like it. To paraphrase the French philosopher Jean-Paul Sartre, I sincerely think that freedom is all about fixing your goals and trying to reach them by all means necessary; as long, of course, as those means don't hinder other people's liberty. And the hard part of trying to be free in that sense of the word involves being able to move aside even the most seductive obstacles, including girls.

•

I must admit here that my relationships with girls, then with women, without being turbulent, didn't bring me that far. As a young teenager, I loved to attract their attention, of course, but I was far too shy to start anything. Moreover, with sports on my mind, I wouldn't see girls as my priority, but more as potential obstacles.

I was sixteen when I first found love. I would have given her the moon, but the moon wasn't what she wanted. She preferred to have one of my best friends, and she left me for him. Like every other boy experiencing his first breakup, I swore I would never fall in love again. That separation had been responsible for my first and last suicidal ideation. Even today, the bitter taste that abrupt finale left in my mouth comes back every time I start a new romance.

After that I had girlfriends, of course, but I wasn't in love. During my years in the junior league, everything was easy in that respect. I was extremely popular with girls and had no questions to ask myself. Still, I wasn't chasing girls even then. I had a girlfriend whom I adored. Our relationship lasted a little over a year.

My relationships couldn't last or be taken seriously during those years. My only goal was to play in the NHL. Teenage love can't support the kind of self-sacrifice I was imposing on myself. Girls would grow tired and, sometimes disappointed, often upset, would simply leave me. They would move away even faster when I made them feel they were a threat to my dream.

When I arrived in the NHL, I was sad to see all those players leaving their wives and sometimes their kids behind them to throw themselves into a new season. They wouldn't be there for the magic moments that are the first words or the first steps of their babies. When these moments would happen, they'd be stuck in a hotel room somewhere far from home.

I had promised myself that this wouldn't happen to me, that I would be an ever-present father. I was going to live out my career, and then start a family. But life decided otherwise ...

•

I met Erin Kathan in Edmonton, in one of the fitness centres in which I was a partner. She was working there as a physical trainer. Over three years we had developed a great friendship, nothing more, although her energy and her personality had seduced me at first sight.

After years of friendship, we each got out of a confrontational love relationship almost at the same time. Without even thinking about it, we started going out together on a more and more regular basis. The seeds of love had been sown a long time ago; now was the time to let them bloom and blossom. At least, that was my impression.

A few days before I left for Montreal to attend my first training camp with the team, Erin told me she was pregnant. The surprise was total; the joy, boundless! I was going to be a father! I hadn't planned it that way, but for once I put my plans aside and fully tasted the joy of that news.

A few weeks later, medical tests revealed that Erin was awaiting twins, a girl and a boy. I was so happy and shocked at the same time. I started thinking immediately about how to prepare myself for the arrival of my two angels.

The fabulous news also made me forget for a couple of months what a great friend Erin was, but not necessarily the woman of my life. She was strong, stubborn, and independent, just like me. As friends, the meeting of those two personalities would create joyful fireworks; as lovers, the sparks were incendiary.

She came to Montreal to live with me for the last months of her pregnancy. Because of my crazy agenda, I had hired a nanny so that she could take care of Erin on a full-time basis and stay on after the birth of our sweet twins.

On March 30, 2009, Milayna Julia Laraque and Marcus Oliver Laraque were born. I saw them coming out and was exultant. Those two beautiful and magnificent gifts of God instantly became my reason to live and the inspiration for everything I would accomplish in the future. It was the most touching, moving moment of my life.

•

In the following months, the relationship between Erin and me started to gradually unravel. We tried by any means we could to save our little family, but the conflicts between the two of us kept on growing, moving us away from each other a little bit more every day.

That was when we took a difficult but necessary decision. To stay together on the same road wouldn't have served in any way the future of our beloved children. Neither Erin nor I believed in the idea of sticking together because of the children. Parents who don't get along—that's something kids can feel at a pretty young age, and it can mark them negatively for the rest of their lives.

About a year after Milayna Julia and Marcus Oliver were born, Erin and I decided that our roads should take different directions. I bought a house for Erin and the children in Edmonton. Since my house is very close to theirs, I would visit them as often as I could.

Erin and I acted as mature adults. We both decided that Milayna Julia and Marcus Oliver would be the centre of our lives at all times. We promised ourselves to forget about our differences to better concentrate on their education and well-being.

I'm a very present father and will continue to accept my responsibilities as a father to the best of my capacities as long as God keeps me on this earth. I also know that Milayna Julia and Marcus Oliver couldn't dream of having a better mother than Erin.

Just like everybody else when they become parents, I would have loved my children to live under the same roof with both their parents still being together. Fate decided otherwise, but I'm persuaded today that their balance will be reinforced by the situation. I know these words will sound strange to some of my readers, but my family background proves to me that I'm right to think that way.

Speaking of my family, my parents reacted quite differently to the news of our separation. Évelyne had a very maternal reaction. She was disappointed, of course, but her main worry was whether she would still see her grandchildren in the future. Today, she has no fear about that.

As for my father, I still don't know what got into him when he learned the news, but his reaction hurt me deeply. He was still living in Edmonton when it happened. Instead of supporting me like any father would, he started badmouthing me to some of my friends. He was so narcissistic, I simply decided not to talk to him anymore.

•

When I look at my beloved twins today, I can't help seeing myself when I was a child. The road ahead of them won't be easy, and my biggest wish is to give them the best weapons to fight the adversity and the ignorance they will encounter while growing up.

I remember the little Georges I was, facing racism in the hockey world. I was helpless then. I was living in a world dominated by whites and in a sport made for whites. A black kid's place wasn't in the rink—that's what I was being told repeatedly.

It took me years to learn that the very first black professional hockey player was named Willie O'Ree and that he debuted at the Montreal Forum with the Boston Bruins on January 18, 1958.

Better still, it wasn't until the end of 2010 that I learned something amazing about the relationship between black people and hockey. Just a few weeks before Christmas, a friend emailed me a link to a short video available on YouTube. Watching it, I learned that while the game of hockey was invented by the First Nations, all the basic rules of modern hockey were created at the beginning of the nineteenth century by black people in Nova Scotia.

I was stunned by the news, which shouldn't have been news if history had been written objectively. I did some research, and finally found a book entitled *Black Ice*, written by two (white) historians, George and Darril Fosty.

Reading that book was a very emotional experience for me. The Fosty brothers show, with archival documents and photos as evidence, that as early as 1820, descendants of slaves had created a hockey league in Nova Scotia. They were playing according to rules that for the most part are still operative all around the hockey world.

I couldn't believe it. Hockey, played almost entirely by whites, had been invented by black people. I wish I'd known that when players, parents, coaches, and referees were telling me I didn't belong in the sport.

I started talking to NHL officials about that incredible story. After having done some research on their own, they came to the conclusion that everything the Fosty brothers had written in their book was the plain truth. They decided to include that part of history in their official archives and to rewrite the official version of the birth of hockey in North America. I thank them for that.

I tried to do the same thing with the Hockey Hall of Fame, an institution totally independent of the NHL. They never returned my calls. They probably thought the whole affair would tarnish their image. They would have had to change so many things that they chose to close their ears. Difficult for them, indeed, to publicly say today, for instance, that Bernard "Boom Boom" Geoffrion wasn't the father of the slapshot after all. But I won't give up ...

•

As a kid, I was raised thinking that everything adults would say was the truth and was to be accepted as such. I wasn't to doubt in any way what people responsible for my education were telling me. Everything I needed to know, all the essential things, I would learn from the ones who knew better, the responsible adults. It would have been pointless for me to look anywhere else; I would simply have wasted my time.

Since then I've understood that that predetermined road, even when it's paved with the best intentions in the world, will always make us miss beautiful, enlightening, rich experiences if we don't dare leaving it from time to time. I know for certain now that to doubt is one of the best virtues you can teach your children. The second one has to be curiosity; the curiosity to go and see what's hiding behind those certainties we're taught to take for granted.

Throughout my youth, I prayed to God to help me reach my dream. In return I promised Him that I would involve myself in causes that I believed were right; that I would always open myself to others; that I would trust the knowledge I gained through my own experiences to build my own judgment instead of letting others decide things for me.

The first impulse that drove me to involve myself in various humanitarian, social, and charity causes came from my will to give back to God what He had given me. Then I could see for myself the immediate impact my actions could have on people and the society surrounding me. I started involving myself in trying, modestly, to influence for the better the course of the world in which I lived.

Today, since my beautiful children were born, I try to work for the future. I want to give them everything my own experiences have given me and will still be giving me in the years to come. In the meantime, I involve myself so that tomorrow's world, the one in which they'll live their adult life, happens to be better than the one I knew then and know now.

•

Writing those last words, I'm in Tanzania. This trip was to take place from July 20 to August 10, 2011. It was planned in support of the Lani Foundation, a non-profit organization that helps projects promoting life and the prevention of suicide among twelve- to twenty-five-year-old youths.

Together, the ten of us who agreed to do the journey raised more than $50,000 for the Lani Foundation. None of us had ever been to Africa before.

Our itinerary was exciting. We would participate in three safaris in three days, climb Mount Meru at an altitude of 4566 metres, and then ascend the breathtaking Mount Kilimanjaro at 5896 metres. We were all in top condition for the challenge, but none of us knew what to expect.

The Maasai tribe visit was definitely the most interesting, and one of the most amazing learning experiences for me. This nation's people are all over Africa, and often these men are paid to guard villages or hotels. People from this nation eat cow meat and drink three litres of cow blood mixed with milk every day. They are strong. They can kill lions. They're very tall, dress in red, and walk all around the country with their cows looking for fields to feed their herd. The more cows a Maasai has, the more wives he can have. That's what defines how rich a man is. When we were greeted in their village, I was happy to dance and jump around with them. Because of my personality, pretty much everyone I met adopted me quickly, and soon my Maasai name became "Layza." From now on, I'll be called by this name in Africa.

After the safaris and the visit, it was time to start climbing. For the first climb, up Mount Meru, there was quite a team with us. Everything was planned to a T by the Karavanier group from Montreal. We had porters who carried our bags and our own cook who prepared every meal. I don't think I need to tell you how awesome it was to eat African vegan meals. I even got some of my colleagues to try some of them—I don't know if it was because they were sick of eating chicken or of listening to me lecturing them about veganism. But we all found the food amazing.

The ascent of the first mountain was planned in three stages, averaging five hours a day of climbing. We had a ranger at the front for security reasons: there was always the possibility of coming across wild animals. We were, in fact, invading their habitat. The higher we climbed, the less air we got to breathe and the colder it got. After the first two stages, at 3500 metres, we were already on top of the clouds. What a view! Everyone was doing great because we had a fantastic guide. The key was to go slowly in order to avoid altitude sickness. The climb was pretty quiet most of the time, since in the thin air we were focussed on putting one foot in front of the other. I had a lot of time to think about things.

Because I was in excellent shape, the altitude didn't bother me. I felt strong even though at night I wouldn't sleep much. I didn't take any medication and was convinced that, because I'm a vegan, my immune system was pretty strong. I was telling everyone not to eat any dairy because it can clog up your lungs, which are even more essential up above the clouds. On the third day of climbing Mount Meru, we had to go up another kilometre. This mountain, which is unknown to many people, is much harder to climb than Kilimanjaro. Only four out of the ten of us did it, and man, did they ever suffer.

But the strangest thing happened to me. At the beginning of our climb that day, the mountain started to become very steep. It was like climbing to the top of a pyramid with a small path to walk on—and you can see all the way down. I started to suffer from vertigo. I was getting dizzy, and my body kept leaning towards the ravine. I couldn't walk straight; I was leaning towards the edge even though I was using both my walking sticks to hold on. The higher I got, the worse it was. As you must know by now, I have a big ego and it would be very hard for me to turn around. However, I knew that if I kept going I would probably faint, fall down the ravine, and die. I started thinking about my twins and figured it wasn't worth the risk, so I went back to the camp.

Since childhood, I've always been afraid of heights. I remember when our whole family would go to La Ronde in Montreal. I would never go on the roller coasters and had to wait for hours for my brother and sister to get off the rides. All I could do was the haunted house, the bumper cars, and the merry-go-round, but that was too embarrassing. I tried for years to conquer this fear. I did bungee jumping once; I almost died and would never do it again. While I was at the top, after looking down for an hour, I decided not to do it—and then I fell by accident. I even hated going up the CN Tower in Toronto. But I've never experienced anything like I did on Mount Meru. I have vertigo, and I'll have to seek help so that I don't miss out on other opportunities I may have in the future.

Because of my condition, I cut my trip short and didn't go to Mount Kilimanjaro. I knew that, even though we were going to do the stages in seven days, I'd be able to do only the first five before it got too steep. Just thinking about it made me dizzy. And if I know I can't do something all the way, it'll never make me happy to come home with a consolation prize, saying that I did the first five days and was only one stage away. It's like losing in the Stanley Cup finals. Does any player write "I *nearly* won the Stanley Cup" on his resumé? I wrote it in this book only to make clear how terrible that experience feels. There was no way I was going to come up short on purpose.

But one of my fellow climbers was every bit as fiercely committed as I ever was. Julie Gauthier, who came with her sister Caroline and her dad, Charles, showed the group the greatest act of courage I've even seen. What is amazing is that she's blind, but Julie was ready to do anything. There wasn't a quitting bone in her body, as difficult and challenging as the road was. Her mental strength would have made you cry. The effort it took her, her sister, and her dad to do that trip was something I will never forget. Her journey is an inspiration. If she can accomplish this feat, then anything is possible. You always have to believe in yourself. Every dream is achievable when you live your life to the fullest for yourself and not for anyone else.

I may have succumbed to my vertigo in Africa, but I can't end this book with a story of how I backed down—especially since one of the accomplishments I am most proud of came only weeks earlier. On June 3, 2011, I took part in the Esprit de Corps foundation's run from downtown Montreal to the Empire State Building in New York City, a relay run of 609 kilometres. The foundation organizes that run every year to raise money for single-parent families.

I love a challenge, but this one was at the very limit of what I could do. The way the run goes is simple. There are twenty runners, grouped in pairs. The first pair runs ten kilometres, then stops and waits for the other nine to run their ten-kilometre share. In other words, you run ten kilometres every seven hours, for a total of eighty-five kilometres.

In May, before the run, we went through a special training session. Twenty of us had to run from Montreal to Mont Tremblant, with each pair doing five eight-kilometre runs before we all ran the last two kilometres together.

At the time, I tipped the scales at about three hundred pounds and had not been training at all, since I was too busy with the Green Party in the federal election. Needless to say, I struggled. There were times when other runners had to push me in the back to help me up hills. My considerable ego was shattered. The only reason I didn't quit was that news of Derek Boogaard's death came right at the beginning of that training run. I tweeted that I was dedicating the run to him, and people supported me with their messages.

After that gruelling run, I understood I had to practise a lot before the event, because no one was allowed to stop running and walk. If one runner were to do that, another was to take his or her place. It was going to be a three-day-long challenge. I trained hard, ran a lot of stairs, and lost about thirty pounds. There was no way I could fail.

Physically speaking, that run was the hardest thing I have done in my entire life. My knees were a mess. After each ten-kilometre run, I needed ice for my knees, which were swelling because I have no cartilage left. I had to take anti-inflammatory pills after every run, but I'm just glad my back held up. At 275 pounds, I proudly did the eighty-five kilometres without walking and without any help. The fact that we had such a great team made the experience fantastic, and even though it was mentally and physically the hardest thing ever, I'm already excited to join the group and do it again next year.

As I write this, I realize I have been telling the same story again and again throughout this book. Whether it is something as big as a career in hockey or as a short as a run; whether it is something you just stumble into, like my efforts in figure skating, or something you devote your life to, like my work with charity, there is really only one way to do things—with all your heart.

Writing these words, I'm thinking about you, Milayna Julia and Marcus Oliver.

I love you.

EPILOGUE

I hope you have enjoyed the story of my life. I have certainly enjoyed living it.

Looking back, what still surprises me is how impossible it would have been to guess how things would turn out for me for those who knew me only as a little kid in Sorel-Tracy, or those who knew me playing hockey in the Q.

And looking back on my career, on the hundreds of fights, there is absolutely no clue as to how one thing would lead to another to take me so far from the lights of the NHL and push me towards the greatest honour of my life. All through my youth, I dreamed of only one thing, and I was lucky enough to achieve it. And I was even luckier that there were more dreams to come true for me.

In 2011, I was approached by the Canada-Tibet Committee and asked to introduce the Dalai Lama, who was going to be in Montreal to speak about global citizenship. I asked whether the person on the phone was joking. The idea of me, former NHL heavyweight, introducing His Holiness was more than I could believe.

But the committee didn't think of me as a tough guy. They thought of all the hospital visits, my love for children, my constant fight for animals rights, my work for Haiti. They thought of me as an activist, not a pugilist.

So on September 7, 2011, there I was in front of a crowd in Montreal with the Dalai Lama. I couldn't even express how much gratitude I felt for being asked to grace the stage with such an embodiment of love, compassion, and the infinite potential of each human being. Prior to that event, I was reminded of a quote that I had come across from His Holiness: "My religion is very simple, my religion is kindness."

In a world that has bred more war and more hate because of religious differences, His Holiness' only sword is compassion. I have seen in my own life how deep that dagger can reach into my heart. Immediately following the September 11 attacks, I tuned into the television footage with much apprehension and fear. As I looked at channel after channel, the shock began to set in, and I found myself not focusing on the act or devastation itself, but instead was overwhelmed by the images of grown men falling to the ground weeping over the loss of friends and loved ones as perfect strangers extended their arms to embrace the pain and share the burden. And the sword was driven deeper as I gazed blankly at the screen, breathless, as I watched the lifeless bodies of babies being cradled in the arms of dusty, unrecognizable firemen. It was in that moment that I felt the uncontrollable urge of human compassion to reach out and embrace all others that needed to be embraced.

Then ten years later, there I was onstage with the man whose life is devoted to that message of compassion and responsibility to others. He walked up to me, his eyes sparkling like someone who could see all the good in the world, and reached out to take my hand. Even though I am accustomed to being in the spotlight, in front of thousands, in that moment I could not believe I was there. I felt so lucky.

What His Holiness talked about was the way we look at our communities. What he made me see is that my ability to extend love and compassion is not limited to this city or even this country. I have been given the gift of infinite wisdom, potential, and love. We all have. The biggest disservice that I can do to this world is to withhold these gifts. Without borders, colours, or languages, our community extends to each and every human being occupying this beautiful planet. And as you should all know today, the only language and the only currency required is that of unbounded love, compassion, and kindness.

I know this may sound fanatical coming from me. And I know that we all have our everyday lives that make unbounded compassion for others seem impossible. But it's not. We love our kids this way. The luckiest know what it means to be loved this way by parents. As I stood on the stage in the presence of His Holiness, and he put the *khata* (Tibetan scarf) around my neck, he looked me in the eyes and took my hands. I felt blessed—an exhilaration and humility I had never experienced.

More than ever, I knew that how you start out does not determine where you end up.

ACKNOWLEDGMENTS

Ever since reading Jackie Robinson's autobiography as a kid, it's been my dream to tell my own story someday. Just short of my thirty-fifth birthday, my dream came true. As much as Jackie's book changed my life, I hope to inspire many of you with my story.

First off though, I would like to dedicate this book to my children, Milayna Julia Laraque and Marcus Oliver Laraque. Your daddy loves you with all his heart and hopes someday, when you're old enough to read his book, you'll be proud of him and inspired to pursue your own dreams. To their mother, Erin Kathan, thank you for delivering our two angels into this world and doing such a great job raising them mostly alone. To June and Darrel Rousel, my mom, Évelyne Toussaint, and my best friend, brother, and soulmate Don Radomski, thank you for being the best godparents ever and for always being there for the twins. To my parents, thanks for everything. Without you, I would not be the person I am today. To my sister, Daphney, and my brother, Jules, who have had such a huge impact on my life, thanks for your constant support and love. To my brothers Marc Filion, Michael Schayer, Brett Klawitter, Shafin Devji, David Ettedgui, Nick Brusatore, Tuffy Ballas, and Jeremy Roenick, and my cousins Philip and Stefan Charles-Pierre, Thierry and Steve Jean-Louis, and Patrick Raphael, as well as all my other friends, thank you for always being there for me throughout the good and tough times. Finally, thanks to my editor at Penguin Canada, Nick Garrison, for publishing my book and making my dream come true. As well, a big thank-you to Pierre Thibeault, who spent so many hours with me—and without me!—working to make this possible. Pierre, I could not have picked a better person to help me tell my story.

Finally, I'd like to say a solemn thank you to Sid Terrabain, who died tragically in August 2011. Sid and his family welcomed me into their Edmonton home when I was just a scared kid, and he became like an older brother to me. I'll never forget that generosity.

May God bless you all.
Much love,
Georges Laraque

INDEX